Interpersonal Skills

Custom Edition for James Madison University

Taken from:

Human Relations: Interpersonal Job-Oriented Skills, Ninth Edition
by Andrew J. DuBrin

Guide to Meetings
by Mary Munter and Michael Netzley

Guide to Managerial Communication: Effective Business Writing and Speaking, Seventh Edition
by Mary Munter

Workplace Communication: Process and Product
by Sharon J. Gerson and Steven M. Gerson

Guide to Business Etiquette
by Roy A. Cook, Gwen O. Cook and Laura J. Yale

D1307886

COLLEGE OF
BUSINESS
JAMES MADISON UNIVERSITY®

Custom Publishing

New York   Boston   San Francisco
London   Toronto   Sydney   Tokyo   Singapore   Madrid
Mexico City   Munich   Paris   Cape Town   Hong Kong   Montreal

Taken from:

Human Relations: Interpersonal Job-Oriented Skills, Ninth Edition
by Andrew J. DuBrin
Copyright © 2007, 2005, 2000, 1994, 1990 by Pearson Education, Inc.
Published by Prentice Hall, Inc.
Upper Saddle River, New Jersey 07458

Guide to Meetings
by Mary Munter and Michael Netzley
Copyright © 2002 by Pearson Education, Inc.
Published by Prentice Hall, Inc.

Guide to Managerial Communication: Effective Business Writing and Speaking, Seventh Edition
by Mary Munter
Copyright © 2006, 2003, 2000, 1997, 1992 by Pearson Education, Inc.
Published by Prentice Hall, Inc.

Workplace Communication: Process and Product
by Sharon J. Gerson and Steven M. Gerson
Copyright © 2007 by Pearson Education, Inc.
Published by Prentice Hall, Inc.

Guide to Business Etiquette
by Roy A. Cook, Gwen O. Cook and Laura J. Yale
Copyright © 2005 by Pearson Education, Inc.
Published by Prentice Hall, Inc.

This special edition published in cooperation with Pearson Custom Publishing.

Printed in the United States of America

10   9

2008560085

DE

Pearson
Custom Publishing
is a division of

www.pearsonhighered.com

ISBN 10: 0-536-77822-1
ISBN 13: 978-0-536-77822-2

Table of Contents

Interpersonal Skills

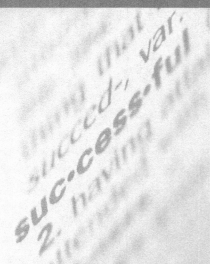

Understanding Individual Differences

Learning Objectives

After reading and studying this chapter and doing the exercises you should be able to

1. Take into account the individual differences among people in dealing with them on the job.
2. Develop insight into how your personality, mental ability, emotional intelligence, and values differ from others.
3. Respond to personality differences among people.
4. Respond to mental ability differences among people.
5. Respond to differences in values among people.

How old is too old to be flying hundreds of passengers has long been a difficult question. Right now, the United States kicks commercial airline pilots out of the cockpit before they hit their 60th birthday. But that may change. As pensions erode, there is a growing push to raise that age to 65, and there's an increased likelihood that travelers will start seeing older captains in the cockpit. Some other nations are already moving in this direction, and in Congress, lawmakers have introduced legislation that would bump up the age. Even the Air Line Pilots Association, which in the past has successfully blocked attempts to raise the age, now says it is studying whether a change makes sense.

Gray-haired pilots have the advantage of extensive and wide-ranging experience at the controls, enabling smart, well-informed decision making—which is just what you want, if, say, a plane runs into trouble. Consider that in 1989, United Airlines Captain David Cronin flew a Boeing 747 back to Honolulu after a large section of the fuselage blew out, sucking nine passengers to their death. Two of four engines quit and wing flaps were damaged, but Cronin's flying skills saved 327 passengers. Then, within a month, he was deemed too old to fly.

Yet older pilots may also run a greater risk of sudden incapacitation, slower reactions, or declining mental facilities. While medical studies provide no clear-cut answers, many show that skills do deteriorate with aging.

Discussion Question

1. What should the Federal Aviation Administration do about potential differences in flying ability based on age?

Source: Scott McCartney, "How Old Is too Old to Fly an Airliner?" February 22, 2005, pp. D1, D4. *The Wall Street Journal.* Reprinted with permission.

It might be true that in general people 60 and younger have the top vision and quick reaction time necessary to perform satisfactorily as a commercial airline pilot. However, there is still a wide variation in these abilities with different age groups. Some younger people have poor vision, poor reaction time, and poor judgment to boot. In general, individual differences exert a profound effect on job performance and behavior. Such differences refer to variations in how people respond to the same situation based on personal characteristics. One of hundreds of possible examples is that some people can concentrate longer and harder on their work, thereby producing more and higher quality work, than others.

individual differences Variations in how people respond to the same situation based on personal characteristics.

This chapter describes several of the major sources of individual differences on the job. It also gives you the chance to measure your standing on several key dimensions of behavior and helps you develop skill in responding to individual differences. Knowing how to respond to such differences is the cornerstone of effective interpersonal relations.

PERSONALITY

◄ Learning Objective 1

◄ Learning Objective 2

"We're not going to promote you to department head," said the vice president to the analyst. "Although you are a great troubleshooter, you've alienated too many people in the company. You're too blunt and insensitive." As just implied, most successes and failures in people-contact jobs are attributed largely to interpersonal skills. And personality traits are important contributors to interpersonal, or human relations, skills.

Personality refers to those persistent and enduring behavior patterns and tend to be expressed in a wide variety of situations. A person who is brash and insensitive in one situation is likely to behave similarly in many other situations. Your personality is what makes you unique. Your walk, your talk, your appearance, your speech, and your inner values and conflicts all contribute to your personality. Have you ever noticed that when you know a person well you can identify that person by his or her footsteps even though you do not see the individual? This is true because many people have a distinctive gait.

personality Persistent and enduring behavior patterns that tend to be expressed in a wide variety of situations.

I will illustrate the importance of personality to interpersonal relations in organizations by describing eight key personality traits and psychological types related to cognitive styles. In addition, you will be given guidelines for dealing effectively with different personality types.

EIGHT MAJOR PERSONALITY FACTORS AND TRAITS

Many psychologists believe that the basic structure of human personality is represented by five broad factors, known as the Five Factor Model (or Big Five): neuroticism, extraversion (the scientific spelling of *extroversion*), openness, agreeableness, and conscientiousness. Three more key personality factors—self-monitoring of behavior, risk taking and thrill seeking, and optimism—are so important for human relations to be considered here.

All eight factors have a substantial impact on interpersonal relations and job performance. The interpretations and meanings of these factors provide useful information because they help you pinpoint important areas for personal development. Although these factors are partially inherited, most people can improve them providing they exert much conscious effort over a period of time. For example, it

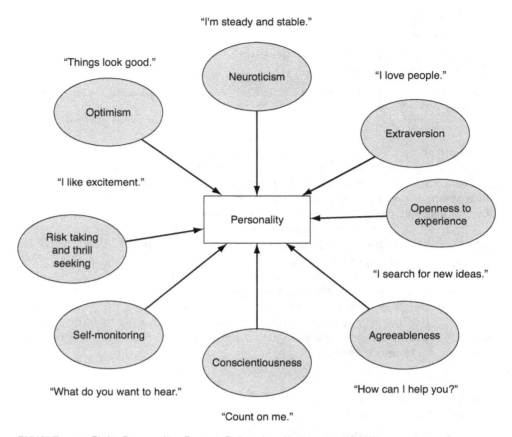

FIGURE 1–1 Eight Personality Factors Related to Interpersonal Skills

usually takes a minimum of three months of effort before a person is perceived to be more agreeable. The eight factors, shown in Figure 1-1, are described in the following list.

1. *Neuroticism* reflects emotional instability and identifies people prone to psychological distress and coping with problems in unproductive ways. Traits associated with this personality factor include being anxious, insecure, angry, embarrassed, emotional, and worried. A person of low neuroticism—or high emotional stability—is calm and confident, and usually in control.

2. *Extraversion* reflects the quantity or intensity of social interactions, the need for social stimulation, self-confidence, and competition. Traits associated with extraversion include being sociable, gregarious, assertive, talkative, and active. An outgoing person is often described as extraverted, whereas introverted persons are described as reserved, timid, and quiet.

3. *Openness* reflects the proactive seeking of experience for its own sake. Traits associated with openness include being creative, cultured, intellectually curious, broadminded, and artistically sensitive. People low on this personality factor are practical, with narrow interests.

4. *Agreeableness* reflects the quality of one's interpersonal orientation. Traits associated with the agreeableness factor include being courteous, flexible, trusting, good-natured, cooperative, forgiving, softhearted, and tolerant. The other end of the continuum includes disagreeable, cold, and antagonistic people.

5. *Conscientiousness* reflects organization, self-restraint, persistence, and motivation toward attaining goals. Traits associated with conscientiousness include being hardworking, dependable, well organized, and thorough. The person low in conscientiousness is lazy, disorganized, and unreliable.

6. *Self-monitoring* of behavior refers to the process of observing and controlling how we are perceived by others. High self-monitors are pragmatic and even chameleonlike actors in social groups. They often say what others want to hear. Low self-monitors avoid situations that require them to adapt to outer images. In this way their outer behavior adheres to their inner values. Low self-monitoring can often lead to inflexibility.

7. *Risk taking and thrill seeking* refers to the propensity to take risks and pursue thrills. Persons with high standing on this personality trait are sensation-seekers who pursue novel, intense, and complex sensations. They are willing to take risks for the sake of such experiences. The search for giant payoffs and daily thrills motivates people with an intense need for risk taking and thrill seeking.[1] Take Self-Assessment Quiz 1-1 to measure your propensity for risk taking and thrill seeking.

SELF-ASSESSMENT QUIZ 1-1

THE RISK-TAKING SCALE

Directions: Answer true or false to the following questions to obtain an approximate idea of your tendency to take risks, or your desire to do so:

	True	False
1. I eat sushi or other raw fish.	☐	☒
2. I think that amusement park roller coasters should be abolished.	☐	☒
3. I don't like trying foods from other cultures.	☐	☒
4. I would choose bonds over growth stocks.	☐	☒
5. I like to challenge people in positions of power.	☒	☐
6. I don't always wear a seat belt while driving.	☐	☒
7. I sometimes talk on my cell phone while driving at highway speeds.	☒	☐
8. I would love to be an entrepreneur (or I love being one).	☐	☒
9. I would like helping out in a crisis such as a product recall.	☐	☒
10. I would like to go cave exploring (or already have done so).	☒	☐
11. I would be willing to have at least one-third of my compensation based on a bonus for good performance.	☒	☒
12. I would be willing to visit a maximum security prison on a job assignment.	☒	☐

Scoring and Interpretation: Give yourself one point each time your answer agrees with the key. If you score 10–12, you are probably a high risk taker; 6–9, you are a moderate risk taker; 3–5, you are cautious; 0–2, you are a very low risk taker.

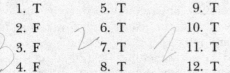

1. T	5. T	9. T
2. F	6. T	10. T
3. F	7. T	11. T
4. F	8. T	12. T

Source: The idea of a test about risk-taking comfort, as well as several of the statements on the quiz, comes from psychologist Frank Farley.

8. *Optimism* refers to a tendency to experience positive emotional states, and to typically believe that positive outcomes will be forthcoming from most activities. The other end of the scale is *pessimism*—a tendency to experience negative emotional states, and to typically believe that negative outcomes will be forthcoming from most activities. Optimism versus pessimism is also referred to in more technical terms as positive affectivity versus negative affectivity, and is considered a major personality trait. A person's tendency toward having positive affectivity (optimism) versus negative affectivity (pessimism) also influences job satisfaction. Being optimistic, as you would suspect, tends to enhance job satisfaction.[2]

Evidence for the relevance of the Five Factor Model (traits one through five of the previous list) of personality in understanding human behavior comes from a cross-cultural study involving 7,134 individuals. The five-factor structure of the American personality was also found to hold true for German, Portuguese, Hebrew, Chinese, Korean, and Japanese samples when the personality test questions were translated into each of these languages. Based on this extensive study, it was concluded that personality structure is universal, much like the structure of the brain or the body.[3] Another look at the evidence found that extraversion, agreeableness, and conscientiousness are major personality factors in most cultures. Neuroticism and openness are more dependent on the culture and are particularly relevant in the United States.[4]

THE EIGHT FACTORS AND TRAITS AND JOB PERFORMANCE

Depending on the job, any one of the preceding personality factors can be important for success. One explanation for personality being tied to performance is that a particular personality trait gives us a bias or positive spin to certain actions.[5] A person high in conscientiousness, for example, believes that if people are diligent they will accomplish more work and receive just rewards. Conscientiousness relates to job performance for many different occupations, and has proven to be the personality trait most consistently related to success. However, there are a few instances in which being highly conscientious can interfere with job success. If the job requires considerable spontaneity and imagination, a highly conscientious person might perform poorly because he or she dislikes breaking the rules or straying from conventional thinking.[6] For example, a conscientious advertising worker might hesitate to develop a television advertisement that depicted a woman jumping out of a building onto a UPS delivery truck.

Another important research finding is that extraversion is associated with success for managers and sales representatives. The explanation is that managers and salespeople are required to interact extensively with other people.[7] For people who want to advance in their careers, being a high self-monitor is important. An analysis was made of the self-monitoring personality by combining 136 studies involving 23,101 people. A major finding was that high self-monitors tend to receive better performance ratings than low self-monitors. High self-monitors were also more likely to emerge as leaders and work their way into top management positions.[8] Another advantage to being a high self-monitor is that the individual is more likely to help out other workers, even when not required.[9] An example would be helping a worker outside your department with a currency exchange problem even though this was not your responsibility. The willingness to go beyond one's job description is referred to as organizational citizenship behavior. Good organizational citizens are highly valued by employers.

A combination of personality factors will sometimes be more closely associated with job success than one factor alone. A study about personality and job performance ratings was conducted with diverse occupations including clerical workers and wholesale appliance sales representatives. A key finding was that conscientious workers who also scored high on agreeableness performed better than conscien-

organizational citizenship behavior The willingness to go beyond one's job description.

tious workers who were less agreeable.[10] (Being agreeable toward your manager helps elevate performance evaluations!) A study with experienced pharmaceutical sales representatives found that the combination of extraversion and conscientiousness was associated with higher sales. However, being conscientious was the personality factor most closely associated with growth in sales over several years for the experienced sales representatives.[11]

The extent to which a person has a high standing on agreeableness influences whether or not the supervisor perceives him or her as requiring high maintenance (needing a lot of attention). A study with 338 clerical workers in a manufacturing setting found that among employees who had a high standing on conscientiousness, being disagreeable prompted supervisors to rate them as engaging in high-maintenance behavior.[12]

Optimism and pessimism also can be linked to job performance. Optimism can be quite helpful when attempting such tasks as selling a product or service or motivating a group of people. Yet psychologist Julie Normen has gathered considerable evidence that pessimism can sometimes enhance job performance. Pessimists usually assume that something will go wrong, and will carefully prepare to prevent botches and bad luck. A pessimist, for example, will carefully back up computer files or plan for emergencies that might shut down operations.[13]

COGNITIVE STYLES AND PERSONALITY TYPES

People go about solving problems in various ways. You may have observed, for example, that some people are more analytical and systematic while others are more intuitive. The most widely used method of classifying problem-solving styles is the Myers-Briggs Type Indicator (MBTI).[14] Many readers of this book will have already taken the MBTI. Modes of problem solving are referred to as cognitive styles. According to this method of understanding problem-solving styles, your personality traits influence strongly how you approach problems, such as being introverted pointing you toward dealing with ideas. Knowledge of these cognitive styles can help you relate better to people because you can better appreciate how they make decisions.

cognitive style
Mental processes used to perceive and make judgments from situations.

According to the famous psychoanalyst Carl Jung, how people gather and evaluate information determines their cognitive style. Jung's analysis became the basis for the MBTI. Jung reasoned that there are four dimensions of psychological functioning:

1. Introverted versus Extraverted. Introverts are oriented toward the inner world of ideas and feelings, whereas extraverts are oriented toward the outer world of people and objects.

2. Thinking versus Feeling. Thinkers prefer to make decisions logically based on facts and figures, whereas feelers base decisions on subjective information.

3. Sensing versus Intuiting. Sensing individuals prefer to concentrate on details, whereas intuitive individuals prefer to focus on broad issues (the "big picture").

4. Judging versus Perceiving. Judging types seek to resolve issues, whereas perceiving types are relatively flexible and search for additional information.

Combining the four types with each other results in 16 personality types, as shown in Figure 1-2. Research evidence for the MBTI is generally positive with respect to the 16 types, and the fact that people with different cognitive styles prefer different occupations.[15] For example, the ENTP cognitive type is labeled the "conceptualizer." He or she is passionate about new opportunities and dislikes routine, and is more likely to be an entrepreneur than a corporate manager. The ISTJ cognitive type is labeled the "traditionalist," and will often become an accountant or financial analyst. The INJT type is labeled the "visionary." Although a small proportion of the population, these individuals are often chief executives of business firms. One of the most common types among people in general, as well as among managers, is the ESTJ, labeled the "organizer."

ENTP (Conceptualizer)	ISTJ (Traditionalist)	INTJ (Visionary)	ESTJ (Organizer)
Quick, ingenious, will argue either side of issue for fun, may neglect routine assignments. (Good for creative work where deadlines are not crucial.)	Serious, quiet, practical, logical, dependable. (Good for work requiring careful attention to detail such as accountant or auditor.)	Skeptical, critical, independent, determined, original. (Good for major leadership role such as CEO.)	Practical, realistic, has a natural mind for business or mechanics, likes to organize and run activities. (Good for manufacturing supervisor.)

FIGURE 1–2 Four Cognitive Styles of the Myers-Briggs Typology

Note: I = Introvert, *E* = Extrovert, *T* = Thinking, *F* = Feeling, *S* = Sensing, *N* = Intuitive, *J* = Judging, and *P* = Perceiving.

Source: The personality descriptions are based on information from *Meyers-Briggs Type Indicator* by Katharine C. Briggs and Isabel Briggs Myers. Copyright 1983 by Consulting Psychologists Press, Inc. All rights reserved.

Many people who use the Myers-Briggs are unaware that it is an approximate measure, and not a definitive scale such as a measure of physical weight. The most reliable dimension appears to be thinking versus feeling, which is similar to reflecting about details versus jumping to a quick decision based on feel and experience, or being reflective versus impulsive.

If you take the Myers-Briggs Type Indicator, often available in career centers, you will discover your type. You can also study these four types and make a tentative judgment as to whether one of them fits your problem-solving style. Recognizing your problem-solving style can help you identify work that you are likely to perform well, as detailed in Figure 1-2.

GUIDELINES FOR DEALING WITH DIFFERENT PERSONALITY TYPES

Learning Objective 3 ▶ A key purpose in presenting information about a sampling of various personality types is to provide guidelines for individualizing your approach to people. As a basic example, if you wanted to score points with an introvert, you would approach that person in a restrained, laid-back fashion. In contrast, a more gregarious, lighthearted approach might be more effective with an extravert. The purpose of individualizing your approach is to build a better working relationship or to establish rapport with the other person. To match your approach to dealing with a given personality type, you must first arrive at an approximate diagnosis of the individual's personality. The following suggestions are therefore restricted to readily observable aspects of personality.

1. When relating to a person who appears to be neurotic based on symptoms of worry and tension, be laid back and reassuring. Attempt not to project your own anxiety and fears. Be a good listener. If possible, minimize the emphasis on deadlines and the dire consequences of a project's failing. Show concern and interest in the person's welfare.

2. When relating to an extraverted individual, emphasize friendliness, warmth, and a stream of chatter. Talk about people more than ideas, things, or data. Express an interest in a continuing working relationship.

3. When relating to an introverted individual, move slowly in forming a working relationship. Do not confuse quietness with a lack of interest. Tolerate moments of silence. Emphasize ideas, things, and data more heavily than people.

4. When relating to a person who is open to experience, emphasize information sharing, idea generation, and creative approaches to problems. Appeal to his or her intellect by discussing topics of substance rather than ordinary chatter and gossip.

5. When relating to a person who is closed to experience, stick closely to the facts of the situation at hand. Recognize that the person prefers to think small and deal with the here and now.

6. When relating to an agreeable person, just relax and be yourself. Reciprocate with kindness to sustain a potentially excellent working relationship.

7. When relating to a disagreeable person, be patient and tolerant. At the same time, set limits on how much mistreatment you will take. Disagreeable people sometimes secretly want others to put brakes on their antisocial behavior.

8. When relating to a conscientious person, give him or her freedom and do not nag. The person will probably honor commitments without prompting. Conscientious people are often taken for granted, so remember to acknowledge the person's dependability.

9. When relating to a person of low conscientiousness, keep close tabs on him or her, especially if you need the person's output to do your job. Do not assume that because the person has an honest face and a pleasing smile he or she will deliver as promised. Frequently follow up on your requests, and impose deadlines if you have the authority. Express deep appreciation when the person does follow through.

10. When dealing with a person whom you suspect is a high self-monitor, be cautious in thinking that the person is really in support of your position. The person could just be following his or her natural tendency to appear to please others, but not really feel that way.

11. When relating to a person with a high propensity for risk taking and thrill seeking, emphasize the risky and daring aspects of activities familiar to you. Talk about a new product introduction in a highly competitive market, stock options, investment in high-technology startup firms, skydiving, and race car driving.

12. When relating to a person with a low propensity for risk taking and thrill seeking, emphasize the safe and secure aspects of activities familiar to you. Talk about the success of an established product in a stable market (like pencils and paperclips), investment in U.S. Treasury bonds, life insurance, camping, and gardening.

13. When dealing with a sensing-type person, emphasize facts, figures, and conventional thinking without sacrificing your own values. To convince the sensing type, emphasize logic more than emotional appeal. Focus on details more than the big picture.

14. When dealing with an intuiting-type individual, emphasize feelings, judgments, playing with ideas, imagination, and creativity. Focus more on the big picture than details.

To start putting these guidelines into practice, do the role-plays in Skill-Building Exercise 1-1. Remember that a role-player is an extemporaneous actor. Put yourself in the shoes of the character you play and visualize how he or she would act. Because you are given only the general idea of a script, use your imagination to fill in the details.

SKILL-BUILDING EXERCISE 1-1

PERSONALITY ROLE-PLAYS

The Extravert: One student assumes the role of a successful outside sales representative who has just signed a $3 million order for the company. The sales rep comes back to the office elated. The other student assumes the role of a member of the office support staff. He or she decides this is a splendid opportunity to build a good relationship with the triumphant sales rep. Run the role-play for about seven minutes. The people not involved in the role-play will observe and then provide feedback when the role-play is completed. (These directions regarding time, observation, and feedback also apply to the two other role-plays in this exercise and throughout the book.)

Openness: One student plays the role of an experienced worker in the department who is told to spend some time orienting a new co-op student or intern. It appears that this new person is open to experience. Another student plays the role of the co-op student who is open to experience and eager to be successful in this new position.

Sensing and Intuiting Types: One student plays the role of a sensing-type individual who is responsible for reviewing the company expense accounts. The other student plays the role of a manager in whose department many expense account abuses (such as lack of documentation and high expenses) have been uncovered. This manager is an intuitive type. The person in charge of the accounts is visiting the manager in the latter's office to discuss this problem.

MENTAL ABILITY

intelligence The capacity to acquire and apply knowledge, including solving problems.

Mental ability, or intelligence, is one of the major sources of individual differences that affects job performance and behavior. Intelligence is the capacity to acquire and apply knowledge, including solving problems. Intelligent workers can best solve abstract problems. In an exceedingly simple job, such as packing shoes into boxes, having below-average intelligence can be an advantage because the employee is not likely to become bored.

Understanding the nature of intelligence contributes to effective interpersonal relations in the workplace. Your evaluation of a person's intelligence can influence how you relate to that person. For example, if you think a person is intelligent you will tend to seek his or her input on a difficult problem. If you realize that different types of intelligence exist, you are more likely to appreciate people's strengths. You are thus less likely to judge others as being either good or poor problem solvers.

g (general) factor A factor in intelligence that contributes to the ability to perform well in many tasks.

Four important aspects of mental ability include: (1) the components of traditional intelligence, (2) practical intelligence, (3) multiple intelligences, and (4) emotional intelligence. (This fourth type of intelligence can also be regarded as personality, not mental ability.) Knowledge of the four aspects will enrich your understanding of other workers and yourself.

COMPONENTS OF TRADITIONAL INTELLIGENCE

s (special) factors Specific components of intelligence that contribute to problem-solving ability.

Intelligence consists of more than one component. A component of intelligence is much like a separate mental aptitude. Evidence suggests that intelligence consists of a g (general) factor and s (special) factors that contribute to problem-solving ability. Scores of tests of almost any type (such as math, aptitude for spatial relations, or reading skill) are somewhat influenced by the *g* factor. The *g* factor helps explain why some people perform well in so many different mental tasks. Substantial evidence has accumulated over the years that workers with high intelligence tend to perform better. The relationship between *g* and job performance is likely to be strongest for those aspects of jobs involving thinking and knowledge, such as problem solving and technical expertise.[16]

Over the years various investigators have arrived at different special factors contributing to overall mental aptitude. The following seven factors have been identified consistently:

1. **Verbal comprehension.** The ability to understand the meaning of words and their relationship to each other and to comprehend written and spoken information.

2. **Word fluency.** The ability to use words quickly and easily, without an emphasis on verbal comprehension.

3. **Numerical acuity.** The ability to handle numbers, engage in mathematical analysis, and to do arithmetic calculations.

4. **Spatial perception.** The ability to visualize forms in space and manipulate objects mentally, particularly in three dimensions.

5. **Memory.** Having a good rote memory for symbols, words, and lists of numbers, along with other associations.

6. **Perceptual speed.** The ability to perceive visual details, to pick out similarities and differences, and to perform tasks requiring visual perception.

7. **Inductive reasoning.** The ability to discover a rule or principle and apply it in solving a problem and to make judgments and decisions that are logically sound.

Being strong in any of the preceding mental aptitudes often leads to an enjoyment of work associated with that aptitude. The reverse can also be true: enjoying a type of mental activity might lead to the development of an aptitude for the activity. Self-Assessment Quiz 1-2 gives you the opportunity to measure your preferences for numerical information.

PRACTICAL INTELLIGENCE

Many people, including psychologists, are concerned that the traditional way of understanding intelligence inadequately describes mental ability. An unfortunate implication of intelligence testing is that intelligence as traditionally calculated is largely the ability to perform tasks related to scholastic work. Thus, a person who scored very high on an intelligence test could follow a complicated instruction manual, but might not be street smart.

To overcome the limited idea that intelligence mostly involves the ability to solve abstract problems, the triarchic theory of intelligence has been proposed. The theory holds that intelligence is composed of three different subtypes: analytical, creative, and practical. The *analytical* subtype is the traditional intelligence needed for solving difficult problems. Analytical intelligence is required to perform well in most school subjects. The *creative* subtype is the type of intelligence required for imagination and combining things in novel ways. The *practical* subtype is the type of intelligence required for adapting your environment to suit your needs.[17] The idea of practical intelligence helps explain why a person who has a difficult time getting through school can still be a successful businessperson, politician, or athlete. Practical intelligence incorporates the ideas of common sense, wisdom, and street smarts.

A person with high practical intelligence would also have good intuition, an experience-based way of knowing or reasoning in which the weighing and balancing

The best measure of a person's intelligence is the type of life he or she leads.
—David Wechsler, developer of one of the most widely used IQ tests

triarchic theory of intelligence An explanation of mental ability holding that intelligence is composed of three different subtypes: analytical, creative, and practical.

intuition An experience-based way of knowing or reasoning in which the weighing and balancing of evidence are done automatically.

SELF-ASSESSMENT QUIZ 1–2

ATTITUDES TOWARD NUMERICAL INFORMATION

Directions:: Describe how well you agree with each of the following statements, using the following scale: disagree strongly (DS); disagree (D); neutral (N); agree (A); agree strongly (AS). Circle the number in the appropriate column.

	DS	D	N	A	AS
1. I enjoy work that requires the use of numbers.	1	2	3	4	5
2. I think quantitative information is difficult to understand.	5	4	3	2	1
3. I find it satisfying to solve day-to-day problems involving numbers.	1	2	3	4	5
4. Numerical information is very useful in everyday life.	1	2	3	4	5
5. I prefer not to pay attention to information involving numbers.	5	4	3	2	1
6. I think more information should be available in numerical form.	1	2	3	4	5
7. I don't like to think about issues involving numbers.	5	4	3	2	1
8. Numbers are not necessary for most situations.	5	4	3	2	1
9. Thinking is more enjoyable when it does not involve quantitative information.	5	4	3	2	1
10. I like to make calculations involving numerical information.	1	2	3	4	5
11. Quantitative information is vital for accurate decisions.	1	2	3	4	5
12. I enjoy thinking about issues that involve numerical information.	1	2	3	4	5
13. Understanding numbers is as important in daily life as reading or writing.	1	2	3	4	5
14. I easily lose interest in graphs, percentages, and other quantitative information.	5	4	3	2	1
15. I find numerical information to be relevant to most situations.	1	2	3	4	5
16. I think it is important to learn and use numerical information to make well-informed decisions.	1	2	3	4	5
17. Numbers are redundant for most situations.	5	4	3	2	1
18. It is a waste of time to learn information containing a lot of numbers.	5	4	3	2	1
19. I like to go over numbers in my mind.	1	2	3	4	5
20. It helps me think if I put down information as numbers.	1	2	3	4	5

Total Score _____

Scoring and Interpretation: Add the numbers you circled to obtain your total score.

85–100 You have strong positive attitudes toward numerical information and working with quantitative data.

55–84 You have moderately favorable attitudes toward numerical information and working with quantitative data.

20–54 You have very negative attitudes toward numerical information and working with quantitative data. Your dislike for quantitative solutions to problems is so strong that you are quick to distrust statistical analysis.

Source: Table from Madhubalan Viswanathan, "Measurement of Individual Differences in Preference for Numerical Information," *Journal of Applied Psychology,* October 1993, p. 745. Reprinted with permission.

of evidence are done automatically. Examples of good intuition include a merchandiser who develops a hunch that a particular style will be hot next season, a basketball coach who sees the possibilities in a gangly youngster, and a supervisor who has a hunch that a neighbor would be a great fit for her department. Intuition is also required for creative intelligence.

One major reservation some have about practical intelligence is the implication that people who are highly intelligent in the traditional sense are not practical thinkers. In truth, most executives and other high-level workers score quite well on tests of mental ability. These tests usually measure analytical intelligence.

Back to the Opening Case

You will recall the concern about how long to let senior pilots keep flying commercial airplanes. The fact that these experienced flyers currently are allowed to work as pilots up to age 60 shows the importance of practical intelligence. You need good judgment when you have 350 passengers on board. The Federal Aviation Administration maintains that retirement at age 60 has proved to be a safe standard, so why change if you might risk safety? However, as people maintain productive capacity into later years, the FAA might change its position.

MULTIPLE INTELLIGENCES

Another approach to understanding the diverse nature of mental ability is the theory of multiple intelligences. According to Howard Gardner, people know and understand the world in distinctly different ways and learn in different ways. Individuals possess the following eight intelligences, or faculties, in varying degrees:

1. Linguistic. Enables people to communicate through language, including reading, writing, and speaking.
2. Logical-mathematical. Enables individuals to see relationships between objects and solve problems, as in calculus and statistics.
3. Musical. Gives people the capacity to create and understand meanings made out of sounds and to enjoy different types of music.
4. Spatial. Enables people to perceive and manipulate images in the brain and to recreate them from memory, as is required in making graphic designs.
5. Bodily-kinesthetic. Enables people to use their body and perceptual and motor systems in skilled ways such as dancing, playing sports, and expressing emotion through facial expressions.
6. Intrapersonal. Enables people to distinguish among their own feelings and acquire accurate self-knowledge.
7. Interpersonal. Makes it possible for individuals to recognize and make distinctions among the feelings, motives, and intentions of others as in managing or parenting.
8. Naturalist. Enables individuals to differentiate among, classify, and utilize various features of the physical external environment.

multiple intelligences A theory of intelligence contending that people know and understand the world in distinctly different ways and learn in different ways.

Your profile of intelligences influences how you best learn and to which types of jobs you are best suited. Gardner believes that it is possible to develop these separate intelligences through concentrated effort. However, any of these intelligences might fade if not put to use.[18] The components of multiple intelligences might also be perceived as different talents or abilities. Having high general problem-solving ability (g) would contribute to high standing on each of the eight intelligences.

EMOTIONAL INTELLIGENCE

emotional intelligence
Qualities such as
understanding one's
own feelings, empathy
for others, and the
regulation of emotion
to enhance living.

Later research has updated and expanded the idea of practical intelligence, suggesting that how effectively people use their emotions has a major impact on their success. Emotional intelligence refers to qualities such as understanding one's own feelings, having empathy for others, and regulating one's emotion to enhance living. A person with high emotional intelligence would be able to engage in such behaviors as sizing up people, pleasing others, and influencing them. Four key factors included in a recent analysis of emotional intelligence are as follows:[19]

1. **Self-awareness.** The ability to understand your moods, emotions, and needs as well as their impact on others. Self-awareness also includes using intuition to make decisions you can live with happily. (A person with good self-awareness knows whether he or she is pushing other people too far.)

2. **Self-management.** The ability to control one's emotions and act with honesty and integrity in a consistent and acceptable manner. The right degree of self-management helps prevent a person from throwing temper tantrums when activities do not go as planned. Effective workers do not let their occasional bad moods ruin their day. If they cannot overcome the bad mood, they let coworkers know of their problem and how long it might last. (A person with low self-management would suddenly decide to drop a project because the work was frustrating.)

3. **Social awareness.** Includes having empathy for others and having intuition about work problems. A team leader with social awareness, or empathy, would be able to assess whether a team member has enough enthusiasm for a project to assign him to that project. Another facet of social skill is the ability to interpret nonverbal communication, such as frowns and types of smiles.[20] (A supervisor with social awareness, or empathy, would take into account the most likely reaction of group members before making a decision affecting them.)

4. **Relationship management.** Includes the interpersonal skills of being able to communicate clearly and convincingly, disarm conflicts, and build strong personal bonds. Effective workers use relationship management skills to spread their enthusiasm and solve disagreements, often with kindness and humor. (A worker with relationship management skill would use a method of persuasion that is likely to work well with a particular group or individual.)

Emotional intelligence thus incorporates many of the skills and attitudes necessary to achieve effective interpersonal relations in organizations. Most of the topics in this book, such as resolving conflict, helping others develop, and possessing positive political skills, would be included in emotional intelligence. As mentioned earlier, emotional intelligence might also be regarded as a major aspect of personality rather than true intelligence. For example, if you can read the feelings of other people, aren't you just being smart? Self-Assessment Quiz 1-3 gives you an opportunity to measure your emotional intelligence, but you will need persistence to get the information.

GUIDELINES FOR RELATING TO PEOPLE OF DIFFERENT LEVELS AND TYPES OF INTELLIGENCE

Learning Objective 4 ▶

Certainly you cannot expect to administer mental ability and emotional intelligence tests to all your work associates, gather their scores, and then relate to associates differently based on their scores. Yet it is possible to intuitively develop a sense for the mental quickness of people and the types of mental tasks they perform best. For example, managers must make judgments about mental ability in selecting people for

WHAT IS YOUR EMOTIONAL INTELLIGENCE?

Psychologists have developed various measures of emotional intelligence. The EIQ test found by visiting *http://www.myskillsprofile.com* deals with 16 emotional competencies. The feedback report provides a chart of your emotional competencies together with a detailed description of your profile. An advantage of this quiz is that it is based on the work of two of the original researchers in emotional intelligence, not the later popularizers of the concept.

jobs and assigning them to tasks. Following are several guidelines worth considering for enhancing your working relationships with others.

1. If you perceive another worker (your manager included) to be mentally quick, present your ideas in technical depth. Incorporate difficult words into your conversation and reports. Ask the person challenging questions.

2. If you perceive another worker to be mentally slow, present your ideas with a minimum of technical depth. Use a basic vocabulary, without going so far as to be patronizing. Ask for frequent feedback about having been clear.

3. If you perceive a work associate to relish crunching numbers, use quantitative information when attempting to persuade that person. Instead of using phrases such as "most people," say "about 65 percent of people."

4. If you perceive a work associate to have high creative intelligence, solicit his or her input on problems requiring a creative solution. Use statements such as "Here's a problem that requires a sharp, creative mind, so I've come to you."

5. If you perceive a work associate to have low emotional intelligence, explain your feelings and attitudes clearly. The person may not get the point of hints and indirect expressions.

To start putting these guidelines into practice, do the role-play in Skill-Building Exercise 1-2.

VALUES AS A SOURCE OF INDIVIDUAL DIFFERENCES

Another group of factors influencing how a person behaves on the job is that person's values and beliefs. A **value** refers to the importance a person attaches to something. Values are also tied to the enduring belief that one's mode of conduct is better than another mode of conduct. If you believe that good interpersonal relations are the most important part of your life, your humanistic values are strong. Similarly, you may think that people who are not highly concerned about interpersonal relations have poor values.

Values are closely tied in with **ethics,** or the moral choices a person makes. A person's values influence which kinds of behaviors he or she believes are ethical. Ethics convert values into action. An executive who strongly values profits might not find it unethical to raise prices higher than needed to cover additional costs. Another executive who strongly values family life might suggest that the company invest money in an on-site childcare center. Ethics is such an important part of interpersonal relations in organizations that the topic receives separate mention in Chapter 6.

value The importance a person attaches to something.

ethics The moral choices a person makes. Also, what is good and bad, right and wrong, just and unjust, and what people should do.

ADAPTING TO PEOPLE OF
DIFFERENT MENTAL ABILITY

The Mentally Sharp Coworker: One student plays the role of a worker who needs to learn a new software package in a hurry. You intend to approach a particular coworker who is known for having a sharp mind. You wonder whether this highly intelligent person will be interested in your problem. The other person plays the role of the computer whiz who ordinarily does not like to solve problems for people that they should be able to solve themselves. The first worker meets with the second to discuss loading the software.

The Mentally Average Team Member: One student plays the role of a supervisor who needs to explain to a team member how to calculate discounts for customers. To the supervisor's knowledge, the team member does not know how to calculate discounts, although it will be an important part of the team member's new job. The supervisor and the team member get together for a session on calculating discounts.

Differences in values among people often stem from age, or generational, differences. Workers over age 50, in general, may have different values than people who are much younger. These age differences in values have often been seen as a clash between Baby Boomers and members of Generation X and Generation Y. According to the stereotype, Boomers see Generation Xers and Yers as disrespectful of rules, not willing to pay their dues, and being disloyal to employers. Generation Xers and Yers see Boomers as worshipping hierarchy (layers of authority), being overcautious, and wanting to preserve the status quo.

Table 1-1 summarizes these stereotypes with the understanding that massive group stereotypes like this are only partially accurate because there are literally millions of exceptions. For example, many Baby Boomers are fascinated with technology, and many Generation Yers like hierarchy.

HOW VALUES ARE LEARNED

People acquire values in the process of growing up, and many values are learned by the age of four. One important way we acquire values is through observing others, or modeling. Models can be teachers, friends, brothers, sisters, and even public figures. If we identify with a particular person, the probability is high that we will develop some of his or her major values.

Derek, a restaurant owner, was known for his ability to offer employment to troubled teenagers and then help them get back on their feet. Asked why he put so much effort into helping youths in trouble, he explained, "I was greatly influenced as a boy by my Uncle Clarence. I was going through troubled times—stealing from a variety store and getting drunk on beer.

"Uncle Clarence took me under his wing and spent hours listening to my problems. He would take me fishing and ask if there was anything he could do to help me. Finally, I straightened out. I decided that I would be like Uncle Clarence if someday I had a chance to help young people."

Another major way values are learned is through the communication of attitudes. The attitudes that we hear expressed directly or indirectly help shape our values. Assume that using credit to purchase goods and services was considered an evil

TABLE 1-1 Value Stereotypes for Several Generations of Workers

Baby Boomers (1946–1964)	Generation X (1965–1977)	Generation Y (1978–1984)
Use technology as necessary tool	Techno-savvy	Techno-savvy
Appreciate hierarchy	Teamwork very important	Teamwork very important
Tolerate teams but value independent work	Dislike hierarchy	Dislike hierarchy
Strong career orientation	Strive for work–life balance but will work long hours for now	Strive for work–life balance but will work long hours for now
More loyalty to organization	Loyalty to own career and profession	Believe in informality
		Want to strike it rich quickly
Favor diplomacy	Candid in conversation	Ultracandid in conversation
Favor old economy	Appreciate old and new economy	Prefer the new economy
Expect a bonus based on performance	Would appreciate a signing bonus	Expected a signing bonus before the dot-com crash
Believe that issues should be formally discussed	Believe that feedback can be administered informally	Believe that feedback can be given informally, even on the fly

Sources: Several of the ideas in this table are from Robert McGarvey, "The Coming of Gen X Bosses," *Entrepreneur,* November 1999, pp. 60–64; Joanne M. Glenn, "Teaching the Net Generation," *Business Education Forum,* February 2000, pp. 6–14; Anita Bruzzese, "There Needn't Be a Generation Gap," Gannett News Service, April 22, 2002.

practice among your family and friends. You might therefore hold negative values about installment purchases. Unstated but implied attitudes may also shape your values. If key people in your life showed no enthusiasm when you talked about work accomplishments, you might not place such a high value on achieving outstanding results. If, however, your family and friends centered their lives on their careers, you might develop similar values. (Or you might rebel against such a value because it interfered with a more relaxed lifestyle.) Many key values are also learned through religion and thus become the basis for society's morals. For example, most religions emphasize treating other people fairly and kindly. To "knife somebody in the back" is considered immoral both on and off the job.

CLARIFYING YOUR VALUES

The values that you develop early in life are directly related to the kind of person you are and to the quality of the relationships you form.[21] Recognition of this fact has led to exercises designed to help people clarify and understand some of their own values. Self-Assessment Quiz 1-4 gives you an opportunity to clarify your values.

THE MESH BETWEEN INDIVIDUAL AND JOB VALUES

Under the best of circumstances, the values of employees mesh with those required by the job. When this state of congruence exists, job performance is likely to be higher. Suppose that Jacquelyn strongly values giving people with limited formal education an opportunity to work and avoid being placed on welfare. So she takes a job as a manager of a dollar store that employs many people who would ordinarily

SELF-ASSESSMENT QUIZ 1–4

CLARIFYING YOUR VALUES

Directions: Rank from 1 to 20 the importance of the following values to you as a person. The most important value on the list receives a rank of 1; the least important a rank of 20. Use the space next to "Other" if the list has left out an important value in your life.

11	Having my own place to live
15	Having one or more children
13	Having an interesting job and career
9	Owning a car
16	Having a good relationship with coworkers
1	Having good health
17	Sending and receiving e-mail messages, and using the Web
14	Being able to stay in frequent contact with friends by cell phone
19	Watching my favorite television shows
12	Participating in sports or other pastimes
18	Following a sports team, athlete, music group, or other entertainer
2	Being a religious person
8	Helping people less fortunate than myself
6	Loving and being loved by another person
10	Having physical intimacy with another person
7	Making an above-average income
4	Being in good physical condition
3	Being a knowledgeable, informed person
5	Completing my formal education
	Other

1. Discuss and compare your ranking of these values with the person next to you.
2. Perhaps your class, assisted by your instructor, can arrive at a class average on each of these values. How does your ranking compare to the class ranking?
3. Look back at your own ranking. Does it surprise you?
4. Are there any surprises in the class ranking? Which values did you think would be highest and lowest?

have limited opportunity for employment. Jacquelyn is satisfied because her employer and she share a similar value.

When the demands made by the organization or a superior clash with the basic values of the individual, that person suffers from **person–role conflict**. The individual wants to obey orders, but does not want to perform an act that seems inconsistent with his or her values. A situation such as this might occur when an employee is asked to produce a product that he or she feels is unsafe or of no value to society.

A manager of a commercial weight-reduction center resigned after two years of service. The owners pleaded with her to stay, based on her excellent performance. The man-

person–role conflict
The situation that occurs when the demands made by the organization clash with the basic values of the individual.

ager replied, "Sorry, I think my job is immoral. We sign up all these people with great expectations of losing weight permanently. Most of them do achieve short-term weight reduction. My conflict is that over 90 percent of our clientele regain the weight they lost once they go back to eating standard food. I think we are deceiving them by not telling them up front that they will most likely gain back the weight they lose."

GUIDELINES FOR USING VALUES TO ENHANCE INTERPERSONAL RELATIONS

◀ Learning Objective 5

Values are intangible and abstract, and thus not easy to manipulate to help improve your interpersonal relations on the job. Despite their vagueness, values are an important driver of interpersonal effectiveness. Ponder the following guidelines:

1. Establish the values you will use in your relationships with others on the job, and then use those values as firm guidelines in working with others. For example, following the Golden Rule, you might establish the value of treating other people as you want to be treated. You would then not lie to others to gain personal advantage, and you would not backstab your rivals.

2. Establish the values that will guide you as an employee. When you believe that your values are being compromised, express your concern to your manager in a tactful and constructive manner. You might say to your manager, "Sorry, I choose not to tell our customers that our competitor's product is inferior just to make a sale. I choose not to say this because our competitor makes a fine product. But what I will say is that our service is exceptional."

3. Remember that many values are a question of opinion, not a statement of being right versus wrong. If you believe that your values are right, and anybody who disagrees is wrong, you will have frequent conflict. For example, you may believe that the most important value top managers should have is to bring shareholders a high return on their investment. Another worker believes that profits are important, but providing jobs for as many people as possible is an equally important value. Both of you have a good point, but neither is right or wrong. So it is better to discuss these differences rather than hold grudges because of them.

To help you put these guidelines into practice, do Skill-Building Exercise 1-3. Remember, however, that being skilled at using your values requires day-by-day monitoring.

SKILL-BUILDING EXERCISE 1-3

THE VALUE-CONFLICT ROLE-PLAY

One student plays the role of a company president who makes an announcement to the group that the company must soon lay off 10 percent of the workforce in order to remain profitable. The president also points out that the company has a policy against laying off good performers. He or she then asks four of the company managers to purposely give below-average performance ratings to 10 percent of employees. In this way, laying them off will fit company policy.

Four other students play the role of the company managers who receive this directive. If such manipulation of performance evaluations clashes with your values, engage in a dialogue with your manager expressing your conflict. Remember, however, that you may not want to jeopardize your job.

Conduct this group role-play for about seven minutes, with other class members observing and being prepared to offer feedback.

SUMMARY

Individual differences are among the most important factors influencing the behavior of people in the workplace. Knowing how to respond to such differences is the cornerstone of effective interpersonal relations.

Personality is one of the major sources of individual differences. The eight major personality factors described in this chapter are neuroticism, extraversion, openness, agreeableness, conscientiousness, self-monitoring of behavior, risk taking and thrill seeking, and optimism. Depending on the job, any one of these personality factors can be important for success, and they also affect interpersonal relations.

Personality also influences a person's cognitive style, or the mental processes used to perceive and make judgments from information. According to the Myers-Briggs Type Indicator (MBTI), four dimensions of psychological functioning are as follows: introverted versus extraverted; thinking versus feeling; sensing versus intuiting; and judging versus perceiving. Combining the four types with each other results in 16 personality types, such as a person being a conceptualizer, traditionalist, visionary, or organizer. For example, the organizer (ESTJ) scores high on extraversion, sensing, thinking, and judging.

Mental ability, or intelligence, is one of the major sources of individual differences that affects job performance and behavior. Understanding the nature of intelligence contributes to effective interpersonal relations in organizations. For example, understanding that different types of intelligence exist will help a person appreciate the strengths of people.

Intelligence consists of many components. The traditional perspective is that intelligence includes a general factor *(g)* along with special factors *(s)* that contribute to problem-solving ability. A related perspective is that intelligence consists of seven components: verbal comprehension, word fluency, numerical acuity, spatial perception, memory, perceptual speed, and inductive reasoning.

To overcome the idea that intelligence involves mostly the ability to solve abstract problems, the triarchic theory of intelligence has been proposed. According to this theory, intelligence has three subtypes: analytical, creative, and practical (street smarts included). Another approach to understanding mental ability contends that people have multiple intelligences, or faculties, including linguistic, logical-mathematical, musical, spatial, bodily-kinesthetic, intrapersonal, interpersonal, and naturalist.

Emotional intelligence refers to factors other than traditional mental ability that influence a person's success. The four components of emotional intelligence are (1) self-awareness, (2) self-management, (3) social awareness, and (4) relationship management.

Values and beliefs are another set of factors that influence behavior on the job, including interpersonal relations. Values are closely tied in with ethics. People acquire values in the process of growing up and modeling others. The values a person develops early in life are directly related to the kind of adult he or she becomes and to the quality of relationships formed. Values-clarification exercises help people identify their values. Person–role conflict occurs when the demands made by an organization or a superior clash with the basic values of an individual.

QUESTIONS FOR DISCUSSION AND REVIEW

1. Why is responding to individual differences considered to be the cornerstone of effective interpersonal relations?

2. How can knowledge of major personality factors help a person form better interpersonal relations on the job?

3. In what way might the personality trait of optimism versus pessimism be relevant for job performance?

4. Suppose a high self-monitoring person is attending a company-sponsored social event and that person dislikes such events. How is he or she likely to behave?

5. Identify two business occupations for which a high propensity for risk taking and thrill seeking would be an asset.

6. What kind of problems would a *sensing* type individual prefer to tackle?

7. Which of the seven components of traditional intelligence represents your best mental aptitude? What is your evidence?

8. How could you use the concept of multiple intelligences to raise the self-esteem of people who did not consider themselves to be very smart?

9. Why is emotional intelligence so important for success in business?

10. How can you use information about a person's values to help you relate more effectively to him or her?

GO TO THE WEB

http://www.iVillage.com
(See the quizzes relating to memory loss because they provide clues to keeping your mental ability in top form.)

http://www.queendom.com
(This site provides many tests and quizzes related to cognitive factors and personality.)

AN INTERPERSONAL RELATIONS CASE PROBLEM

MULTIPLE INTELLIGENCES IN THE OFFICE

Liz Russo is the general manager of the Student Loan Division of a major bank. She prides herself on being a modern manager who searches continuously for new ways to manage the student loan business and to manage people. Recently she attended a talk by Harvard University psychologist Howard Gardner given to the management group at the bank. Russo and the other managers listened intently as Gardner explained his theories of intelligence.

The psychologist emphasized that managers must discard the notion that there is only one kind of intelligence. Most of the managers nodded in agreement. Gardner explained that he wants people in charge of managing human resources to recognize that there are at least eight different kinds of intelligence. People with linguistic intelligence are really good at communicating with words. If you have logical-mathematical intelligence, you can deal with abstract relationships like formulating new ideas for products. People with musical intelligence can do wonders with sounds. Those who have spatial intelligence can work well with images and designs.

People who have bodily-kinesthetic intelligence can move their bodies easily, like dancers and athletes. Individuals gifted with intrapersonal intelligence can understand their own feelings well. People with interpersonal intelligence can read other people well. And finally, people with naturalist intelligence can understand and make good use of the environment.

During a lunch following the talk, Russo said to one of the other managers, "What liberating thoughts. The way I interpret Dr. Gardner's theories, people who are talented athletes or dancers are just as intelligent as computer whizzes. It's just that they have a different kind of intelligence."

(Continued)

"Why stop there?" responded the other manager. "One of my kids is a great banjo player, but we're wondering if he'll ever make it through high school. His mom and I used to think he was mentally challenged. Now we know his intelligence is the musical type, not the logical type."

Gardner's ideas kept spinning through Russo's mind. She bought a copy of one of his books for each of her managers and asked them all to study the book carefully. Later she scheduled a half-day meeting in a hotel to discuss how to apply the idea of eight human intelligences to the Student Loan Division. Russo said to her management team, "You all seem to agree with the idea that there are eight human intelligences. Now I want us to figure out how to apply Dr. Gardner's theories to make us a more productive business."

Molly Gerbrach, the head of information systems, said with a smirk on her face, "I have a suggestion. If I hire a programmer who proves to be poor at programming, I'll just ask him or her to be the department's official musician!"

"I appreciate the humor, Molly," said Russo, "but now let's get down to business. Let's figure out how to implement these great ideas about different human intelligences."

Case Questions

1. Is Liz Russo being realistic about applying the concept of eight human intelligences to the office setting?

2. Suggest at least two ways in which the theory of eight human intelligences could be applied to improving productivity in the Student Loan Division.

AN INTERPERSONAL RELATIONS CASE PROBLEM

"WE'VE GOT TO MAKE OUR NUMBERS"

Bruce Malone works as an account manager for an office-supply company with branches in most cities of the United States. The company has two lines of business, retail and commercial. Among the many products the company sells are computers and related equipment, office furniture, copy paper, and other basic office supplies.

The retail trade is served by customers walking directly into the store or ordering online. Many of the customers are small business owners or corporate employees who work at home part of their work week. The commercial trade also does some walk-in purchasing and online ordering. However, each large customer is also assigned an account manager who calls on them periodically to discuss their needs for larger purchases such as office furniture and multiple copiers and desktop computers.

Malone is meeting his sales targets for the year despite a flat economy in the city where the office supplier is located. Shortly before Thanksgiving, Malone was analyzing his sales to estimate his performance for the year. According to his projections, his total sales would be 1 percent beyond his quota, giving him a satisfactory year. Making his quota would qualify him for a year-end bonus.

The Friday after Thanksgiving, Malone received an e-mail message from his boss Lucille Whitman requesting that the two meet Monday morning before Bruce began working with his customers. At the start of the meeting, Whitman told Malone that she had something very important to discuss with him. "Bruce, we are getting a lot of heat from corporate headquarters," Whitman began. "If we don't make our numbers [attaining the sales goals] the stock price could dip big time, and the home office executives will be in trouble. Even their bonuses will be at risk"

"I've done what I can," responded Malone. "I'm going to make my quota for the year plus a little extra margin. So I guess I'm covered. There isn't much I can do about the company as a whole."

"Let me be a little more specific," replied Whitman. "The company is in trouble, so we all have to pitch in and show better numbers for the year. What we need our account managers to do is to pump up the sales figures a little. Maybe you could count as December sales a few of the purchases your customers have planned for early January. Or maybe you could ship extra-large orders at a discount, and tell your customers they can pay as late as February or March.

"You're smart, Bruce. Beef up your sales figures for the year a little because we have got to make our numbers."

"Lucille, maybe I could work extra hard to pull in a few more sales in the next four weeks. But I would feel rotten faking my sales figures for December. I'm a professional."

With an angry tone, Whitman responded, "I don't care what you call yourself; we have got to make our numbers. Get back to me soon with your plan for increasing your numbers for December."

Case Questions

1. What is the nature of the conflict Bruce Malone is facing?
2. What type of values is Lucille Whitman demonstrating?
3. What do you recommend Bruce should have done to work his way out of the problem he was facing?
4. Is Bruce too naïve for a career in business?

INTERPERSONAL SKILLS ROLE-PLAY

The "Making the Numbers" Conundrum

Here is an opportunity to practice dealing with the type of conflict facing Bruce Malone. One person plays Bruce who has a follow-up conversation with Lucille Whitman about improving his December sales figures by less than straightforward means. Another student plays the role of Lucille Whitman who is focused on the corporate demands of "making the numbers." Bruce wants to communicate clearly how uncomfortable he feels about fudging the facts, while Lucille feels enormous pressure to meet the demands of the executive group. Ideally, the two role-players will reach a solution acceptable to both sides.

CHAPTER 2

Developing Teamwork Skills

Learning Objectives

After reading and studying this chapter and doing the exercises you should be able to

1. Identify several types of teams in organizations.
2. Understand the advantages and disadvantages of teams.
3. Identify various team member roles.
4. Be ready to apply interpersonal-related tactics for effective team play.
5. Be ready to apply task-related tactics for effective team play.

Baltimore's Chesapeake Habitat for Humanity (CHH) is a nonprofit organization that renovates vacant houses and sells them at noninterest mortgage rates to low-income home buyers. This year, the nonprofit's 11 employees will oversee 2,000 local volunteers renovating 11 homes.

But CHH is renovating much more than houses; it's also updating its business model. In June, CHH launched its own for-profit venture called Team-Builds, where corporate teams pay $7,500 for an all-day team-building session with an organization development consultant while working together to rebuild an old house. Amid nail guns and drywall, teams will work out their problems and increase their competitiveness.[1]

Discussion Question

1. Why would companies spend so much time and money developing teamwork skills? Doesn't everybody know how to be a team player?

The enthusiasm of companies to send groups of workers to TeamBuilds illustrates the importance of teamwork in organizations. Many firms rely more on teamwork than on individuals acting alone to accomplish work. To be successful in the modern organization, it is therefore necessary to be an effective team player. You have to work smoothly with other members of the team to accomplish your goals. Teamwork is more important as people work their way up through the organization. Executives, such as CEOs, preach teamwork but tend to dominate meetings and make more decisions by themselves.[2]

The challenges a team member faces come to light when the true nature of a team is recognized. A team is a special type of group. Team members have complementary skills and are committed to a common purpose, a set of performance goals, and an approach to the task. In other words, the members of a team work together smoothly, and all pull in the same direction. A workplace team should be more like an effective athletic team than a group of individuals out for individual glory.[3]

This chapter gives you the information, insights, and preliminary practice necessary to develop effective teamwork skills. Self-Assessment Quiz 2-1 will help you assess your current mental readiness to be a contributing team member.

> **Team** A small number of people with complementary skills who are committed to a common purpose, set of performance goals, and approach for which they hold themselves mutually accountable.

SELF-ASSESSMENT QUIZ 2-1

TEAM PLAYER ATTITUDES

Directions: Describe how well you agree with each of the following statements, using the following scale: disagree strongly (DS); disagree (D); neutral (N); agree (A); agree strongly (AS). Circle the number in the appropriate column.

	DS	D	N	A	AS
1. I am at my best when working alone.	5	4	3	2	1
2. I have belonged to clubs and teams ever since I was a child.	1	2	3	4	5
3. It takes far too long to get work accomplished with a group.	5	4	3	2	1
4. I like the friendship of working in a group.	1	2	3	4	5
5. I would prefer to run a one-person business than to be a member of a large firm.	5	4	3	2	1
6. It's difficult to trust others in the group on key assignments.	5	4	3	2	1
7. Encouraging others comes to me naturally.	1	2	3	4	5
8. I like the give-and-take of ideas that is possible in a group.	1	2	3	4	5
9. It is fun for me to share responsibility with other group members.	1	2	3	4	5
10. Much more can be accomplished by a team than by the same number of people working alone.	1	2	3	4	5

Total Score _____

Scoring and Interpretation: Add the numbers you circled to obtain your total score.

41–50 You have strong positive attitudes toward being a team member and working cooperatively with other members.

30–40 You have moderately favorable attitudes toward being a team member and working cooperatively with other members.

10–29 You much prefer working by yourself to being a team member. To work effectively in a company that emphasizes teamwork, you may need to develop more positive attitudes toward working jointly with others.

TYPES OF TEAMS

Learning Objective 1 ▶ All teams in the workplace have the common element of people working together cooperatively and members possessing a mix of skills. Nevertheless, many specific types of work teams can be identified. Successful people will usually have the opportunity to be a member of several different types of teams.

Four representative work teams are self-managing work teams, cross-functional teams, virtual teams and crews. Projects, task forces, and committees are similar in design to cross-functional teams, so they do not receive separate mention here. No matter what label the team carries, its broad purpose is to contribute to a *collaborative workplace* in which people help each other achieve constructive goals. The idea is for workers to collaborate (a high level of cooperation) rather than compete with or prevent others from getting their work done.

As teams have become more common in the workplace, effort has been directed toward specifying the skills and knowledge a person needs to function effectively on a team, particularly a self-managing work team. Self-Assessment Quiz 2-2 presents a representative listing of team skills as perceived by employers.

SELF-MANAGING WORK TEAMS

The best-known work team is a group of workers who take much of the responsibility for managing their own work. The same type of team is referred to as a self-managing work team, a self-directing work team, a production work team, or a team. A **self-managing work team** is a small group of employees responsible for managing and performing technical tasks to deliver a product or service to an external or internal customer.[4] The vast majority of large- and medium-size firms make some use of self-managing work teams. Work teams are used in a wide variety of activities including producing motorcycles, telephone directories, or a major component for a large computer.

self-managing work team A small group of employees responsible for managing and performing technical tasks to deliver a product or service to an external or internal customer.

Members of a self-managing work team typically work together on an ongoing, day-by-day basis, thus differentiating it from a task force or a committee. The work team is often given total responsibility for or "ownership" of an entire product or service, such as producing a telephone directory. At other times, the team is given responsibility for a major chunk of a job, such as building an airplane engine (but not the entire airplane).

A major hurdle in forming self-managing teams is to help employees overcome the attitude reflected in the statement "I'm not paid to think." Work teams rely less on supervisors and more on the workers assuming more responsibilities for managing their own activities. For example, work team members may be required to discipline other team members who have attendance, performance, or behavioral problems.[5]

As with all teams, mutual trust among members contributes to team effectiveness. A study conducted with business students, however, showed that if the members trust each other too much they may not monitor (check up on) each other's work enough. As a result, group performance will suffer. This problem of too much trust surfaces primarily when the team members have individual assignments that do not bring them into frequent contact with each other.[6] An example of an individual, or autonomous, project would be preparing a statistical report that would later be given to the group.

cross-functional team A work group composed of workers from different specialties, and about the same organizational level, who come together to accomplish a task.

CROSS-FUNCTIONAL TEAMS

It is common practice for teams to be composed of workers from different specialties. A **cross-functional team** is a work group composed of workers from different specialties, who come together to accomplish a task. The purpose of the cross-functional team is to get workers from different specialties to blend their talents toward accomplishing a task that requires such a mix.

SELF-ASSESSMENT QUIZ 2-2

TEAM SKILLS

A variety of skills are required to be an effective member of various types of teams. Several different business firms use the skill inventory here to help guide team members toward the competencies they need to become high-performing team members.

Directions: Review each team skill listed and rate your skill level for each one using the following classification:

   S = strong (capable and comfortable with effectively implementing the skill)

   M = moderate (demonstrated skill in the past)

   B = basic (minimum ability in this area)

   N = not applicable (not relevant to the type of work I do)

Communication skills	*Skill level (S, M, B, or N)*
Speak effectively	_____
Foster open communications	_____
Listen to others	_____
Deliver presentations	_____
Prepare written communication	_____
Self-management skills	
Act with integrity	_____
Demonstrate adaptability	_____
Engage in personal development	_____
Strive for results	_____
Display a commitment to work	_____
Thought process skills	
Innovate solutions to problems	_____
Use sound judgment	_____
Analyze issues	_____
Think "outside the box"	_____
Organizational skills	
Know the business	_____
Use technical/functional expertise	_____
Use financial/quantitative data	_____
Strategic (broad business perspective) skills	
Recognize "big picture" impact	_____
Promote corporate citizenship	_____
Focus on customer needs	_____
Commit to quality	_____
Manage profitability	_____

Interpretation: There is no scoring key for this questionnaire. Its purpose is to raise your awareness of the types of skills that are required to be a successful team member in business.

A typical application of a cross-functional team would be to develop a new product such as a video cell phone. Among the specialties needed on such a team would be computer science, engineering, manufacturing, industrial design, marketing, and finance. (The finance person would help guide the team toward producing a video cell phone that could be sold at a profit.) When members from different specialties work together, they can take into account each other's perspectives when making their contribution. For example, if the manufacturing representative knows that a video cell phone must sell for about one-half the price of a plasma screen TV, then he or she will have to build the device inexpensively. A major advantage of cross-functional teams for product development is that they enhance communication across groups, thereby saving time. In addition to product development, cross-functional teams are used for such purposes as improving quality, reducing costs, and running a company (in the form of a top management team).

To perform well on a cross-functional team a person would have to think in terms of the good of the larger organization, rather than in terms of his or her own specialty. For example, a manufacturing technician might say, "If I proposed using expensive components for the video phone, would the product cost too much for its intended market?"

VIRTUAL TEAMS

virtual team A small group of people who conduct almost all of their collaborative work by electronic communication rather than face-to-face meetings.

Some teams conduct most of their work by sending electronic messages to each other rather than conducting face-to-face meetings. A **virtual team** is a small group of people who conduct almost all of their collaborative work by electronic communication rather than face-to-face meetings. E-mail, including IM (instant messaging), is the usual medium for sharing information and conducting meetings. *Groupware* is another widely used approach to conducting an electronic meeting. Using groupware, several people can edit a document at the same time, or in sequence. Desktop videoconferencing is another technological advance that facilitates the virtual team. Electronic brainstorming, as described in Chapter 3, is well suited for a virtual team.

Most high-tech companies make some use of virtual teams and electronic meetings. Strategic alliances in which geographically dispersed companies work with each other are a natural for virtual teams. It is less expensive for the field technician in Iceland to hold an electronic meeting with her counterparts in South Africa, Mexico, and California than it is to bring them all together in one physical location. Virtual teams are sometimes the answer to the challenge of hiring workers with essential skills who do not want to relocate. With team members geographically dispersed, precise communications are all the more important for virtual teams. The virtual team members usually need a formal document outlining the objectives, job responsibilities, and team goals. Another communication problem takes place when the virtual team is composed of both in-house workers and those in remote locations. The office-bound members become jealous of the seemingly cushy setup enjoyed by the telecommuters. One solution to this problem is for every member of the team to be given a chance to prove he or she can work off-site.[7]

Despite the efficiency of virtual teams, there are times when face-to-face interaction is necessary to deal with complex and emotional issues. Negotiating a new contract between management and a labor union, for example, is not well suited to an electronic meeting.

CREWS

crew A group of specialists each of whom have specific roles, perform brief events that are closely synchronized with each other, and repeat these events under different environmental conditions.

We are all familiar with common usage of the term *crew* in relation to such groups as those who operate airplanes, boats, and firefighting equipment. The technical meaning of the term means virtually the same thing. A **crew** is a group of specialists each of who have specific roles, perform brief events that are closely synchronized with each other, and repeat these events under different environmental conditions. A crew is identified by the technology it handles, such as an aircraft crew, or a deep-sea salvage operation. The crewmembers rarely rotate specialties, such as the flight attendant taking over for the chief pilot. (Special training and licensing would be required.) The following are several criteria of a group qualifying as a crew:[8]

- Clear roles and responsibilities
- Workflow well established before anyone joins the team
- Careful coordination required with other members in order to perform the task
- Group needs to be in a specific environment to complete its task
- Different people can join the group without interfering with its operation or mission

Because of the specialized roles they play, and the essential tasks they perform, much is expected of crews. The future of crews is promising. For example, computer-virus-fighting crews would be a welcome addition to business and society. Mutual trust is especially important in a crew because good cooperation could save one's life, such as in a firefighting crew.

THE ADVANTAGES AND DISADVANTAGES OF TEAMS AND TEAMWORK

Groups have always been the building blocks of organizations. Yet groups and teams have recently grown in importance as the basic unit for organizing work. In an attempt to cope with numerous changes in the outside world, many organizations have granted teams increased independence and flexibility. Furthermore, teams are often required to work more closely with customers and suppliers. ◀ Learning Objective 2

The increased acceptance of teams suggests that group work offers many advantages. Nevertheless, it is useful to specify several of these advantages and also examine the potential problems of groups. Being aware of these potential pitfalls can often help a person avoid them. These same advantages and disadvantages also apply to group decision making, to be described in Chapter 3.

ADVANTAGES OF GROUP WORK AND TEAMWORK

Group work and group decision making offer several advantages over individual effort. If several knowledgeable people are brought into the decision-making process, a number of worthwhile possibilities may be uncovered. It is also possible to gain synergy, whereby the group's total output exceeds the sum of each individual's contribution. For example, it would be a rare person working alone who could build a racing car.

synergy A situation in which the group's total output exceeds the sum of each individual's contribution.

Group decision making is also helpful in gaining acceptance and commitment. The argument is that people who contribute to making a decision will feel some ownership about implementing the decision. Team members often evaluate each other's thinking, so the team is likely to avoid major errors. An advertising specialist was developing an advertising campaign to attract seniors to live in a retirement community. The proposed ads had photographs of senior citizens engaged in playing shuffleboard, visiting the pharmacy, and sleeping in a hammock. Another team member on the project pointed out that many seniors perceive themselves to be energetic and youthful. Ads emphasizing advanced age might therefore backfire. A successful advertising campaign was then developed that featured seniors in more youthful activities such as jogging and dancing.

Working in teams and groups also enhances the job satisfaction of members. Being a member of a work group makes it possible to satisfy more needs than working alone. Among these needs are affiliation, security, self-esteem, and self-fulfillment. (Chapter 9 provides more details about psychological needs.)

DISADVANTAGES OF GROUP WORK AND TEAMWORK

Group activity has some potential disadvantages for both individuals and the organization. Teams and other groups often waste time because they talk too much and act too little. Committees appear to suffer from more inaction than teams. Abigail Johnson, president of Fidelity Investments, the financial services giant, says that committees are not effective decision makers. "They have tended to be slow and overly risk averse. Even worse, I believe, they can drain an organization of talent, because the group can only be as good as the average."[9] A major problem is that members face pressures to conform to group standards of performance and conduct, as just implied. Some teams might shun a person who is much more productive than his or her coworkers. Shirking of individual responsibility is another problem frequently noted in groups. Unless work is assigned carefully to each team member, an under-motivated person can often squeeze by without contributing his or her fair share to a group effort.

social loafing The psychological term for shirking individual responsibility in a group setting.

Social loafing is the psychological term for shirking individual responsibility in a group setting. The social loafer risks being ostracized (shunned) by the group but may be willing to pay the price rather than work hard. Loafing of this type is sometimes found in groups such as committees and project teams. Have you ever encountered a social loafer on a group project at school?

At their worst, teams and other groups foster conflict on the job. People within the work group often bicker about such matters as doing a fair share of the undesirable tasks within the department. Cohesive work groups can also become xenophobic (fearful of outsiders). As a consequence, they may grow to dislike other groups and enter into conflict with them. A customer service group might put considerable effort into showing up a sales group because the latter makes promises to customers that the customer service group cannot keep. For example, a sales representative might promise that a customer can get a loaner if his or her equipment needs repair, although customer service has no such policy.

groupthink A deterioration of mental efficiency, reality testing, and moral judgment in the interest of group solidarity.

A well-publicized disadvantage of group decision making is groupthink, a deterioration of mental efficiency, reality testing, and moral judgment in the interest of group solidarity. Simply put, groupthink is an extreme form of consensus. The group atmosphere values getting along more than getting things done. The group thinks as a unit, believes it is impervious to outside criticism, and begins to have illusions about its own invincibility. As a consequence, the group loses its powers of critical analysis.[10] Groupthink appears to have contributed to several of the major financial scandals of the previous decade. Members of top management got together to vote themselves huge bonuses just before filing bankruptcy for their company. Several of the executives, including a few from Enron Corporation, were later sent to prison for their outrageous decisions.

Two conditions are important for overcoming the potential disadvantages of teams and groups. First, the members must strive to act like a team,[11] following some of the suggestions given in the upcoming pages. Second, the task given to the group should require collective effort instead of being a task that could better be performed by individuals. For example, an international business specialist would probably learn to conjugate verbs in a foreign language better by working alone than on a team. What is your opinion on this issue? Figure 2-1 presents more information about key factors associated with effective work teams and groups. The more of these factors that are present, the more likely it is that a given team or group will be productive.

- The team has clear-cut goals linked to organizational goals so that group members feel connected to the entire organization. Group members are empowered so they learn to think for themselves rather than expecting a supervisor to solve all the difficult problems. At the same time, the group believes it has the authority to solve a variety of problems without first obtaining approval from management.

- Group members are assigned work they perceive to be challenging, exciting, and rewarding. As a consequence, the work is self-rewarding.

- Members depend on one another to accomplish tasks, and work toward a common goal.

- Members learn to think "outside the box" (are creative).

- Members receive extensive training in technical knowledge, problem-solving skills, and interpersonal skills.

- Members inspect their own work for quality.

- Members receive part of their pay related to team or group incentives rather than strictly based on individual performance.

- Group size is generally about 6 people, rather than 10 or more.

- Team members have good intelligence and personality factors, such as conscientiousness and pride that contribute to good performance.

- There is honest and open communication among group members and with other groups in the organization.

- Members have the philosophy of working as a team—25 brains, not just 50 hands.

- Members are familiar with their jobs, coworkers, and the work environment. This experience adds to their expertise. The beneficial effects of experience may diminish after awhile because the team needs fresh ideas and approaches.

- The team has emotional intelligence in the sense that it builds relationships both inside and outside the team. Included in emotional intelligence are norms that establish mutual trust among members, a feeling of group identity, and group efficacy.

FIGURE 2-1 Key Characteristics of Effective Teams and Work Groups

Sources: Ben Nagler, "Recasting Employees into Teams," *Workforce,* January 1998, p. 104; Gerben S. Van Der Vegt et al., "Patterns of Interdependence in Work Teams: A Two-Level Investigation of the Relations with Job and Team Satisfaction," *Personnel Psychology,* Spring 2001, pp. 51–69; Shawn L. Berman, Vanessa Urch Druskat, and Steven B. Wolff, "Building the Emotional Intelligence of Groups," *Harvard Business Review,* March 2001, pp. 80–90; Claus W. Langred, "Too Much of a Good Thing? Negative Effects of High Trust and Individual Autonomy in Self-Managing Work Teams," *Academy of Management Journal,* June 2004, pp. 385–389.

TEAM MEMBER ROLES

A major challenge in learning to become an effective team member is to choose the ◄ Learning Objective 3 right roles to occupy. A role is a tendency to behave, contribute, and relate to others in a particular way. If you carry out positive roles, you will be perceived as a contributor to team effort. If you neglect carrying out these roles, you will be perceived as a poor contributor. Self-Assessment Quiz 2-3 will help you evaluate your present inclinations toward occupying effective roles as a team member. In this section we describe a number of the most frequently observed positive roles played by team members. [12] We will also mention a group of negative roles. The description will be followed by an activity in which the roles can be practiced.

SELF-ASSESSMENT QUIZ 2-3

TEAM PLAYER ROLES

Directions: For each of the following statements about team activity, check *mostly agree* or *mostly disagree*. If you have not experienced such a situation, imagine how you would act or think if placed in that situation. In responding to the statements, assume that you are taking the questionnaire with the intent of learning something about yourself.

	Mostly agree	*Mostly disagree*
1. It is rare that I ever miss a team meeting.	_____	_____
2. I regularly compliment team members when they do something exceptional.	_____	_____
3. Whenever I can, I avoid being the notetaker at a team meeting.	_____	_____
4. From time to time, other team members come to me for advice on technical matters.	_____	_____
5. I like to hide some information from other team members so I can be in control.	_____	_____
6. I welcome new team members coming to me for advice and learning the ropes.	_____	_____
7. My priorities come first, which leaves me with very little time to help other team members.	_____	_____
8. During a team meeting, it is not unusual for several other people at a time to look toward me for my opinion.	_____	
9. If I think the team is moving in an unethical direction, I will say so explicitly.	_____	_____
10. Rarely will I criticize the progress of the team even if I think such criticism is deserved.	_____	_____
11. It is typical for me to summarize the progress in a team meeting, even if not asked.	_____	_____
12. To conserve time, I attempt to minimize contact with my teammates outside our meetings.	_____	_____
13. I intensely dislike going along with a consensus decision if the decision runs contrary to my thoughts on the issue.	_____	_____
14. I rarely remind teammates of our mission statement as we go about our work.	_____	_____
15. Once I have made up my mind on an issue facing the team, I am unlikely to be persuaded in another direction.	_____	_____
16. I am willing to accept negative feedback from team members.	_____	_____
17. Just to get a new member of the team involved, I will ask his or her opinion.	_____	_____
18. Even if the team has decided on a course of action, I am not hesitant to bring in new information that supports another position.	_____	_____
19. Quite often I talk negatively about one team member to another.	_____	_____

	Mostly agree	Mostly disagree
20. My teammates are almost a family to me because I am truly concerned about their welfare.	_____	_____
21. When it seems appropriate, I joke and kid with teammates.	_____	_____
22. My contribution to team tasks is as important to me as my individual work.	_____	_____
23. From time to time I have pointed out to the team how we can all improve in reaching our goals.	_____	_____
24. I will fight to the last when the team does not support my viewpoint and wants to move toward consensus.	_____	_____
25. I will confront the team if I believe that the members are thinking too much alike.	_____	_____
Total Score	_____	

Scoring and Interpretation: Give yourself one point ($+1$) for each statement you gave in agreement with the keyed answer. The keyed answer indicates carrying out a positive, as opposed to a negative, role.

Question number	Positive role answer	Question number	Positive role answer
1.	Mostly agree	14.	Mostly disagree
2.	Mostly agree	15.	Mostly disagree
3.	Mostly disagree	16.	Mostly agree
4.	Mostly agree	17.	Mostly agree
5.	Mostly disagree	18.	Mostly agree
6.	Mostly agree	19.	Mostly disagree
7.	Mostly disagree	20.	Mostly agree
8.	Mostly agree	21.	Mostly agree
9.	Mostly agree	22.	Mostly agree
10.	Mostly disagree	23.	Mostly agree
11.	Mostly agree	24.	Mostly disagree
12.	Mostly disagree	25.	Mostly agree
13.	Mostly disagree		

20–25 You carry out a well-above-average number of positive team roles. Behavior of this type contributes substantially to being an effective team player. Study the information in this chapter to build upon your already laudable sensitivity to occupying various positive roles within the team.

10–19 You carry out an average number of positive team roles. Study carefully the roles described in this chapter to search for ways to carry out a greater number of positive roles.

0–9 You carry out a substantially above average number of negative team roles. If becoming an effective team player is important to you, you will have to diligently search for ways to play positive team roles. Study the information in this chapter carefully.

According to the role theory developed by R. Meredith Belbin and his group of researchers, there are nine frequent roles occupied by team members. All of these roles are influenced to some extent by an individual's personality.

1. **Plant.** The plant is creative, imaginative, and unorthodox. Such a person solves difficult problems. A potential weakness of this role is that the person tends to ignore fine details and becomes too immersed in the problem to communicate effectively.

2. **Resource investigator.** The resource investigator is extroverted, enthusiastic, and communicates freely with other team members. He or she will explore opportunities and develop valuable contacts. A potential weakness of this role is that the person can be overly optimistic and may lose interest after the initial enthusiasm wanes.

3. **Coordinator.** The coordinator is mature, confident, and a natural team leader. He or she clarifies goals, promotes decision making, and delegates effectively. A downside to occupying this role is that the person might be seen as manipulative and controlling. Some coordinators delegate too much by asking others to do some of the work they (the coordinators) should be doing.

4. **Shaper.** The shaper is challenging, dynamic, and thrives under pressure. He or she will use determination and courage to overcome obstacles. A potential weakness of the shaper is that he or she can be easily provoked and may ignore the feelings of others.

5. **Monitor-evaluator.** The monitor-evaluator is even tempered, engages in strategic (big picture and long-term) thinking, and makes accurate judgments. He or she sees all the options and judges accurately. A potential weakness of this role occupant is that he or she might lack drive and the ability to inspire others.

6. **Team worker.** The team worker is cooperative, focuses on relationships, and is sensitive and diplomatic. He or she is a good listener who builds relationships, dislikes confrontation, and averts friction. A potential weakness is that the team worker can be indecisive in a crunch situation or crisis.

7. **Implementer.** The implementer is disciplined, reliable, conservative, and efficient. He or she will act quickly on ideas, and convert them into practical actions. A potential weakness is that the implementer can be inflexible and slow to see new opportunities.

8. **Completer-Finisher.** The completer-finisher is conscientious and eager to get the job done. He or she has a good eye for detail, and is effective at searching out errors. He or she can be counted on for finishing a project and delivering on time. A potential weakness is that the completer-finisher can be a worrier and reluctant to delegate.

9. **Specialist.** The specialist is a single-minded self-starter. He or she is dedicated and provides knowledge and skill in rare supply. A potential weakness of the specialist is that he or she can be stuck in a niche with little interest in other knowledge and may dwell on technicalities.

The weaknesses in the first nine roles point to problems the team leader or manager can expect to emerge, and therefore an allowance should be made. Belbin refers to these potential problems as *allowable weaknesses* because an allowance should be made for them. To illustrate, if a team worker has a tendency to be indecisive in a crisis, the team should not have high expectations of the team worker when faced with a crisis. Team workers will be the most satisfied if the crisis is predicted and decisions involving them are made before the pressure mounts.[13]

Another perspective on team roles is that team members will sometimes engage in *self-oriented roles*. Members will sometimes focus on their own needs rather than those of the group. The individual might be overly aggressive because of a personal need such as wanting a bigger budget for his or her project. The individual might hunger for recognition or power. Similarly the person might attempt to dominate the meeting, block others from contributing, or serve as a distraction. One of the ploys used by distracters recently is to engage in cell phone conversations during a meeting, blaming it on "those people who keep calling me."

The many roles just presented overlap somewhat. For example, the implementer might engage in specialist activities. Do not be concerned about the overlap. Instead, pick and choose from the many roles as the situation dictates—whether or not overlap exists. Skill-Building Exercise 2-1 gives you an opportunity to observe these roles in action. The behavior associated with the roles just described is more important than remembering the labels. For example, remembering to be creative and imaginative is more important than remembering the specific label *plant*.

SKILL-BUILDING EXERCISE 2-1

TEAM MEMBER ROLES

A team of approximately six people is formed to conduct a 20-minute meeting on a significant topic of their choosing. The possible scenarios follow:

Scenario A: Management Team.   A group of managers are pondering whether to lay off one-third of the workforce in order to increase profits. The company has had a tradition of caring for employees and regarding them as the company's most precious asset. However, the CEO has said privately that times have changed in our competitive world, and the company must do whatever possible to enhance profits. The group wants to think through the advisability of laying off one-third of the workforce, as well as explore other alternatives.

Scenario B: Group of Sports Fans.   A group of fans have volunteered to find a new team name to replace "Redskins" for the local basketball team. One person among the group of volunteers believes that the name "Redskins" should be retained because it is a compliment, rather than an insult to Native Americans. The other members of the group believe that a name change is in order, but they lack any good ideas for replacing a mascot team name that has endured for over 50 years.

Scenario C: Community Group.   A community group is attempting to launch an initiative to help battered adults and children. Opinions differ strongly as to what initiative would be truly helpful to battered adults and children. Among the alternatives are establishing a shelter for battered people, giving workshops on preventing violence, and providing self-defense training. Each group member with an idea strongly believes that he or she has come up with a workable possibility for helping with the problem of battered people.

While the team members are conducting their heated discussion, other class members make notes on which team members carry out which roles. Students should watch for the different roles as developed by Belbin and his associates, as well as the self-oriented roles. For example, students in the first row might look for examples of the plant. Use the role worksheet that follows to help make your observations. Summarize the comment that is indicative of the role. An example would

(Continued)

be noting in the shaper category: "Linda said naming the team the 'Washington Rainbows' seems like too much of an attempt to be politically correct."

Plant _____

Resource Investigator _____

Coordinator _____

Shaper _____

Monitor-Evaluator _____

Team Worker _____

Implementer _____

Completer-Finisher _____

Specialist _____

Self-Oriented Roles _____

GUIDELINES FOR THE INTERPERSONAL ASPECTS OF TEAM PLAY

Learning Objective 4 ▶ The purpose of this and the following section is to help you enhance your effectiveness as a team player by describing the skills, actions, and attitudes required to be an effective team player. You can regard these behaviors (the collective term for skills, actions, and attitudes) as goals for personal improvement. Identify the actions and attitudes for which you need the most improvement, and proceed accordingly with self-development.

One convenient method for classifying team activities in pursuit of goals is to categorize them as people-related or task-related. Remember, however, that the categorization of people- versus task-related activities is not entirely accurate. For example, if you are challenging your teammates with a difficult goal, are you focusing more on the people (offering them a motivational challenge) or the task (achieving the goal)? We begin first with people-related actions and attitudes, followed in the next section by task-related actions and attitudes.

Back to the Opening Case

Companies spend enormous amounts of time and money in developing the teamwork skills of employees who work on teams, including a variety of outdoor activities. Although almost everybody has had some experience with teams in school or athletics, most people are not natural team players—they need to develop skills. Workers who rebuild old houses to help homeless or low-income people often find the experience educational and morally uplifting. Teamwork is dramatized because working alone, for example, it is almost impossible to install a new roof.

TRUSTING TEAM MEMBERS

The cornerstone attitude of an outstanding team player is to trust team members, including the leader. Working on a team is akin to a small-business partnership. If you do not believe that the other team members have your best interests at heart, it will be difficult for you to share opinions and ideas. You will fear that others will make negative statements behind your back.

Trusting team members also includes believing that their ideas are technically sound and rational until proven otherwise. Another manifestation of trust is taking risks with others. You can take a risk by trying out one of their unproved ideas. You can also take a risk by submitting an unproved idea and not worrying about being ridiculed.

DISPLAYING A HIGH LEVEL OF COOPERATION AND COLLABORATION

Cooperation and collaboration are synonymous with teamwork. If you display a willingness to help others by working cooperatively with them, you will be regarded as a team player. If you do not cooperate with other team members, the team structure breaks down. Collaboration at a team level refers to working jointly with others to solve mutual problems. Although working with another person on a given problem may take longer than working through a problem alone, the long-term payoff is important. You have established a climate favorable to working on joint problems where collective action is necessary.

Achieving a cooperative team spirit is often a question of making the first move. Instead of grumbling about poor teamwork, take the initiative and launch a cooperative spirit in your group. Target the most individualistic, least cooperative member of the group. Ask the person for his or her input on an idea you are formulating. Thank the person, then state that you would be privileged to return the favor.

Another way of attaining good cooperation is to minimize confrontations. If you disagree with the opinion of another team member, patiently explain the reasons for your differences and look for a workable way to integrate both your ideas. A teammate might suggest, for example, that the team stay until midnight to get a project completed today. You have plans for the evening and are angered by the suggestion. Instead of lashing out at your teammate, you might say, "I agree we need to put in extra time and effort to get the job done. But why can't we spread out this extra effort over a few days? In this way those of us who cannot work until midnight this evening can still contribute."

Skill-Building Exercise 2-2 is a widely used technique for demonstrating the importance of cooperation and collaboration.

SKILL-BUILDING EXERCISE 2-2

THE SCAVENGER HUNT

The purpose of this teamwork exercise is to demonstrate the importance of cooperation and collaboration in accomplishing a task under pressure. The class is divided into teams of about five students. How much time you can devote to the task depends upon your particular class schedule. The instructor will supply each team with a list of items to find within a prescribed period of time—usually about 35 minutes. Given the time constraints, the group will usually have to conduct the hunt on campus. Following is a representative list of items to find in an on-campus scavenger hunt:

- A fountain pen
- A tie
- A brick

- A cap from a beer bottle
- A pocket knife
- A flash drive

When the groups return within 30 minutes, you hold a public discussion about what you learned about teamwork and what insights you acquired.

RECOGNIZING THE INTERESTS AND ACHIEVEMENTS OF OTHERS

A fundamental tactic for establishing yourself as a solid team player is to actively recognize the interests and achievements of others. Let others know you care about their interests. After you make a suggestion during a team meeting, ask: "Would my suggestion create any problems for anybody else?" or "How do my ideas fit into what you have planned?"

Recognizing the achievements of others is more straightforward than recognizing interests. Be prepared to compliment any tangible achievement. Give realistic compliments by making the compliment commensurate with the achievement. To do otherwise is to compromise your sincerity. For example, do not call someone a genius just because he or she showed you how to compute an exchange rate from one currency to another. Instead, you might say, "Thank you. I am very impressed by your knowledge of exchange rates."

A technique has been developed to enable the entire team to recognize the interests and achievements of others. Playing the anonymous praise game, each team member lists what he or she admires about a specific coworker. The team leader collects the responses and sends each team member the comments made about him or her. Using this technique, team members see a compilation of praise based on how coworkers perceive them. The anonymous praise game helps overcome the hesitancy some people have to praise another person face-to-face. [14]

GIVING HELPFUL CRITICISM

The outstanding team player offers constructive criticism when needed, but does so diplomatically. To do otherwise is to let down the team. A high-performance team demands sincere and tactful criticism among members. No matter how diplomatic you are, keep your ratio of criticism to praise small. Keep two time-tested principles in mind. First, attempt to criticize the person's work, not the person. It is better to say "The conclusion is missing from your analysis" than "You left out the conclusion." (The latter statement hurts because it sounds like your teammate did something wrong.)

Another key guideline for criticism is to ask a question rather than to make a declarative statement. By answering a question, the person being criticized is involved in improving his or her work. In the example at hand, it would be effective to ask, "Do you think your report would have a greater impact if it contained a conclusion?" In this way, the person being criticized contributes a judgment about the conclusion. The person has a chance to say, "Yes, I will prepare a conclusion."

SHARING THE GLORY

An effective team player shares praise and other rewards for accomplishment even if he or she is the most deserving. Shared praise is usually merited to some extent because teammates have probably made at least some contribution to the achievement that received praise. For example, if a team member comes up with a powerful suggestion for cutting costs, it is likely that somebody else in the group sparked his or her thinking. Effective examples of sharing glory are easy to find. Think back to watching athletes and other entertainers who win a title or an award. Many of them are gracious enough to share the glory. Shortly after he retired, hockey legend Wayne Gretzky told a television reporter, "I never would have accomplished what I did if I hadn't played with such a great group of guys."

TAKING CARE NOT TO RAIN ON ANOTHER PERSON'S PARADE

As teamwork specialist Pamela Lovell observes, we all have achievements and accomplishments that are sources of pride. Belittling the achievements of others for no legitimate reason brings about tension and anger. Suppress your feelings of petty jealousy.[15] An example would be saying to someone who is proudly describing an accomplishment, "Don't take too much credit. It looks to me like you were at the right place at the right time." If you support teammates by acknowledging their accomplishments, you are more likely to receive their support when needed.

GUIDELINES FOR THE TASK ASPECTS OF TEAM PLAY

The task aspects of team play also make a key contribution to becoming an effective team player. Here we describe six major task-related tactics. As mentioned earlier, a task aspect usually has interpersonal consequences. ◄ Learning Objective 5

PROVIDING TECHNICAL EXPERTISE (OR KNOWLEDGE OF THE TASK)

Most people are selected for a work team primarily because of their technical expertise. *Technical* refers to the intimate details of any task, not just tasks in engineering, physical science, and information technology. The sales promotion specialist on a product development team has technical expertise about sales promotion, whether or not sales promotion requires knowledge of engineering or computers.

As team consultant Glenn Parker observes, to use your technical expertise to outstanding advantage you must have the willingness to share that expertise.[16] Some experts perceive their esoteric knowledge as a source of power. As a consequence, they are hesitant to let others share their knowledge for fear of relinquishing power. It is also necessary for the technical expert to be able to communicate with team members in other disciplines who lack the same technical background. The technical person who cannot explain the potential value of his or her contribution may fail to receive much attention.

ASSUMING RESPONSIBILITY FOR PROBLEMS

The outstanding team player assumes responsibilities for problems. If a problem is not yet assigned to anybody, he or she says, "I'll do it." One team member might note that true progress on the team's effort is blocked until the team benchmarks (compares itself) with other successful teams. The effective team player might say, "You are right, we need to benchmark. If it's okay with everybody else, I'll get started on the benchmarking project tomorrow. It will be my responsibility." Taking responsibility must be combined with dependability. The person who takes responsibility for a task must produce, time after time.

SEEING THE BIG PICTURE

Effective team players need to think conceptually, or see the big picture. A trap in team effort is that discussion can get bogged down in small details and the team might lose sight of what it is trying to accomplish. The team player (including the team leader) who can help the group focus on its broader purpose plays a vital role. The following case history illustrates what it means to see the big picture.

> *A sales process improvement team was asked to make it easier for customers to purchase office equipment when they visited the company's retail center. Under the existing process, five different people had to handle the sales transaction. The customer was often kept waiting for up to an hour. During its second meeting, the team vented its hostility toward the warehouse specialists. As the conversation became more heated, several team members discussed documenting all the problems created by the warehouse personnel and then reporting them to the vice president of marketing. As emotions intensified, several team members ridiculed the warehouse workers.*

Beth, the store manager and one of the team members, helped the group step back and see the big picture. She challenged the group in these words: "Hold on. Why are we here? Is our purpose to improve the sales process or to attack the very people who keep items for sale in stock?" The team accepted the suggestion and praised Beth for her contribution. The team then refocused its effort on reducing the paperwork required to complete a sales transaction.

BELIEVING IN CONSENSUS

consensus General acceptance by the group of a decision.

A major task-related attitude for outstanding team play is to believe that consensus has merit. Consensus is general acceptance of a decision by the group. Every member may not be thrilled about the decision, yet they are unopposed and are willing to support the decision. Believing that consensus is valuable enables you to participate fully in team decisions without thinking that you have sacrificed your beliefs or the right to think independently. To believe in consensus is to believe that the democratic process has relevance for organizations and that ideal solutions are not always possible.

FOCUSING ON DEADLINES

A notable source of individual differences among work group members is how much importance they attach to deadlines. Some work group members may regard deadlines as a moral contract, to be missed only in case of emergency. Others may view deadlines as an arbitrary date imposed by someone external to the group. Other work group members may perceive deadlines as moderately important. Differences in perception about the importance of deadlines influence the group's ability to meet deadlines.[17]

Keeping the group focused on the deadline is a valuable task behavior because meeting deadlines is vital to team success. Discussing the importance of the deadlines is helpful because of the varying attitudes about deadlines likely to be found among group members.

HELPING TEAM MEMBERS DO THEIR JOBS BETTER

Your stature as a team player will increase if you take the initiative to help coworkers make needed work improvements. Helping other team members with their work assignments is a high-level form of cooperation. Make the suggestions in a constructive spirit rather than displaying an air of superiority. Identify a problem that a coworker is having, and then suggest alternatives he or she might be interested in exploring. Avoid saying to team members that they "should" do something, because many people become defensive when told what they should do. The term *should* is usually perceived as a moral judgment given to one person by another, such as being told that you should save money, should learn a second language, or should improve your math skills.

BEING A GOOD ORGANIZATIONAL CITIZEN

A comprehensive way of carrying out the task aspects of team play (as well as relationship aspects) is to help out beyond the requirements of your job description. As discussed in Chapter 1, such extra-role activity is referred to as organizational citizenship behavior—working for the good of the organization even without the promise of a specific reward. As a result of many workers being good organizational citizens, the organization functions more effectively in such ways as improved product quantity and quality.[18] Good citizenship on the job encompasses many specific behaviors, including helping a coworker with a job task and refraining from complaints or petty grievances. A good organizational citizen would carry out such specific acts as picking up litter in the company parking lot. He or she would also bring a reference to the office that could help a coworker solve a job problem. Most of

SKILL-BUILDING EXERCISE 2-3

HABITAT FOR HOMELESS PEOPLE

Organize the class into teams of about six people. Each team takes on the assignment of formulating plans for building temporary shelters for homeless people. The task will take about one hour and can be done inside or outside the class. The dwellings you plan to build, for example, might be two-room cottages with electricity and indoor plumbing.

During the time allotted to the task, formulate plans for going ahead with Habitat for Homeless People. Consider dividing up work by assigning certain roles to each team member. Sketch out tentative answers to the following questions:

1. How will you obtain funding for your venture?
2. Which homeless people will you help?
3. Where will your shelters be located?
4. Who will do the actual construction?

After your plan is completed, evaluate the quality of the teamwork that took place within the group. Specify which teamwork skills were evident and which ones did not surface. Search the chapter for techniques you might use to improve teamwork. The skills used to accomplish the habitat task could relate to the team skills presented in Self-Assessment Quiz 2-2, the interpersonal aspects of team play, the task aspects of team play, or some team skill not mentioned in this chapter. Here is a sampling of the many different skills that might be relevant in this exercise:

* Speaks effectively
* Listens to others
* Innovates solutions to problems
* Thinks outside the box

* Displays a high level of cooperation and collaboration
* Provides knowledge of the task
* Sees the big picture
* Focuses on deadlines

the other team player tactics described here are related to organizational citizenship behavior.

Skill-Building Exercise 2-3 will help you integrate the many suggestions presented here for developing teamwork skills.

SUMMARY

To be successful in the modern organization it is necessary to be an effective team player. Team members have complementary skills and are committed to a common purpose. All teams have some elements in common, but four key types of teams are self-managing work teams, cross-functional teams, virtual teams, and crews. (A virtual team does most of its work electronically instead of in face-to-face meetings.)

Groups and teams offer such advantages as gaining synergy, avoiding major errors, and gaining increased acceptance of and commitment to decisions. Working in groups can also enhance job satisfaction. Groups and teams also have disadvantages, such as more talk than action, conformity in thinking and action, social loafing, and the creation of conflict. A serious potential problem is groupthink, whereby bad decisions are made as a by-product of strong consensus. Key characteristics of effective work groups are outlined in Figure 2-1.

An important part of being an effective team player is to choose effective roles. The roles studied here are: plant, resource investigator, coordinator, shaper, monitor-evaluator, team worker, implementer, completer-finisher, and specialist. Self-oriented roles are less effective and detract from group productivity.

Guidelines for effectively contributing to the interpersonal aspects of team play include (1) trusting team members, (2) displaying a high level of cooperation and collaboration, (3) recognizing the interests and achievements of others, (4) giving helpful criticism, (5) sharing the glory, and (6) taking care not to rain on another person's parade.

Guidelines for effectively contributing to the task aspects of team play include (1) providing technical expertise, (2) assuming responsibility for problems, (3) seeing the big picture, (4) believing in consensus, (5) focusing on deadlines, and (6) helping team members do their jobs better.

QUESTIONS FOR DISCUSSION AND REVIEW

1. Part of being a good team player is helping other members. How can members of a workplace team help each other?

2. How do team members know when they have achieved synergy?

3. What should the other team members do when they uncover a social loafer?

4. What is the potential downside of heavily emphasizing the *specialist* role?

5. How can the *monitor-evaluator* role backfire for a person?

6. Assume that you are a team member. What percent of your pay would you be willing to have based on a group reward? Explain your reasoning.

7. How effective do you think the scavenger hunt really is in building cooperation among team members?

8. A number of companies have sent employees to a team-building exercise in which they literally walk over hot coals. The participants receive appropriate training. (*Caution:* Many participants in this exercise do suffer serious burns.) Why would walking over hot coals help build teamwork?

9. The "little picture" in studying this chapter is learning details about teamwork skills. What is the "big picture"?

10. How can a person achieve individual recognition yet still be a team player?

GO TO THE WEB

http://content.monster.com/tools/quizzes/teamplayer/
(Take the quiz Are You a Team Player?)

http://www.skydivingmagazine.com/
(Find the article "How to Be a Team Player" written by a skydiver.)

AN INTERPERSONAL RELATIONS CASE PROBLEM

TEAM BUILDING GONE WILD AT USPS

They bark like a pack of dogs, quack like a flock of ducks and hiss like a nest of vipers. They wrap each other from head to toe in paper toweling and aluminum foil and pipe cleaners. They build sandcastles and gingerbread houses and practice picking up oranges while blindfolded. These are professional auditors and investigators who police the United States Postal Service.

The mission of the USPS Office of Inspector General is to make the mail more efficient and cost-effective by rooting out waste, fraud, abuse and mismanagement. Yet hundreds of IG staffers were taking part in bizarre bonding and team-building exercises and playing goofy games that burn up millions of dollars—and appear to do little or nothing to curb postal inefficiencies, a *New York Daily News* investigation found.

As stamp prices and postal deficits soared over the past few years, the agency's well-paid, highly trained employees got a lesson in scat singing, took an outing to a racetrack—and delved into the history of the Civil War during a $100,000 retreat to the battlefield at Gettysburg. On USPS time, they've composed Christmas Carols, belted out "We Are Family" at sing-alongs, conducted mock trials in which witnesses were paraded before a judge and jury—and played children's games like follow the leader.

Under the supervision of Postal Inspector General Karla Corcoran, civil servants have been paid to emit animal sounds, embark on treasure hunts, dress in cat costumes and seek the counsel of make-believe wizards, magicians and mad scientists at mass gatherings of the workforce.

They've been jetting into the capital from 15 field offices around the nation for "annual recognition conferences" that celebrated the organization and its values. The tab for the last three confabs: $3.6 million, including planning and salary costs. At one such event at the Renaissance Washington D.C. Hotel, a blindfolded and barefoot Corcoran was swaddled in a blue blanket and hoisted into the air above a hotel ballroom on colored ropes and strings manipulated by some 500 of her 725 employees. The point of lifting the boss skyward was to show that by working together as a team, they could accomplish a task that would have been impossible to perform alone.

"Touchy-feely bonding exercises, management retreats at first-class hotels and annual celebratory events all divert resources that could be better invested in audits and investigations," said Debra Ritt, the agency's former No 1 auditor.

"I question whether spending tens of thousands of dollars for an afternoon of treasure hunting sets the gold standard for prudence," said Senate Finance Committee Chairman Chuck Grassley.

In written responses to questions, the agency said its audits and probes of postal operations have identified $2.2 billion in potential, projected and actual savings during the past six years. Its team-and-leadership development programs mirror those offered by corporate giants and consume only minimal resources, officials claim. They help workers learn more about each other, and themselves, so they can discover novel ways to think and work together.

The exercises also teach acceptance of five core workplace values that the agency instills in all staffers: teamwork, leadership, communication, creativity and conceptualization. Wrapping people in paper toweling, for instance displayed teamwork; building sandcastles showed creativity; mimicking animals involved conceptualization. Besides, said agency spokesperson Laura Whitaker, when "fun and humor" are integrated into the workplace, people become more productive and creative and absenteeism and downtime plummet.

Fun and humor, however, is now how ex-employees such as John Rooney, a former special assistant to Corcoran, describe the organization. "We were forced to play silly games, build gingerbread houses and sing songs praising Karla, and I found the whole thing humiliating, demoralizing and nonproductive," Rooney said.

A spokeswoman for Karla Corcoran said that their undoubtedly had a positive effect on the Postal Service's bottom line. Corcoran announced her retirement in August 2003, following a 274-page report by the President's Council in Integrity and Efficiency. She rebutted all the criticism made by the Council, saying that the investigators sat down with all her enemies, and said "Tell me all your dirt."

Case Questions

1. How might Karla Corcoran have accomplished the development of teamwork without triggering so much criticism of her efforts?

2. What defense might you offer for Corcoran's efforts at building teamwork in the U.S. Postal Service?

3. What does this case tell us about the importance Corcoran placed on teamwork?

Sources: Douglas Feiden, "Bizarre Postal Bonding: Goofy Games Cost Public Millions as Stamp Prices Soar," *http://www.nydailynew.com/news/story/*, March 9, 2003; "CAGW Calls for Postal IG's Removal," *http://www.cagw.org/site/*, May 1, 2003; Larry Margasak, "Employees Harshly Criticize Retiring Postal Service Inspector General," Associated Press, August 20, 2003. New York Daily News, L.P. Reprinted with permission.

AN INTERPERSONAL RELATIONS CASE PROBLEM

SHOWBOAT BRENT

Mary Tarkington, CEO of one of the major dot-com retailers, became concerned that too many employees at the company were stressed out and physically unhealthy. Tarkington said, "I have walked through our distribution center at many different times of the day and night, and I see the same troublesome scene. The place is littered with soft-drink cans and fast-food wrappers. Loads of our workers have stomachs bulging out of their pants. You always see a few workers huddled outside the building smoking. The unhealthiness around the company is also reflected in high absenteeism rates, and health insurance costs that are continually rising.

"I want to see a big improvement in the health of our employees. It makes sense from the standpoint of being a socially responsible company, and from the standpoint of becoming more profitable. With this in mind, I am appointing a project team to study how we can best design and implement a company wellness program. Each member of the team will work about five hours per week on the project. I want to receive a full report in 45 days, and I expect to see progress reports along the way."

Five people were appointed to the wellness task force: Ankit, a programmer; Jennifer, a Web site designer; Brent, a systems analyst; Derek, a logistics technician; and Kristine, a human resource specialist. During the first meeting, the group appointed Kristine as the wellness task force head because of her professional specialty. Ankit, Jennifer, and Derek offered Kristine their congratulations, and wished her the best. Brent offered a comment with a slightly different tone: "I can see why the group chose you to head our task force. I voted for you also, but I think we should be starting with a blank tablet. We are making no assumptions that anybody's ideas carry more professional weight than anybody else."

The next time the group met, each member reported some preliminary findings about wellness programs they had researched. Ankit summarized a magazine article on the topic, Jennifer reported on a friend's experience with his company wellness program, Derek presented some data on how wellness programs can boost productivity and morale, and Kristine reported on *workforce.com*, a human resource Web site that carries information about

wellness programs. Each spent about six minutes on his or her presentation.

Brent then walked up to the front of the conference room and engaged his laptop computer. He began a 25-minute PowerPoint presentation about what he thought the committee should be doing, along with industry data about wellness programs. At the end of Brent's presentation, Kristine commented with a quizzical look, "Thanks Brent, but I thought we agreed to around a 5-minute presentation this first time around."

Brent replied, "Good point Kristine, yet I'm only doing what I consider best for getting our mission accomplished."

Ten days later, CEO Tarkington visited the task force to discuss its progress. Kristine, as the task force head, began the progress report. She pointed out that the group had gathered substantial information about corporate wellness programs. Kristine also noted that so far, establishing one at the company looked feasible and worthwhile. She commented that the group was beginning to assemble data about the physical requirements for having a wellness program, and the cost of implementation.

With a frown Brent said, "Not so fast, Kristine. Since we last met I have taken another look at the productivity figures about wellness centers. People who run wellness programs apparently supplied these figures, so the information could be tainted. I say that we are rushing too fast to reach a decision. Let's get some objective data before making a recommendation to the company."

Kristine groaned as she looked at Mary Tarkington and the task force members. She whispered to Jennifer to her right, "There goes Brent, showboating again."

Case Questions

1. Which team player roles is Brent attempting to occupy?

2. In what way is Brent occupying self-oriented roles?

3. Which team player roles is Kristine attempting to occupy?

4. What actions, if any, should the other task force members take to make Brent a better team player?

CHAPTER 3

Group Problem Solving and Decision Making

Learning Objectives

After reading and studying this chapter and doing the exercises you should be able to

1. Understand the difference between rational and political decision making.

2. Use the general approach to problem-solving groups.

3. Make effective use of brainstorming.

4. Recognize the potential contribution of electronic brainstorming.

5. Make effective use of the nominal group technique.

6. Understand how to increase the efficiency of group problem solving through e-mail and groupware.

Jim Graf has his sights set on a target 100 million miles away. Sometimes it's closer. Sometimes it's farther. Mars. The target is moving. So is he. Each morning he leads a team of several managers in a standup meeting in his office at NASA's Jet Propulsion Laboratory on the top floor of a sprawling, four-story building tucked into the foothills above Pasadena, California. Sitting is not allowed. All the meeting's participants are constantly in motion, changing positions with respect to one another, even as their target changes position with respect to Earth.

"We have a daily standup so we can talk about things," said Graf. "We physically stand up here. I want everybody a little uncomfortable so they get right to the point." Usually these meetings last about 15 minutes. Some mornings, they go longer.

"It's important to communicate," said Graf. "You wouldn't think a team member working on one thing would need to know about another team working on another thing, until suddenly you hear someone say, 'Wow, that impacts me!' The standup meetings are essential to our success."[1]

Discussion Question

1. Do you think people at the Jet Propulsion Laboratory can make major decisions standing up? Or would standup meetings just be good for building team spirit and deciding on what to eat for lunch?

Standup meetings are but one way in which groups solve many key problems. Part of having high-level interpersonal skills is the ability to work closely with others in solving problems and making decisions. This chapter will enhance your group problem-solving and decision-making skills. You will receive guidelines for applying several major group problem-solving methods. As a starting point in studying these techniques, first think through your present level of receptiveness toward group problem solving by doing Self-Assessment Quiz 3-1.

SELF-ASSESSMENT QUIZ 3-1

MY PROBLEM-SOLVING TENDENCIES

Directions:: Describe how well you agree with the following statements, using the following scale: disagree strongly (DS); disagree (D); neutral (N); agree (A); agree strongly (AS). Circle the number in the appropriate column.

	DS	D	N	A	AS
1. Before reaching a final decision on a matter of significance, I like to discuss it with one or more other people.	1	2	3	4	5
2. If I'm facing a major decision, I like to get away from others to think it through.	5	4	3	2	1
3. I get lonely working by myself.	1	2	3	4	5
4. Two heads are better than one.	1	2	3	4	5
5. A wide range of people should be consulted before an executive makes a major decision.	1	2	3	4	5
6. To arrive at a creative solution to a problem it is best to rely on a group.	1	2	3	4	5
7. From what I've seen so far, group decision making is a waste of time.	5	4	3	2	1
8. Most great ideas stem from the solitary effort of great thinkers.	5	4	3	2	1
9. Important legal cases should be decided by a jury rather than by a judge.	1	2	3	4	5
10. Individuals are better suited than groups to solve technical problems.	5	4	3	2	1

Total Score _____

Scoring and Interpretation: Add the numbers you circled to obtain your total score.

46–50 You have strong positive attitudes toward group problem solving and decision making. You will therefore adapt well to the decision-making techniques widely used in organizations. Be careful, however, not to neglect your individual problem-solving skills.

30–45 You have neutral attitudes toward group problem solving and decision making. You may need to remind yourself that group problem solving is well accepted in business.

10–29 You much prefer individual to group decision making. Retain your pride in your ability to think independently, but do not overlook the contribution of group problem solving and decision making. You may need to develop more patience for group problem solving and decision making.

RATIONAL VERSUS POLITICAL DECISION MAKING IN GROUPS

◄ Learning Objective 1

Group decision making is the process of reaching a judgment based on feedback from more than one individual. Most people involved in group problem solving may share the same purpose in agreeing on a solution and making a decision. Nevertheless, they may have different agendas and use different methods. Two such different approaches to group decision making are the rational model and the political model.

The **rational decision-making model** is the traditional, logical approach to decision making, based on the scientific method. It is grounded in establishing goals, establishing alternatives, examining consequences, and hoping for optimum results. The search for optimum results is based on an economic view of decision making—the idea that people hope to maximize gain and minimize loss when making a decision. For example, a work team would choose the lowest cost, highest quality supplier even though the team leader may be a good friend of the sales representative of a competitor.

The rational model also assumes that each alternative is evaluated in terms of how well it contributes to reaching the goals involved in making the decision. For example, if one of the goals in relocating a factory were to reduce energy costs and taxes, each alternative would be carefully examined in terms of its tax and energy consequences. A team member might say, "Setting up a factory in the Phoenix area sounds great. It's true that taxes are low, the labor market is wonderful, and we won't lose any days to snow emergencies. But did you know that the energy costs are very high because of the amount of air conditioning required?"

The **political decision-making model** assumes that people bring preconceived notions and biases into the decision-making situation. Because the decision makers are politically motivated (a focus on satisfying one's own interests), the individuals often do not make the most rational choice. In the relocation example at hand, two of the members may say "Thumbs up to Phoenix" for reasons that satisfy their own needs. One team member might be fascinated with the American Indian culture so prevalent in Arizona and therefore want to move to Phoenix. Another member might have retired parents living in Phoenix and be interested in living near them.

People who use the political model may operate on the basis of incomplete information. Facts and figures that conflict with personal biases and preferences might get blocked out of memory or rationalized away. A team member might say, "Those air conditioning costs are exaggerated. I have heard that if you use thermal pumps in a factory, the cooling costs go way down."

In practice, it is sometimes difficult to determine whether a decision maker is being rational or political. Have you ever noticed that many hotels do not have a 13th floor? The reason is both rational and political. The hotel manager might say rationally, "Many people are superstitious about the number 13, so they will refuse to take a room on the 13th floor. So if we want to maximize room use, the rational decision for us is to label the 13th floor as 14. In this way we will avoid the irrational [political] thinking of guests."

group decision making The process of reaching a judgment based on feedback from more than one individual.

rational decision-making model The traditional, logical approach to decision making based on the scientific method.

political decision-making model The assumption about decision making that people bring preconceived notions and biases into the decision-making situation.

GUIDELINES FOR USING GENERAL PROBLEM-SOLVING GROUPS

◄ Learning Objective 2

Solving problems effectively in groups requires skill. Here we examine three aspects of group problem solving useful in making more effective decisions: working through the group problem-solving steps, managing disagreement about the decision, and aiming for inquiry rather than advocacy.

WORKING THROUGH THE GROUP PROBLEM-SOLVING STEPS

When team members get together to solve a problem, they typically hold a discussion rather than rely on formal problem-solving techniques. Several team members might attempt to clarify the true nature of the problem, and a search then begins for an acceptable solution. Although this technique can be effective, the probability of solving the problem well (and therefore making the right decision) increases when the team follows a systematic procedure. The following guidelines represent a time-tested way of solving problems and making decisions within a group.[2] You may recognize these steps as having much in common with the scientific method. The same steps are therefore ideal for following the rational decision-making model. Two other aspects of group decision making will be described here: managing disagreement and inquiry versus advocacy. Assume that you are a team member of a small business that distributes food supplies to hospitals, nursing homes, and schools. Your business volume is adequate, but you have a cash-flow problem because some of your customers take over 30 days to pay their bills. Here is how problem solving would proceed following the steps for effective group problem solving and decision making:

Step One. *Identify the problem.* Describe specifically what the problem is and how it manifests itself. The surface problem is that some customers are paying their bills late. Your company's ultimate problem is that it does not have enough cash on hand to pay expenses.

Step Two. *Clarify the problem.* If group members do not see the problem the same way, they will offer divergent solutions to their own individual perceptions of the problem. To some team members, late payments may simply mean the company has less cash in the bank. As a result, the company earns a few dollars less in interest. Someone else on the team might perceive the problem as mostly an annoyance and inconvenience. Another person may perceive late payers as being immoral and therefore want to penalize them. The various perceptions of the problem solvers contribute to their exercising a political model of decision making. It is important for the group to reach consensus that the ultimate problem is not enough cash on hand to run the business, as explained in Step 1.

Step Three. *Analyze the cause.* To convert what exists into what they want, the group must understand the cause of the specific problems and find ways to overcome the causes. Late payment of bills (over 30 days) can be caused by several factors. The customers may have cash-flow problems of their own, they may have slow-moving bureaucratic procedures, or they may be understaffed. Another possibility is that the slow-paying customers are dissatisfied with the service and are holding back on payments in retaliation. Research, including interviewing customers, may be needed to analyze the cause or causes.

Step Four. *Search for alternative solutions.* Remember that multiple alternative solutions can be found to most problems. The alternative solutions you choose will depend on your analysis of the causes. Assume that you did not find customers to be dissatisfied with your service, but that they were slow in paying bills for a variety of reasons. Your team then gets into a creative mode by developing a number of alternatives. Among them are offering bigger discounts for quick payment, dropping slow-paying customers, sending out your own bills more promptly, and using follow-up phone calls to bring in money. For regular customers, you might try for automatic withdrawals from their checking account. Another possibility would be to set up a line of credit that would enable your firm to make short-term loans to cover expenses until your bills were paid.

Step Five. *Select alternatives.* Identify the criteria that solutions should meet; then discuss the pros and cons of the proposed alternatives. No solution should be laughed at or scorned. Specifying the criteria that proposed solutions should meet requires you to think deeply about your goals. For example, your team might establish the following criteria for solutions: that they (a) improve cash flow, (b) do not lose customers, (c) do not cost much to implement, and (d) do not make the company appear desperate. The pros and cons of each proposed alternative can be placed on a flip chart, board, or computer screen.

Step Six. *Plan for implementation.* Decide what actions are necessary to carry out the chosen solution to the problem. Suppose your group decides that establishing a bank line of credit is the most feasible alternative. The company president or the chief financial officer might then meet with a couple of local banks to apply for a line of credit at the most favorable rate. Your group also chooses to initiate a program of friendly follow-up telephone calls to encourage more rapid payment.

Step Seven. *Clarify the contract.* The contract is a restatement of what group members have agreed to do and deadlines for accomplishment. In your situation, several team members are involved in establishing a line of credit and initiating a system of follow-up phone calls.

Step Eight. *Develop an action plan.* Specify who does what and when to carry out the contract. Each person involved in implementing alternatives develops an action plan in detail that stems logically from the previous steps.

Step Nine. *Provide for evaluation and accountability.* After the plan is implemented, reconvene to discuss progress and to hold people accountable for results that have not been achieved. In the situation at hand, progress will be measured in at least two objective ways. You can evaluate by accounting measures whether the cash-flow problem has improved and whether the average cycle time on accounts receivable has decreased.

The steps for effective group problem solving are best applied to complex problems. Straightforward problems of minor consequence (such as deciding on holiday decorations for the office) do not require all the steps. Nevertheless, remember that virtually every problem has more than one feasible alternative. A classic example of searching for the best alternative to a problem is as follows:

At one time complaints of late room service were plaguing a Ritz-Carlton hotel, a chain known for its superior service. To solve the problem, president Horst Schulze dispatched a team composed of a room-service order taker, a waiter, and a cook. Everything seemed fine except that the service elevator took a long time. Next, the group consulted with the engineers in charge of the elevator. Neither the engineers nor the elevator company representative could find a technical problem with the elevator.

Next, team members took turns riding the elevators at all hours for a week. Finally, one of them observed that every time the elevator made its trip from the first floor to the twenty-fourth, it stopped four or five times. At each step, housemen (who assisted the housekeepers) got on the elevators to different floors. The housemen were taking towels from other floors to bring them to housekeepers on their own floors who were short of towels. Foraging for towels was slowing down the elevators.

The team discovered that the Ritz-Carlton didn't really have a room-service problem or an elevator problem; it had a towel shortage. As the hotel bought more towels, room-service complaints dropped 50 percent.[3]

For practice in using the problem steps described above, do Skill-Building Exercise 3-1.

SKILL-BUILDING EXERCISE 3-1

A GENERAL PROBLEM-SOLVING GROUP

The class is divided into groups of about six people. Each group takes the same complicated problem through the nine steps for effective group decision making. Several of the steps will be hypothetical because this is a simulated experience. Pretend you are a task force composed of people from different departments in the company. Choose one of the following possibilities:

Scenario 1: Your company wants your task force to decide whether to purchase a corporate jet for members of senior management or require them to continue flying on commercial airlines.

Scenario 2: You are employed by Eastman Kodak Company, the film and digital imaging giant. Data supplied by the marketing research department indicates that the consumption of film by consumers worldwide is declining more rapidly than anticipated. At the same time, digital photography is increasing at a pace much faster than forecasted. Your task force is asked to recommend a plan for increasing the consumption of film.

MANAGING DISAGREEMENT ABOUT GROUP DECISION MAKING

A major reason that group decision making does not proceed mechanically is that disagreement may surface. Such disagreement is not necessarily harmful to the final outcome of the decision because those who disagree may have valid points and help prevent groupthink. The idea is to manage disagreement so the decision-making process does not break down, and the dissenters are not squelched. Conflicts about decisions were studied among 43 cross-functional teams engaged in new product development. Disagreeing about major issues led to positive outcomes for team performance (as measured by ratings made by managers) under two conditions.[4]

First, the dissenters have to feel they have the freedom to express doubt. To measure such freedom, participants in the study responded to such statements as "I sometimes get the feeling that others are not speaking up although they harbor serious doubts about the direction being taken." (Strongly disagreeing with this statement would suggest that group members had the freedom to express doubt.)

Second, doubts must be expressed collaboratively (trying to work together) rather than contentiously (in a quarrelsome way). An example of collaborative communication would be having used the following statement during decision making: "We will be working together for a while. It's important that we both [all] feel comfortable with a solution to this problem." An example of contentious communication would be high agreement with the statement, "You're being difficult and rigid."

Conflict-resolution techniques, as described in Chapter 5, are another potentially useful approach to managing disagreement about decision making.

AIMING FOR INQUIRY VERSUS ADVOCACY IN GROUP DECISION MAKING

Another useful perspective on group decision making is to compare the difference between group members involved in *inquiry* (looking for the best alternative) versus *advocacy* (or fighting for one position). Inquiry is an open process designed to generate multiple alternatives, encourage the exchange of ideas, and produce a well-reasoned solution. Decision makers who care more about the good of the firm than personal gain are the most likely to engage in inquiry. According to David A. Garvin and Michael A. Roberto, this open-minded approach doesn't come easily to most people.[5]

Instead, most groups charged with making a decision tend to slip into the opposite mode, called advocacy. The two approaches look similar because under either mode the group members are busily immersed in work and appear to be searching for the best alternative. Yet the results from the two modes are quite different. Using an advocacy approach, participants approach decision making as a contest with the intent of selecting the winning alternative. One member of the group might be trying to gain the largest share of the budget, and become so passionate about winning budget share that he loses objectivity. Advocates might even withhold important information from the group, such as not revealing that their budget is big enough considering their decreased activity.

With an advocacy approach, the disagreements that arise tend to separate the group, and are antagonistic. Personality conflicts come into play, and one person might accuse the other side of not being able to see the big picture. In contrast, an inquiry-focused group carefully considers a variety of alternatives and collaborates to discover the best solution.

Conflict-resolution methods can be useful in helping the decision makers overcome the advocacy approach. As part of resolving the conflict, the group leader must make sure everyone knows that his or her viewpoint is being carefully considered.

GUIDELINES FOR BRAINSTORMING

In many work situations, groups are expected to produce creative and imaginative solutions to problems. When the organization is seeking a large number of alternatives for solving the problems, brainstorming is often the technique of choice. Brainstorming is a group problem-solving technique that promotes creativity by encouraging idea generation through noncritical discussion. Alex Osborn, who developed the practice of brainstorming, believed that one of the main blocks to organizational creativity was the premature evaluation of ideas.[6] The basic technique is to encourage unrestrained and spontaneous participation by group members. The term *brainstorm* has become so widely known that it is often used as a synonym for a clever idea.

◄ Learning Objective 3

brainstorming A group problem-solving technique that promotes creativity by encouraging idea generation through noncritical discussion.

Brainstorming is used both as a method of finding alternatives to real-life problems and as a creativity-training program. In the usual form of brainstorming, group members spontaneously call out alternative solutions to a problem facing them. Any member is free to enhance or "hitchhike" upon the contribution of another person. At the end of the session, somebody sorts out the ideas and edits the more unrefined ones.

Brainstorming is widely used to develop new ideas for products, find names for products, develop advertising slogans, and solve customer problems. For instance, the idea for luxury sport utility vehicles (SUVs) emerged from a brainstorming session. Brainstorming has also been used to develop a new organizational structure in a government agency, and it is now widely used in developing software.

Adhering to a few simple rules or guidelines helps ensure that creative alternative solutions to problems will be forthcoming. The brainstorming process usually falls into place without frequent reminders about guidelines. Nevertheless, here are nine rules to improve the chances of having a good session. Unless many of these rules are followed, brainstorming becomes a free-for-all, and is not brainstorming in its original intent.

1. **Group size should be about five to seven people.** If there are too few people, not enough suggestions are generated; if there are too many people,

the session becomes uncontrolled. However, brainstorming can be conducted with as few as three people.

2. **Everybody is given the chance to suggest alternative solutions.** Members spontaneously call out alternatives to the problem facing the group. (Another approach is for people to speak in sequence.)

3. **No criticism is allowed.** All suggestions should be welcome; it is particularly important not to use derisive laughter.

4. **Freewheeling is encouraged.** Outlandish ideas often prove quite useful. It's easier to tame a wild idea than to originate one.

5. **Quantity and variety are very important.** The greater the number of ideas put forth, the greater the likelihood of a breakthrough idea.

6. **Combinations and improvements are encouraged.** Building upon the ideas of others, including combining them, is very productive. Hitchhiking or piggybacking is an essential part of brainstorming.

7. **Notes must be taken during the session by a person who serves as the recording secretary.** The session can also be taped, but this requires substantial time to retrieve ideas.

8. **Invite outsiders to the brainstorming session.** Inviting an outsider to the brainstorming session can add a new perspective the "insiders" might not think of themselves. (Such is the argument for having a diverse problem-solving group.)

9. **Do not overstructure by following any of the above eight ideas too rigidly.** Brainstorming is a spontaneous group process.

According to one observer, the most productive brainstorming sessions take place in physically stimulating environments as opposed to a drab conference room. Natural light may stimulate thinking, so work in a room with windows or outside if weather permits. Changing from a seated position to walking around from time to time can be mentally stimulating. Food and drink also contribute to an enhanced environment for brainstorming.[7]

Brainstorming is an effective technique for finding a large number of alternatives to problems, particularly when the list of alternatives is subsequently refined and edited. Brainstorming in groups is also valuable because it contributes to job satisfaction for many people. Skill-Building Exercise 3-2 gives you an opportunity to practice a commercially useful application of brainstorming.

A curious feature of brainstorming is that individuals working alone typically produce more useful ideas than those placed in a group. Brainstorming by individuals working alone is referred to as brainwriting. When electronic brainstorming is described in the next section, we will analyze why some people generate fewer ideas in a group setting. Skill-Building Exercise 3-3 gives you a chance to compare brainstorming with brainwriting.

brainwriting
Brainstorming by individuals working alone.

GUIDELINES FOR ELECTRONIC BRAINSTORMING

Learning Objective 4 ▶ A promising electronic procedure has been developed to overcome the limitations of conventional brainstorming in groups. First, we will examine problems with brainstorming more carefully; then we will describe electronic brainstorming.

LIMITATIONS TO SPOKEN BRAINSTORMING

The full potential of brainstorming has been held back by three forces that block production of ideas: evaluation apprehension, free riding, and inhibiting procedures.[8] Being aware of these production-blocking mechanisms can help you improve your skill in brainstorming.

SKILL-BUILDING EXERCISE 3-2

1-800-I INSIGHT

Using conventional brainstorming, huddle in small groups. Your task is to develop 800, 888, or 900 numbers for firms in various enterprises. Keep in mind that the best 800, 888, or 900 numbers are easy to memorize and have a logical connection to the goods or services provided. After each group makes up its list of telephone numbers (approximately five for each firm on the list), compare results with the other groups. Here is the list of nationwide enterprises:

- A chain of funeral homes
- A pest-control firm whose service emphasizes termites
- A software problem help line for Microsoft® Corporation
- A student-loan company
- A dial-a-prayer service (a 900 number)
- An introduction (dating) service (a 900 number)

SKILL-BUILDING EXERCISE 3-3

BRAINSTORMING VERSUS BRAINWRITING

Half the class is organized into brainstorming groups of about six people. The rest of the class works by themselves. Groups and individuals then work on the same problems for 10 minutes. The brainstorming groups follow the aforementioned guidelines. Individuals jot down as many alternatives as come to mind without interacting with other people. After the problem-solving sessions are completed, compare the alternatives developed by the groups and individuals. Groups and individuals choose one of the following problems so that solutions can be compared to the same problems:

1. How might we effectively utilize the senior citizens in our community?
2. How can we earn extra money, aside from holding a regular job?
3. How can we find new people to date?
4. How can we save money on food costs?
5. How can we save money on gasoline?

Evaluation apprehension means that many people are unwilling to come forth with some of their ideas because they fear being critically evaluated. This fear may be intensified when people are told that the group is being observed and rated or that experts are in the group. (Did you notice any evaluation apprehension in the brainstorming exercise?) When people work by themselves—and do not have to present their ideas to the larger group—they will have less evaluation apprehension.

Free riding is just about the same behavior as social loafing. Free riders do not work as hard in a group as they would if they worked alone. They are willing to let the next person do the heavy thinking. A reason offered for free riding is that being an outstanding contributor in a group carries no larger reward than being a noncontributor. A person generating ideas alone would not have the opportunity to free ride.

An *inhibiting procedure* in spoken (or verbal) brainstorming is that only one person can speak at a time. This limits the idea generation and production time available to group members. As a result some people forget what they wanted to say because they were listening to others. They might also ignore the ideas of others because they are rehearsing what they want to say. Furthermore, they will hold back on ideas that are redundant.

THE ELECTRONIC BRAINSTORMING PROCEDURE

electronic brainstorming
Method of generating ideas with the aid of a computer. Group members simultaneously and anonymously enter their suggestions into a computer, and the ideas are distributed to monitors of other group members.

A development designed to overcome the problem of production blocking in brainstorming is **electronic brainstorming**. Using this method, group members simultaneously enter their suggestions into a computer, and the ideas are distributed to the screens of other group members. Although the group members do not talk to each other, they are still able to build on each other's ideas and combine ideas.

Electronic brainstorming allows members to enter their ideas whenever they want, while sending along their ideas anonymously. These two features reduce the inhibitions caused by waiting for other people and by fear of negative evaluations.

During electronic brainstorming, individuals work in face-to-face groups, typically seated around a U-shaped table. Each group member has a computer terminal connected to all the other terminals and a monitor. The software enables individuals to enter their ideas anonymously as those ideas occur to them. (Good keyboarding skills are essential to keep up with the group.)

Every time an individual enters an idea, a random set of the group's ideas is entered on the individual's monitor. Individuals can access other random sets of ideas by pressing a specified function key. Accessing the other ideas can stimulate the person's own generation of new ideas and also allows for piggybacking.

Electronic brainstorming researcher Keng L. Siau suggests that brainstorming via e-mail can increase both the quantity and quality of ideas. When participants do not face each other directly, they can concentrate more on the creativity task at hand and less on the interpersonal aspects of interaction.[9] If your school or employer is equipped with an electronic brainstorming capability, you are encouraged to try the procedure. Setting up such a capability is costly, however. Next, we describe a low-cost procedure that offers many of the advantages of electronic brainstorming, but does not require special software. In addition, you will be able to test the procedure yourself.

GUIDELINES FOR THE NOMINAL GROUP TECHNIQUE

Learning Objective 5 ▶

nominal group technique (NGT) A group problem-solving technique that calls people together in a structured meeting with limited interaction.

A team leader or other manager who must make a decision about an important issue sometimes needs to know what alternatives are available and how people will react to them. In such cases, group input may be helpful. Spoken brainstorming is not advisable because the problem is still in the exploration phase and requires more than a list of alternative solutions.

A problem-solving technique called the **nominal group technique (NGT)** was developed to fit the situation. The NGT is a group problem-solving technique that calls people together in a structured meeting with limited interaction. The group is called nominal (in name only) because people first present their ideas without interacting with each other, as they would in a real group. (This aspect of the nominal group technique is incorporated into electronic brainstorming.) However, group discussion does take place at a later stage in the process.

A problem that is an appropriate candidate for NGT is a decision about which suppliers or vendors should be eliminated. Many companies are shrinking their number of suppliers because they believe that working with a smaller number of suppliers can lead to higher quality components. It is easier to train a small number of suppliers, and it is also possible to build better working relationships when fewer people are involved.

A decision of this type can lead to hurt feelings and breaking up of old friendships. Suppose Pedro Ortiz, the team leader, is empowered to make this decision about reducing the number of suppliers. The nominal group technique involves a six-step decision process:

1. Work-team members are assembled because they will all participate in the decision to reduce the number of companies that serve as suppliers to the team. All team members are told in advance of the meeting and the agenda. The meeting is called, and an office assistant is invited to help take care of the administrative details of the meeting.

2. The team leader presents a specific question. Ortiz tells the group, "Top management says we have to reduce our number of suppliers by two-thirds. It's too difficult to keep track of all these different suppliers and train them to meet our quality specs. I dislike terminating a supplier as much as anybody, but I can understand the logic of top management. Right now our team is doing business with 12 suppliers, and we should shrink that number to 4. Your assignment is to develop criteria for choosing which suppliers to eliminate. I also need to know how you feel about the decision you make on supplier reduction and how it might affect the operations of our team."

3. Individual team members write down their ideas independently, without speaking to other members. Using notepads, e-mail, or word processors, the five team members write down their ideas about reducing the number of suppliers by two-thirds.

4. Each team member in turn presents one idea to the group. The group does not discuss the ideas. The office assistant summarizes each idea by writing it on a flip chart. Here are the ideas submitted by each team member:

   Alternative A. We'll carefully study the prices offered by all 12 suppliers. The 8 suppliers with the highest average prices for comparable goods are given the boot. I like this idea because our team will save the company a bundle of money.

   Alternative B. Let's keep the 4 suppliers who have the best quality record. We'll ask each supplier if they have won a quality award. If a supplier has won a quality award, the company is put on the retained list. We'll include awards from their customers or outside standards such as ISO 9000. If we find more than 4 of the suppliers have won awards, we'll retain those with the most impressive awards.

   Alternative C. I say we reward good service. We keep the 4 suppliers among the 12 who have been the most prompt with deliveries. We'll also take into account how good the suppliers have been about accepting returns of damaged or defective merchandise.

   Alternative D. Here's an opportunity to get in good with top management. Stop kidding each other. We know that the plant's general manager [Jake] has his favorite suppliers. Some of them are his fishing and golfing buddies.

The suppliers who are friends with Jake get our vote. In this way, Jake will think our team shows really good judgment.

Alternative E. Let's reward the suppliers who have served us best. We'll rate each supplier on a 1 to 10 scale on three dimensions: the quality of goods they have provided us, price, and service in terms of prompt delivery and returns policy. We could do the ratings in less than one hour.

5. After each team member has presented his or her idea, the group clarifies and evaluates the suggestions. The length of the discussion for each of the ideas varies substantially. For example, the idea about rating suppliers on three criteria might precipitate a 30-minute discussion. The discussion about retaining the plant manager's political connections might last only 5 minutes.

6. The meeting ends with a silent, independent rating of the alternatives. The final group decision is the pooled outcome of the individual votes. The team members are instructed to rate each alternative on a 1 to 10 scale, with 10 being the most favorable rating. The ratings that follow are the pooled ratings (the sum of the individual ratings) received for each alternative. The maximum score is 50 (10 points × 5 raters).

Alternative A, price alone: 35

Alternative B, quality-award record: 30

Alternative C, good service: 39

Alternative D, plant manager's favorites: 14

Alternative E, combination of quality, price, and service: 44

Team leader Ortiz agrees with the group's preference for choosing the 4 suppliers with the best combination of quality, price, and service. He schedules a meeting to decide which suppliers meet these standards. Ortiz brings the team's recommendations to the plant manager, and they are accepted. Although the team is empowered to make the decision, it is still brought to management for final approval. To practice the nominal group technique, do Skill-Building Exercise 3-4.

The Job-Oriented Interpersonal Skills in Action box describes how a medical practice made good use of the nominal group technique.

SKILL-BUILDING EXERCISE 3-4

THE NOMINAL GROUP TECHNIQUE

With a clear understanding of the mechanics of the NGT as described in the text, the technique can be demonstrated in about 30 minutes. The class is divided into groups of about seven. One person plays the role of the team leader, who can also assume the responsibility of the office assistant (recording information on flip charts or a computer).

You are the key member of a motion picture and television film production company. You have a contract to produce a series of four films. The problem you face is which North American (United States, Canadian, or Mexican) city to choose as the film site. The president has ruled out Hollywood because expenses are too high. Solve this problem using the NGT, and make a decision about which city to choose for your film site.

Job-Oriented Interpersonal Skills in Action

FAMILY PRACTICE DOCTOR PRESCRIBES THE NOMINAL GROUP TECHNIQUE FOR HIS OFFICE

Each staff member of a family medical practice sees a different aspect of the practice, from scheduling to vital-signs taking. As a consequence each professional and staff support worker has unique insights into how to strengthen the practice to improve care. Our small group practice (two physicians, a physician assistant, and 8.5 full-time-equivalent support staff) recently used the nominal group technique to answer two important questions:

1. What are five ways we could improve our existing level of customer service?

2. What are five things we should be doing to make our practice superior?

The nominal group technique takes a reasonable amount of time, but we modified the process slightly to make it briefer. Rather than conducting the entire technique in one long meeting, we completed some steps by individuals working alone. We gave each staff member our two questions and asked them to submit their ideas the next business day. We combined their suggestions and ideas into a master list, which we distributed to all employees. The next step was for the group to discuss the ideas in a meeting. We met again to discuss our votes. Later, each person ranked the ideas again and gave the ranks to the physician manager. Finally, we met once again to discuss the result and our next steps.

Our group of 13 people, including full- and part-time employees, came up with 47 different ideas. The 5 top-ranking ideas for improving our current level of customer service were as follows:

1. Work as a team. Teamwork in our context includes helping in whatever way is needed. Examples include cross training individuals and allowing each person to describe at a staff meeting some unknown details of his or her job so that others can gain understanding of his or her role.

2. Reduce chart confusion and scatter. This includes filing more quickly, decreasing

the possible locations for charts, and computerizing patient records.

3. Return phone calls to patients more quickly. Nurses should set aside time to respond to voice mail within an agreed-upon time frame such as 24 hours.

4. Make patients feel more welcome in our office. For example, we would like to spend more time with patients, and provide coffee and nutritious snacks for them in the lobby.

5. Reduce paperwork. We want to decrease the amount of paperwork patients need to complete, including the amount of information required of first-time patients.

The top five ideas for making our practice superior were as follows:

1. Have health providers phone patients with their test results. Patients should receive timely feedback from the person most able to give them the information they need.

2. Enhance nonmedical contact with patients. We could easily send cards for birthdays and other special events in our patients' lives and make social phone calls to homebound patients.

3. Improve the effectiveness of the referral process. For example, we should send a copy of the medical chart note from the patient's last visit, including the problem list, with each referral. We should also note any precautions, such as allergic reactions to medication.

4. Schedule longer appointments for new patients. New patients require extra time from all of us, and their first impression is critical. We should emphasize relationship building during the first visit.

5. Decorate the office for various seasons of the year, including holidays. The patients

(Continued)

will be more comfortable and staff members will feel better about their workplace. Our decorations will reflect the cultural diversity of our patient base.

In addition to generating these ideas, the nominal group technique has helped build commitment or buy-in by all workers in the practice. My observation is that group members have developed a sense of ownership as we have moved forward with each area of improvement. What in the past would have been considered "the doctors' ideas" by certain staff members are now *our ideas,* such as returning calls to patients promptly.

Questions

1. From your standpoint as a patient, or potential patient, do you think the NGT produced any useful results?
2. Was the NGT, as used here, any better than just getting the staff together for a 30-minute traditional brainstorming session?

USING STANDUP MEETINGS TO FACILITATE PROBLEM SOLVING

The meeting is part training, part operations, part philosophy—all conducted with drill-like efficiency. We work in a 7-days-a-week, 24-hours-a-day business, and our customers are diverse. Employees need to know how to think on their feet to solve a problem.
—Horst Schulze, president and COO of the Ritz-Carlton hotel chain, talking about standup meetings[11]

Problem solving and decision making can sometimes be improved by conducting meetings while standing up instead of sitting down. The general idea is that participants standing up in the problem-solving group are likely to be more alert and will come to a decision more quickly. Some people solve problems better when standing because they literally "think well on their feet." Few people would be willing to stand for several hours, so they reach a decision quickly.

Many meeting leaders who use standup meetings are pleased with the results in terms of reaching high-quality decisions rapidly. At the Ritz-Carlton hotels, corporate executives hold standup meetings to start the business day. A team of researchers investigated the effectiveness of standup meetings.[10] Study participants were 555 students in an introduction to management course who were offered extra credit for participating in the study. The students were randomly assigned to five-person groups, producing 111 groups. They were divided almost equally into standup and sit-down groups.

All groups were assigned the Lost on the Moon exercise, which presents a scenario involving a crash on the moon. Participants were asked to rank 15 pieces of equipment that survived the crash in terms of their importance for survival. Correct answers to the problem were the ranking of the equipment given by NASA astronauts and scientists. The major results of the experiment were as follows:

1. Sit-down meetings lasted about 34 percent longer than the standup meetings (788 seconds versus 589 seconds).
2. Sit-down and standup meetings made decisions of equal quality.
3. More suggestions about task accomplishment were used by groups in the sit-down meetings than in the standup meetings.
4. Participants in the sit-down meetings were more satisfied than participants in the standup meetings.

One implication for this study is that people make decisions more quickly when standing up, without sacrificing decision quality. However, people prefer to sit down. In general, if you think that a task can be performed in 30 minutes or less, a standup meeting is likely to be effective.

Back to the Opening Case

Indeed, the rocket scientists and other workers at the Jet Propulsion Lab use standup meetings to make major decisions. At one standup meeting Graf challenged the group to come up with an alternative method for covering the spacecraft deck so they could avoid potential heat loss while operating the radar antenna. The current plan could cost the orbiter to lose 15 watts of power as wasted heat, and every watt of power and every ounce of heat counts in space. So the group thrashed out a complicated solution to the problem of a minor heat loss.

To learn more about the heavy-duty problem solving that takes place standing up at the Jet Propulsion Lab, visit http://mars. jpl.nasa.gov/.

USING E-MAIL AND GROUPWARE TO FACILITATE GROUP DECISION MAKING

The presence of so many teams in the workplace means that people must work col-   ◀ Learning Objective 6
lectively and that they must make decisions together. Collective effort usually translates into meetings. Without any meetings, people are working primarily on their own and thus are not benefiting from working in teams. Yet with too many meetings it is difficult to accomplish individual work such as dealing with e-mail, making telephone calls, analyzing information, and preparing reports.

Appropriate use of e-mail and groupware can facilitate interaction among team members and group decision making, while at the same time minimizing the number of physical meetings. Such use of e-mail and other electronic tools makes possible the virtual teams described in the previous chapter.

USING E-MAIL TO FACILITATE MEETINGS

By using e-mail, team members can feed important information to all other members of the team without the ritual of entering a meeting and passing around handouts.[12] Using e-mail, many small details can be taken care of in advance of the meeting. During the meeting, major items can be tackled. The typical use of e-mail is to send brief memos to people on a distribution list. A more advanced use of e-mail is to distribute word processing documents as well as spreadsheets and graphics, including photographs, as attachments.

Think back to the decision reached by the team using the nominal group technique. As a follow-up to the meeting, the team was to get together to rate all 12 suppliers on quality, price, and service. Using e-mail, the group could cut down substantially on the amount of time they would have to spend in a group meeting. They might even be able to eliminate a group meeting. Pedro Ortiz might instruct the team members to send their ratings and explanations to each other within 10 working days.

Each team member would then rate all 12 suppliers on quality, service, and price. The ratings would then be sent to all other team members by e-mail. Ortiz could tally the results and report the final tally to each team member by e-mail. Since all team members could have performed the same calculation themselves, there would be no claims of a biased decision. A team meeting could be called to discuss the final results if Ortiz or the other team members thought it was necessary.

Pushing the use of e-mail too far can inhibit rather than enhance group decision making and teamwork. If people communicate with each other almost exclusively by e-mail, the warmth of human interaction and facial expressions is lost. Piggybacking of ideas is possible by reading each other's ideas on a computer monitor. Nevertheless, the wink of an eye, the shared laughter, and the encouraging smiles that take place in a traditional meeting make an important contribution to team effort, including group problem solving. Also, face-to-face interaction facilitates creativity as people exchange ideas.

USING GROUPWARE TO FACILITATE GROUP PROBLEM SOLVING

The application of e-mail just described can be considered part of groupware because e-mail was used to facilitate work in groups. Electronic brainstorming also relies on groupware because software is applied to facilitate group decision making. At its best, groupware offers certain advantages over single-user systems. Some of the most common reasons people use groupware are as follows:[13]

- To facilitate communication by making it faster, clearer, and more persuasive
- To communicate when it would not otherwise be possible
- To enable telecommuting (working from home)
- To reduce travel costs
- To bring together multiple perspectives and expertise
- To assemble groups with common interests where it would not be possible to gather a sufficient number of people face-to-face
- To facilitate group problem solving

Another example of groupware is a *shared whiteboard* that allows two or more people to view and draw on a common drawing surface even when they are at a distance. The link to group decision making is that drawing sketches and diagrams might be an important part of the decision making. An example would be a sales team suggesting ways of dividing a geographic territory for selling.

Despite all these potential applications and benefits of groupware, the system will break down unless almost all the parties involved use the software successfully. For example, all members of the virtual team must be willing to get online at the same time to have a successful meeting.

SUMMARY

An important aspect of interpersonal relations in organizations is that groups solve many key problems. Group problem solvers and decision makers often use the rational model or the political model. The rational decision-making model is the traditional, logical approach to decision making based on the scientific method. The model assumes that each alternative is evaluated in terms of how well it contributes to reaching the goals involved in making the decision.

The political decision-making model assumes that people bring preconceived notions and biases into the decision-making situation. Because the decision makers are politically motivated, the individuals often do not make the most rational choice. Instead, the decision makers attempt to satisfy their own needs.

General problem-solving groups are likely to arrive at better decisions when they follow standard steps or guidelines for group problem solving. The steps are as follows: (1) identify the problem, (2) clarify the problem, (3) analyze the cause, (4) search for alternative solutions, (5) select alternatives, (6) plan for implementation, (7) clarify the contract, (8) develop an action plan, and (9) provide for evaluation and accountability. Disagreements about group decisions can be managed by giving dissenters the freedom to express doubt, and expressing doubts collaboratively rather than contentiously. Group decision making is more productive when group members are involved in inquiry, or looking for the best alternative. Advocacy, or fighting for one position, leads to poorer decisions.

When the organization is seeking a large number of alternatives to problems, brainstorming is often the technique of choice. Brainstorming is used as a method of finding alternatives to real-life problems and as a creativity-training program. Using the technique, group members spontaneously call out alternative solutions to the problem. Members build on the ideas of each other, and ideas are not screened or evaluated until a later stage. The right physical environment, such as sunlight, facilitates brainstorming. Brainstorming by working alone, or brainwriting, is also effective in generating alternative solutions.

Electronic brainstorming is a recent development designed to overcome the problem of production blocking in brainstorming, such as free riding. Using electronic brainstorming, group members simultaneously enter their suggestions into a computer, and the ideas are transmitted to the screens of other group members. Building on each other's ideas is allowed. Experiments with electronic brainstorming have been favorable.

The nominal group technique (NGT) is recommended for a situation in which a leader needs to know what alternatives are available and how people will react to them. In the NGT, a small group of people contributes written solutions to the problem. Other members respond to their ideas later. Members rate each other's ideas numerically, and the final group decision is the sum of the pooled individual votes.

Problem solving and decision making can sometimes be improved by conducting meetings while standing up instead of sitting down. The general idea is that participants who are standing up are more likely to be alert and come to a decision quickly. An experiment with management students indicated that standup groups made decisions more quickly, but that decision makers who sat down were more satisfied.

Electronic mail can be used to facilitate group decision making because members can feed information to each other without having to meet as a group. Memos, spreadsheet analyses, and graphics can be distributed through the network. Too much emphasis on e-mail, however, results in losing the value of face-to-face human interaction.

Various types of groupware, including e-mail and electronic brainstorming, can facilitate group decision making. Also, a shared whiteboard allows two or more people to view and draw on a common drawing surface even when they are at a distance.

QUESTIONS FOR DISCUSSION AND REVIEW

1. Why are group decisions more likely to lead to commitment than decisions made by a manager acting alone?

2. Based on any experience you have had at school or at work, what process or method is usually followed in making group decisions?

3. Which personality characteristics described in Chapter 1 do you think would help a person be naturally effective in group problem solving?

4. Identify several problems on or off the job for which you think brainstorming would be effective.

5. What is your opinion of the importance of the physical setting (such as sunlight and refreshments) for stimulating creative thinking during brainstorming?

6. What, if any, accommodations should be made in electronic brainstorming for group members who have poor keyboarding skills?

7. Identify two work-related problems for which the nominal group technique is particularly well suited.

8. Companies have known about standup meetings for many years, and the results have been favorable in terms of productivity. Why, then, are standup meetings still not very popular?

9. How can a team leader apply groupware to help the group become more productive?

10. Which group decision-making technique described in this chapter do you think members of a professional sports team are the most likely to use? Why?

GO TO THE WEB

http://www.thinksmart.com/
(Group problem solving and creativity. Go to Work Out Your Creativity.)

http://www.nova-mind.com/
(Mind mapping for group and individual problem solving. See the demonstration.)

AN INTERPERSONAL RELATIONS CASE PROBLEM

STRUGGLING TO MAKE A DECISION AT BMI

Building Maintenance Inc., a firm of 325 full- and part-time employees, is engaged in the cleaning and general maintenance of offices and shopping plazas. Bud Nyrod founded BMI as "one man and one van" 10 years ago. The four other members of the executive team also have a financial stake in the business.

BMI is headquartered in an old office building scheduled for demolition. The pending demolition has forced the firm to face a relocation decision. Bud called a 10 A.M. meeting of the executive team to address the problem. As he entered the conference room, Karen, Liz, Marty, and Nick were already seated.

Bud: Good to see the whole team here. I assume that you have already given some thought to our relocation decision. Let me review the alternatives I see. We can either relocate to some decent space in one of the newly refurbished downtown buildings, or we can get some slightly better space in a suburban park. Karen, as our financial officer, you must have some relevant facts and figures.

Karen: As you requested a few weeks ago, Bud, I have looked into a variety of possibilities. We can get some decent downtown space at about $35 per square foot. And, we can get first-rate accommodations in a suburban office park for about $38 per square foot. Relocation costs would be about the same.

Marty: Customers are influenced by image. So long as we have a good image, I think the customers will be satisfied. By the way, we are doing something that is negatively affecting our image. Our customer-service representatives are just too rude over the phone. I think these folks should have proper training before we turn them loose on the customer phone. Lots of other companies have good brooms, vacuum cleaners, and power-cleaning equipment. Our only edge is the good service we offer customers.

Bud: Liz, what is your position on this relocation decision?

Liz: As employment director, I have a lot to say about relocation. I agree with Marty that customer service should receive top weight in any decision we make about relocation. Customer service, of course, is a direct result of having an efficient crew of maintenance employees. A suburban office park may sound glamorous, but it could be a disaster in terms of recruiting staff. Maintenance workers can afford to get downtown. The vast majority of them live in the city, and they are dependent on mass transit to get to work.

You typically need private transportation to get to an office park. The vast majority of our permanent and temporary employees do not own cars or trucks. And many of them that do own vehicles usually can't afford to keep them in good repair. Many of the temporary help can put gas in their cars only on payday.

So if we relocate to a suburban park, we'll have to rent a small employment office downtown anyway.

Bud: So you're telling us that maybe we should choose both alternatives. We should open an employment office downtown and move the executive office to a suburban office park.

Liz: Now we're introducing a third alternative. We could have two offices downtown: one for the executive and clerical staff and one for hiring maintenance workers.

Bud: Nick, what do you think? Which location would be best for you as director of maintenance operations?

Nick: I'm not in the office too much. I spend most of my time in the field overseeing our supervisors and their crews. Most of our help never see the office after they are hired unless they have a major problem. They report directly to the site. To them their place of work is the building or shopping plaza where they are assigned. Other things are more important than the location of company headquarters.

One of the most important things we should be considering is a big holiday party for this year. I think a year-end party is a real morale builder. It's cost effective in terms of how much turnover it reduces. Some of the maintenance staff will stay on an extra month just to attend the party.

Marty: It looks like you folks have got the major issues out on the table. I really don't care where we locate so long as the needs of our customers come first. I'm eager to know what you people decide. But right now I have to run. I have a luncheon appointment on the other side of town that could mean a big shopping-plaza contract for us.

Bud: Good luck with the sales call, Marty. However, I think you could have scheduled that luncheon for another day. This is a pretty important issue. I'd like you to stay for five more minutes.

Nick: It seems that it's premature for us to reach a decision on this important matter today. Maybe we should call in an office location consultant to help us decide what to do. In the meantime, let's talk some more about the office party. I kind of like that idea.

Case Questions

1. How effective is the BMI team as a problem-solving group?

2. What recommendations can you make to the BMI team to better solve the problem it is facing?

3. How might the team have used the nominal group technique to help solve the problem of office relocation?

AN INTERPERSONAL RELATIONS CASE PROBLEM

THE GREAT WIPER BLADE MYSTERY

It was a mystery—a mystery with millions of dollars and hundreds of jobs riding on the answer. A huge 6.5 percent of the windshield wiper systems being manufactured at an ITT automotive plant in upstate New York for Daimler-Chrysler's minivans were defective. Nobody could figure out why the defect existed. All the parts met specifications; they were assembled correctly, and engineers found no fault with the design. Yet, in a test run, many wipers failed to make a complete sweep across the windshield—a potential disaster for DaimlerChrysler and for the 3,800 automotive workers in the upstate plant.

Plant management assembled a six-person team including engineers, union members, and manufacturing experts to become a detective force to find the answers. The team felt a lot of pressure to resolve the problem because the livelihood of the plant was threatened. If its major product was defective, the plant might be shuttered.

TECHNICAL ASPECTS OF THE PROBLEM

The new wiper system was the biggest and most complex ever assembled in the plant. Instead of just delivery wiper blades, the local plant was given "black box responsibility" to deliver a perfectly functioning windshield system that DaimlerChrysler workers could just snap into place.

The blades, instead of moving right and left in tandem, came together in the center of the windshield and spread apart again, making timing a crucial issue. "The number of things that could go wrong was exponentially greater than for anything we had ever done before," said Rob Price, manufacturing general supervisor. Just one thing did go wrong, but it was enough to threaten the project.

In 6.5 percent of the wipers, the blade's swing was up to 2.5 degrees short. That's equivalent to less than half a second on the face of a clock, but it was enough to make the blade fall short of sweeping the full area in front of the driver's face—an area that federal regulators insist be kept clear of rain and ice.

THE CROSS-FUNCTIONAL TEAM TACKLES THE PROBLEM

Responsibility for solving the problem fell to the DaimlerChrysler cross-functional team: leader of the plant's DaimlerChrysler team, Craig Hysong; manufacturing general supervisor Rob Price; quality technician Rick Fisher; quality analyst Jeannine Marciano; engineer Mike Kinsky; and Ron Maor, an engineer from a sister plant in Ontario, Canada. Each new ITT automotive product had its cross-functional team drawn from the different departments. The team's goal was to make sure the product was launched flawlessly.

The Chrysler Division team picked the best and worst of the wipers—called "Bob" and "Wow" for the best of the best and the worst of the worst. They thought that by comparing the best with the worst, they might somehow isolate and fix the problem.

The team felt the pressure to perform because unless they solved the mystery, Chrysler would have to find a new supplier for windshield wiper systems. Finally, Fisher, the technician, and Maor, the engineer from the plant that supplies the motors, found the answer: It was in the serrations (rough marks, like those on a serrated knife) on the motor's drive shaft that are meant to hold the crank in place.

Case Questions

1. Which approach to (or method of) group problem solving did the plant team use?

2. To what extent did management make the right move in assigning the flawed windshield wiper problem to a team instead of to one engineer or technician?

3. If by chance you happen to have the right expertise, what would you guess was the problem with the windshield wiper system?

Source: Phil Ebersole, "ITT Automotive Sleuths Solve a Design Mystery," May 4, 1997. Rochester, New York, *Democrat and Chronicle.* Reprinted with permission.

CHAPTER 4

Cross-Cultural Relations and Diversity

Learning Objectives

After reading and studying this chapter and doing the exercises you should be able to

1. Recognize who fits under the diversity umbrella.
2. Describe the major values accounting for cultural differences.
3. Overcome many cross-cultural communication barriers.
4. Specify some of the business implications of being sensitive to cultural differences.
5. Improve your cross-cultural relations.

Joan Weiss is the owner and president of Superior Motors, a dealership that sells a variety of luxury vehicles, both new and previously owned. The average sticker price on new vehicles is over $45,000, and the average price for previously owned vehicles is $26,000. During a year-end strategy meeting with Bill Matteson, the director of marketing, Weiss and Matteson agreed that the dealership needed a way to boost sales.

"It's getting more difficult to cope with the wild discounting in this business, and the fact that many of our potential buyers can invest their discretionary dollars in something other than a $75,000 sports car," said Weiss. "What is your take on this problem, Bill?"

"I'm going to pick on an idea both you and I have talked about before," replied Matteson. "Our sales reps are no longer representative of the clientele we serve. Back when you and your late husband founded the dealership, practically all our customers were white, middle-aged males. Yet our customer mix has changed. Many of our customers are women, African American, Chinese, and Indian. Also, many of our best customers are under age 40.

"So let's join the realities of the market, and recruit a few culturally diverse sales reps. If any existing rep quits, he or she will be replaced by somebody who will help us diversify our sales force. The same goes for employees in our service center."

"Let's start on this plan today," agreed Weiss.

Discussion Question

1. Do you think the initiatives taken by the luxury-car dealership are a publicity stunt to appear more inclusive? Or do you think being culturally diverse actually improves a company's business results?

Top management at business firms continues to recognize the importance of a diverse workforce as well as diverse customers. Minority group members in the United States are growing seven times as fast as the majority population. According to the Bureau of Labor Statistics, women make up about 47 percent of the workforce. Minorities and workers from other countries occupy 26 percent of jobs. Furthermore, white males constitute only 15 percent of new entrants to the workforce.

Not only is the workforce becoming more diverse, but business has also become increasingly international. Small- and medium-size firms, as well as corporate giants, are increasingly dependent on trade with other countries. An estimated 10 to 15 percent of jobs in the United States depend on imports or exports. Furthermore, most manufactured goods contain components from more than one country. Also, more and more work, such as call centers and manufacturing, is subcontracted to companies in other countries.

All this workplace diversity has an important implication for the career-minded individual. To succeed in today's workplace a person must be able to relate effectively to people from different cultural groups from within and outside his or her country. Being able to relate to a culturally diverse customer base is also necessary for success.

This chapter presents concepts and techniques you can use to sharpen your ability to work effectively with people from diverse backgrounds. To get you started thinking about your readiness to work in a culturally diverse environment, take Self-Assessment Quiz 4-1.

THE DIVERSITY UMBRELLA

Learning Objective 1 ▶

In this extreme war for talent, we need to create a culture of inclusion.
—Lynn Weaver, vice president of human resources at Yazaki of North America

Improving cross-cultural relations includes understanding the true meaning of appreciating diversity. To appreciate diversity a person must go beyond tolerating and treating people from different racial and ethnic groups fairly. The true meaning of valuing diversity is to respect and enjoy a wide range of cultural and individual differences. Appreciating these differences is often referred to as *inclusion* to emphasize unity rather than diversity. To be diverse is to be different in some measurable way, even if what is measurable is not visible (such as religion or sexual orientation).

To be highly skilled in interpersonal relations, one must recognize and appreciate individual and demographic (group or category) differences. Some people are more visibly diverse than others because of physical features or disabilities. Yet the diversity umbrella is supposed to include everybody in an organization. To value diversity is therefore to appreciate individual differences among people.

Appreciating cultural diversity in organizations was originally aimed at assisting women and minorities. The diversity umbrella continues to include more people as the workforce encompasses a greater variety of people. For example, in recent years much attention has been paid to the rights of employees included in the group GLBT (gay, lesbian, bisexual, and transsexual). The rights of members of diverse religious groups are also receiving attention. One such group is a Christian employee network that opposes rights for people of nontraditional sexual orientation.[1] The goal of a diverse organization is for persons of all cultural backgrounds to achieve their full potential, not restrained by group identities such as gender, nationality, or race. Another important goal is for these groups to work together harmoniously.

SELF-ASSESSMENT QUIZ 4-1

CROSS-CULTURAL SKILLS AND ATTITUDES

Directions: Listed below are skills and attitudes that various employers and cross-cultural experts think are important for relating effectively to coworkers in a culturally diverse environment. For each of the statements, check *applies to me now* or *not there yet,*

	Applies to me now	Not there yet
1. I have spent some time in another country.	_____	_____
2. At least one of my friends is deaf, blind, or uses a wheelchair.	_____	_____
3. Currency from other countries is as real as the currency from my own country.	_____	_____
4. I can read in a language other than my own.	_____	_____
5. I can speak in a language other than my own.	_____	_____
6. I can write in a language other than my own.	_____	_____
7. I can understand people speaking in a language other than my own.	_____	_____
8. I use my second language regularly.	_____	_____
9. My friends include people of races different from my own.	_____	_____
10. My friends include people of different ages.	_____	_____
11. I feel (or would feel) comfortable having a friend with a sexual orientation different from mine.	_____	_____
12. My attitude is that although another culture may be very different from mine, that culture is equally good.	_____	_____
13. I am willing to eat (or have eaten) food from other countries that are not served in my own country.	_____	_____
14. I would accept (or have already accepted) a work assignment of more than several months in another country.	_____	_____
15. I have a passport.	_____	_____

Interpretation: If you answered *applies to me now* to 10 or more of the preceding questions, you most likely function well in a multicultural work environment. If you answered *not there yet* to 10 or more of the questions, you need to develop more cross-cultural awareness and skills to work effectively in a multicultural work environment. You will notice that being bilingual gives you at least five points on this quiz.

Sources: Several ideas for statements on this quiz are derived from Ruthann Dirks and Janet Buzzard, "What CEOs Expect of Employees Hired for International Work," *Business Education Forum*, April 1997, pp. 3–7; and Gunnar Beeth, "Multicultural Managers Wanted," *Management Review*, May 1997, pp. 17–21.

Figure 4-1 presents a broad sampling of the ways in which workplace associates can differ from one another. Studying this list can help you anticipate the types of differences to understand and appreciate in a diverse workplace. The differences include cultural as well as individual factors. Individual factors are also important because people can be discriminated against for personal characteristics as well as group factors. Many people, for example, believe they are held back from promotion because of their weight-to-height ratio.

- ⊘ Race
- ⊘ Sex (or gender)
- ⊘ Religion
- ⊘ Age (young, middle-aged, and old)
- ⊘ Ethnicity (country of origin)
- ⊘ Education
- ⊘ Abilities
- ⊘ Mental disabilities (including attention deficit disorder)
- ⊘ Physical disabilities (including hearing status, visual status, able-bodied, wheelchair user)
- ⊘ Values and motivation
- ⊘ Sexual orientation (heterosexual, homosexual, bisexual, transsexual)
- ⊘ Marital status (married, single, cohabitating, widow, widower)
- ⊘ Family status (children, no children, two-parent family, single parent, grandparent)
- ⊘ Personality traits
- ⊘ Functional background (area of specialization)
- ⊘ Technology interest (high-tech, low-tech, technophobe)
- ⊘ Weight status (average, obese, underweight, anorexic)
- ⊘ Hair status (full head of hair, bald, wild hair, tame hair, long hair, short hair)
- ⊘ Tobacco status (smoker versus nonsmoker, chewer versus nonchewer)
- ⊘ Styles of clothing and appearance (dress up, dress down, professional appearance, casual appearance)

FIGURE 4–1 The Diversity Umbrella

UNDERSTANDING CULTURAL DIFFERENCES

Learning Objective 2 ▶ The groundwork for developing effective cross-cultural relations is to understand cultural differences. Some researchers think that men and women represent different cultures! One cultural difference between the two groups is that women tend to speak indirectly and soften criticism. Men, in contrast, tend to be more direct in giving criticism. Here we discuss six aspects of understanding cultural differences: (1) cultural sensitivity, (2) cultural intelligence, (3) respect for all workers (4) cultural fluency (5) dimensions of differences in cultural values, and (6) avoidance of cultural bloopers. To work smoothly with people from other cultures, it is important to become competent in all six areas.

CULTURAL SENSITIVITY

cultural sensitivity
An awareness of and willingness to investigate the reasons why people of another culture act as they do.

In order to relate well to someone from a foreign country, a person must be alert to possible cultural differences. When working in another country a person must be willing to acquire knowledge about local customs and learn how to speak the native language at least passably. When working with people from different cultures, even from his or her own country, the person must be patient, adaptable, flexible, and willing to listen and learn. The characteristics just mentioned are part of **cultural sensitivity**, an awareness of and willingness to investigate the reasons why individuals of another culture act as they do.[2] A person with cultural sensitivity will recognize certain nuances in customs that will help build better relationships from cultural backgrounds other than his or her own.

CULTURAL INTELLIGENCE

An advanced aspect of cultural sensitivity is to be able to fit in comfortably with people of another culture by observing the subtle cues they give about how a person should act in their presence. **Cultural intelligence (CQ)** is an outsider's ability to interpret someone's unfamiliar and ambiguous behavior the same way that person's compatriots would.[3] With high cultural intelligence a person would be able to figure out what behavior would be true of all people and all groups, such as rapid shaking of a clenched fist to communicate anger. Also, the person with high cultural intelligence could figure out what is peculiar to this group, and those aspects of behavior that are neither universal nor peculiar to the group. These ideas are so abstract, that an example will help clarify.

cultural intelligence (CQ) An outsider's ability to interpret someone's unfamiliar and ambiguous behavior the same way that person's compatriots would.

> *An American expatriate manager served on a design team that included two German engineers. As other team members floated their ideas, the engineers condemned them as incomplete or underdeveloped. The manager concluded that the Germans in general are rude and aggressive.*
>
> *With average cultural intelligence the American would have realized he was mistakenly equating the merit of an idea with the merit of the person presenting it. The Germans, however, were able to make a sharp distinction between the two. A manager with more advanced cultural intelligence might have tried to figure out how much of the two Germans' behavior was typically German and how much was explained by the fact that they were engineers.*

Similar to emotional intelligence, cultural intelligence encompasses several different aspects of behavior. The three sources of cultural intelligence relate to the cognitive, emotional/motivational, and the physical, explained as follows:[4]

1. **Cognitive (the Head).** The cognitive part of CQ refers to what a person knows and how he or she can acquire new knowledge. Here you acquire facts about people from another culture such as their passion for football (soccer in North America), their business practices, and their promptness in paying bills. Another aspect of this source of cultural intelligence is figuring out how you can learn more about the other culture.

2. **Emotional/Motivational (the Heart).** The emotional/motivational aspect of CQ refers to energizing one's actions and building personal confidence. You need both confidence and motivation to adapt to another culture. A man on a business trip to Africa might say to himself, "When I greet a work associate in a restaurant, can I really pull off kissing him on both cheeks. What if he thinks I'm weird?" With strong motivation, the same person might say, "I'll give it a try. I kind of greet my grandfather the same way back in the United States."

3. **The Body (Physical).** The body aspect of CQ is the action component. The body is the element for translating intentions into actions and desires. Kissing the same-sex African work associates on both cheeks is the *physical* aspect just mentioned. We often have an idea of what we should do, but implementation is not so easy. You might know, for example, that when entering an Asian person's home you should take off your shoes, yet you might not actually remove them—thereby offending your Asian work (or personal life) associate.

To practice high cultural intelligence, the mind, heart, and body have to work together. You need to figure out how to act with people from another culture; you need motivation and confidence to change; and you have to translate your knowledge and motivation into action. So when you are on a business trip to London, go ahead and hold your fork in your left hand!

RESPECT FOR ALL WORKERS AND CULTURES

An effective strategy for achieving cross-cultural understanding is to simply respect all others in the workplace, including their cultures. An important component of respect is to believe that although another person's culture is different from yours, it is equally good. Respect comes from valuing differences. Respecting other people's customs can translate into specific attitudes, such as respecting one coworker for wearing a yarmulke on Friday or another for wearing African clothing to celebrate Kwanzaa. Another way of being respectful would be to listen carefully to the opinion of a senior worker who says the company should never have converted to voice mail in place of assistants answering the phone (even though you disagree).

An aspect of respecting all workers that achieves current attention is the importance of respecting the rights of majorities, particularly white males. Many of these men want to be involved in—not excluded from—bringing about cultural diversity in organizations. For example, they might want to mentor minority group members.

Company policies that encourage respect for the rights of others are likely to create a positive influence on tolerance throughout the firm. An example is that many employers have taken steps to recognize and affirm the existence of gay and lesbian workers. Among these steps are publishing formal statements of nondiscrimination, and the inclusion of issues about sexual orientation in diversity training programs. A major policy change has been to grant same-sex couples the same benefits granted to opposite-sex couples.

A study of 537 gay and lesbian employees working for a variety of organizations demonstrated that the more prevalent policies dealing with respect, the more equitably sexual minorities are likely to be treated at work. More equitable treatment, in turn, was associated with gays and lesbians being more satisfied, and less likely to leave the firm.[5]

CULTURAL FLUENCY

cultural fluency The ability to conduct business in a diverse, international environment.

A high-level goal in understanding cultural differences is to achieve cultural fluency, the ability to conduct business in a diverse, international environment.[6] Achieving cultural fluency includes a variety of skills, such as relating well to people from different cultures and knowing a second language. Cultural fluency also includes knowledge of the international business environment, such as how the exchange rate can affect profits. Having high cultural intelligence would contribute to cultural fluency because such intelligence makes it easier to work well with people from other cultures.

Skill-Building Exercise 4-1 is a warm-up activity for achieving cultural sensitivity, and perhaps respect for all workers.

DIMENSIONS OF DIFFERENCES IN CULTURAL VALUES

One way to understand how national cultures differ is to examine their values. Table 4-1 presents an introduction to the subject by comparing values in the United States to the collective values of many Western and Eastern countries. You can use this information as a general stereotype of how Americans are likely to differ from people in many other countries.

The focus of our attention is a more detailed look at seven different values and how selected nationalities relate to them, based on the work of several researchers.[7] A summary of these values follows.

individualism A mental set in which people see themselves first as individuals and believe that their own interests take priority.

    1. **Individualism versus collectivism.** At one end of the continuum is individualism, a mental set in which people see themselves first as individuals and

SKILL-BUILDING EXERCISE 4-1

DEVELOPING CULTURAL SENSITIVITY

Carefully observe products and services such as tennis shoes, notebooks, bicycles, and banking services, and attempt to find out how they are marketed and sold in other countries. For a convenient reference source, interview foreign students and foreigners outside class about these products and services. Your digging for information might uncover such nuggets as the following:

- In India, cricket champions are celebrities comparable to U.S. basketball stars who endorse soft drinks like Coca-Cola and Pepsi.
- In Hungary, peanut butter is considered a luxury food item.
- In some countries in warm climates, meat is freshly killed and hung on hooks for sale—without refrigeration or freezing.

After conducting these product and service interviews, arrive at some kind of interpretation or conclusion. Share your insights with other class members.

Source: "Teaching International Business," *Keying In,* January 1999, p. 1. *National Business Education Association.* Reprinted with permission.

TABLE 4-1 Comparison of U.S. Values with Those in Many Other Countries

In the United States	*In many other countries*
Time is to be controlled	Time is fluid, malleable
Emphasis is on change	Emphasis is on tradition, continuity
Individualism	Group orientation
Personal privacy	Openness, accessibility
Informality	Formality (not as much as in the past)
Individual competition	Cooperation
Equality/egalitarianism	Hierarchy/authority
Short-term emphasis	Long-term emphasis
Work emphasis ("One lives to work.")	Leisure = work emphasis ("One works to live.")
Task emphasis	People emphasis
Direct/explicit communication style	Indirect/implicit communication style
Action bias or emphasis	Planning and preparation emphasis

Source: Adaptation of chart prepared by International Orientation Resources.

believe that their own interests take priority. Collectivism, at the other end of the continuum, is a feeling that the group and society receive top priority. Members of a society who value individualism are more concerned with their careers than with the good of the firm. Members of a society who value collectivism, in contrast, are typically more concerned with the organization than with themselves.

Highly individualistic cultures include the United States, Canada, Great Britain, Australia, and the Netherlands. Japan, Taiwan, Mexico, Greece, and Hong Kong are among the countries that strongly value collectivism. The heavy emphasis on teamwork on the job and in sports in the United States is moving it inhabitants more toward collectivism.

collectivism A feeling that the group and society should receive top priority, rather than the individual.

materialism An emphasis on assertiveness and the acquisition of money and material objects.

concern for others An emphasis on personal relationships and a concern for the welfare of others.

formality A cultural characteristic of attaching considerable importance to tradition, ceremony, social rules, and rank.

informality A cultural characteristic of a casual attitude toward tradition, ceremony, social rules, and rank.

urgent time orientation A cultural characteristic of perceiving time as a scarce resource and tending to be impatient.

casual time orientation A cultural characteristic in which people view time as an unlimited and unending resource and therefore tend to be patient.

high-context culture A culture that makes extensive use of body language.

2. *Acceptance of power and authority.* People from some cultures accept the idea that members of an organization have different levels of power and authority. In a culture that believes in concentration of power and authority, the boss makes many decisions simply because he or she is the boss. Group members readily comply because they have a positive orientation toward authority. In a culture with less acceptance of power and authority, employees do not readily recognize a power hierarchy. They accept directions only when they think the boss is right or when they feel threatened. Countries that readily accept power and authority include France, Spain, Japan, Mexico, and Brazil. Countries that have much less acceptance of power and authority are the United States and particularly the Scandinavian countries (e.g., Sweden).

3. *Materialism versus concern for others.* In this context, materialism refers to an emphasis on assertiveness and the acquisition of money and material objects. It also means a deemphasis on caring for others. At the other end of the continuum is concern for others, an emphasis on personal relations and a concern for the welfare of others. Materialistic countries include Japan, Austria, and Italy. The United States is considered to be moderately materialistic. Scandinavian nations all emphasize caring as a national value. (In the original, the same dimension was referred to as masculinity versus femininity. Such terms are considered to be sexist today.)

4. *Formality versus informality.* A country that values formality attaches considerable importance to tradition, ceremony, social rules, and rank. At the other extreme, informality refers to a casual attitude toward tradition, ceremony, social rules, and rank. Workers in Latin American countries highly value formality, such as lavish public receptions and processions. Americans, Canadians, and Scandinavians are much more informal.

5. *Urgent time orientation versus casual time orientation.* Individuals and nations attach different importance to time. People with an urgent time orientation perceive time as a scarce resource and tend to be impatient. People with a casual time orientation view time as an unlimited and unending resource and tend to be patient. Americans are noted for their urgent time orientation. They frequently impose deadlines and are eager to get started doing business. Asians and Middle Easterners, in contrast, are patient negotiators.

6. *Work orientation versus leisure orientation.* A major cultural difference is the number of hours per week and weeks per year people expect to invest in work versus leisure, or other nonwork activities. American corporate professionals typically work about 55 hours per week, take 45-minute lunch breaks, and two weeks of vacation. Japanese workers share similar values with respect to time invested in work. In contrast, many European countries have steadily reduced the work week in recent years, while lengthening vacations. In March 2005, France overturned its 35-hour workweek and restored its 39-hour workweek, illustrating that Europeans have a preference for a modest workweek.

7. *High-context versus low-context cultures.* Cultures differ in how much importance they attach to the surrounding circumstances, or context, of an event. High-context cultures make more extensive use of body language. Some cultures, such as the Asian, Hispanic, and African American cultures, are high context. In contrast, northern European cultures are low context and make less use of body language. The Anglo American culture is considered to be medium-low context. People in low-context cultures seldom take time in business dealings to build relationships and establish trust.

How might a person use information about cultural differences to improve his or her interpersonal relations on the job? A starting point would be to recognize that a person's national values might influence his or her behavior. Assume that you wanted to establish a good working relationship with a person from a high-context culture. An effective starting point would be to emphasize body language when communicating with the individual.

Attitudes toward hierarchy and status can make a difference in establishing working relationships. A worker who values deference to age, gender, or title might shy away from offering suggestions to an elder or manager to avoid appearing disrespectful. This worker would need considerable encouragement to collaborate in decision making.[8] *Time-consciousness* may create a conflict if you are committed to making deadlines and a team member has a laid-back attitude toward time. You might explain that although you respect his attitudes toward time, the company insists on getting the project completed on time.

Self-Assessment Quiz 4-2 will help you think about how values might be influencing your interpersonal relations in the workplace.

CULTURAL BLOOPERS

An effective way of being culturally sensitive is to minimize actions that are likely to offend people from another culture based on their values. Cultural bloopers are most likely to take place when you are visiting another country. The same bloopers, however, can also be committed with people from a different culture within your

SELF-ASSESSMENT QUIZ 4-2

CHARTING YOUR CULTURAL VALUE PROFILE

Directions: For each of the seven value dimensions, circle the number that most accurately fits your standing on the dimension. For example, if you perceive yourself to be "highly formal," circle 1 on the fourth dimension (item 4).

1. Individualism						Collectivism
1	2	3	4	5	6	7

2. High acceptance of power and authority				Low acceptance of power and authority		
1	2	3	4	5	6	7

3. Materialism						Concern for others
1	2	3	4	5	6	7

4. Formality						Informality
1	2	3	4	5	6	7

5. Urgent time orientation					Casual time orientation	
1	2	3	4	5	6	7

6. Work orientation					Leisure orientation	
1	2	3	4	5	6	7

7. High-context culture					Low-context culture	
1	2	3	4	5	6	7

Scoring and Interpretation: After circling one number for each dimension, use a felt-tipped pen to connect the circles, thereby giving yourself a profile of cultural values. Do not be concerned if your marker cuts through the names of the dimensions. Compare your profile to others in the class. Should time allow, develop a class profile by computing the class average for each of the seven points and then connecting the points.

own country. To avoid these bloopers, you must carefully observe persons from another culture. Studying another culture through reading is also helpful.

E-commerce and other forms of Internet communication have created new opportunities for creating cultural bloopers. The Web site developers and workers responsible for adding content must have good cross-cultural literacy, including an awareness of how the information might be misinterpreted.

- Numerical date formats can be readily misinterpreted. To an American, 4/9/08 would be interpreted as April 9, 2008 (or 1908!). However, many Europeans would interpret the same numerical expression as September 4, 2008.

- Colors on Web sites must be chosen carefully. For example, in some cultures purple is the color of royalty, whereas in Brazil purple is associated with death.

- Be careful of metaphors that may not make sense to a person for whom your language is a second language. Examples include "We've encountered an ethical meltdown" and "Our biggest competitor is over the hill."

English has become the language of business and science throughout the world, yet communicating in a customer's native tongue has its advantages. International business specialist Rick Borelli says that being able to communicate your message directly in your customer's mother tongue provides a competitive advantage.[9] Furthermore, according to the research firm IDC, consumers are four times more likely to purchase a product online if the Web site is in their preferred language.[10] The translator, of course, must have good knowledge of the subtleties of the language to avoid a blooper. An English-to-French translator used the verb *baiser* instead of *baisser* to describe a program of lowering prices. *Baisser* is the French verb "to lower," whereas *baiser* is the verb "to kiss." Worse, in slang *baiser* is a verb that refers to having intimate physical relationships!

Keep two key facts in mind when attempting to avoid cultural mistakes. One is that members of any cultural group show individual differences. What one member of the group might regard as an insensitive act, another might welcome. Recognize also that one or two cultural mistakes will not peg you permanently as a boor. Skill-Building Exercise 4-2 will help you minimize certain cultural bloopers.

SKILL-BUILDING EXERCISE 4–2

CULTURAL MISTAKES TO AVOID WITH SELECTED CULTURAL GROUPS

EUROPE

Great Britain
- Asking personal questions. The British protect their privacy.
- Thinking that a businessperson from England is unenthusiastic when he or she says, "Not bad at all." English people understate their positive emotion.
- Gossiping about royalty.

France
- Expecting to complete work during the French two-hour lunch.
- Attempting to conduct significant business during August—*les vacances* (vacation time).
- Greeting a French person for the first time and not using a title such as "sir," or "madam," or "miss" (*monsieur, madame,* or *mademoiselle*).

Italy
- Eating too much pasta, as it is not the main course.
- Handing out business cards freely. Italians use them infrequently.

Spain	• Expecting punctuality. Your appointments will usually arrive 20 to 30 minutes late.
	• Making the American sign for "okay" with your thumb and forefinger. In Spain (and many other countries) this is vulgar.
Scandinavia (Denmark, Sweden, Norway)	• Being overly rank conscious. Scandinavians pay relatively little attention to a person's rank in the hierarchy.

ASIA

All Asian countries	• Pressuring an Asian job applicant or employee to brag about his or her accomplishments. Asians feel self-conscious when boasting about individual accomplishments; they prefer to let the record speak for itself. In addition, they prefer to talk about group rather than individual accomplishment.
Japan	• Shaking hands or hugging Japanese (as well as other Asians) in public. Japanese consider these practices to be offensive.
	• Not interpreting "We'll consider it" as a no when spoken by a Japanese businessperson. Japanese negotiators mean no when they say "We'll consider it."
	• Not giving small gifts to Japanese when conducting business. Japanese are offended by not receiving these gifts.
	• Giving your business card to a Japanese businessperson more than once. Japanese prefer to give and receive business cards only once.
China	• Using black borders on stationery and business cards, because black is associated with death.
	• Giving small gifts to Chinese when conducting business. Chinese are offended by these gifts.
	• Making cold calls on Chinese business executives. An appropriate introduction is required for a first-time meeting with a Chinese official.
Korea	• Saying no. Koreans feel it is important to have visitors leave with good feelings.
India	• Telling Indians you prefer not to eat with your hands. If the Indians are not using cutlery when eating they expect you to do likewise.

MEXICO AND LATIN AMERICA

Mexico	• Flying into a Mexican city in the morning and expecting to close a deal by lunch. Mexicans build business relationships slowly.
Brazil	• Attempting to impress Brazilians by speaking a few words of Spanish. Portuguese is the official language of Brazil.
Most Latin American countries	• Wearing elegant and expensive jewelry during a business meeting. Latin Americans think people should appear more conservative during a business meeting

Note: A cultural mistake for Americans to avoid when conducting business in most countries outside the United States and Canada is to insist on getting down to business quickly. North Americans in small towns also like to build a relationship before getting down to business. The preceding suggestions will lead to cross-cultural skill development if practiced in the right setting. During the next 30 days, look for an opportunity to relate to a person from another culture in the way described in these suggestions. Observe the reaction of the other person for feedback on your cross-cultural effectiveness.

OVERCOMING CROSS-CULTURAL COMMUNICATION BARRIERS

Learning Objective 3 ▶ Cultural differences create additional barriers. Here are some guidelines for overcoming cross-cultural communication barriers.

1. **Be sensitive to the fact that cross-cultural communication barriers exist.** If you are aware of these potential barriers, you will be ready to deal with them. When you are dealing with a person in the workplace with a different cultural background than yours, solicit feedback in order to minimize cross-cultural barriers to communication. Being aware of these potential barriers will help you develop cultural sensitivity.

2. **Show respect for all workers.** The same behavior that promotes good cross-cultural relations in general helps overcome communication barriers. A widely used comment that implies disrespect is to say to another person from another culture, "You have a funny accent." Should you be transposed to that person's culture, you, too, might have a "funny accent."

3. **Use straightforward language and speak slowly and clearly.** When working with people who do not speak your language fluently, speak in an easy-to-understand manner. Minimize the use of idioms and analogies specific to your language. A computer analyst from Greece left confused after a discussion about a software problem with her manager. The manager said, "Let's talk about this another time because *I can't seem to get to first base with you.*" (The manager was referring to the fact that the conversation was headed nowhere because he couldn't come to an agreement with the analyst.) The computer analyst did not ask for clarification because she did not want to appear uninformed.

4. **Observe cultural differences in etiquette.** Violating rules of etiquette without explanation can erect immediate communication barriers. A major rule of etiquette in many countries is that people address superiors by their last name unless they have worked together for a long time. Or, the superior might encourage being on a first-name basis with him or her. Be aware that an increasing number of cultures are moving toward addressing each other and customers by using the first name only. Yet, it is best to error on the side of formality.

5. **Be sensitive to differences in nonverbal communication.** Stay alert to the possibility that a person from another culture may misinterpret your nonverbal signal. An engineer for a New Jersey company was asked a question by a German coworker. He signaled okay by making a circle with his thumb and forefinger. The German worker stormed away because in his country the same gesture is a personal insult and a vulgar gesture.

   Another key area of cross-cultural differences in nonverbal communication is the handshake. In some cultures, a woman is expected to extend her hand first to shake with a man. In other cultures, people, hug, embrace, or bow instead of shaking hands.[11] (With good cultural sensitivity and cultural intelligence you can figure out what to do when meeting another person.)

6. **Do not be diverted by style, accent, grammar, or personal appearance.** Although these superficial factors are all related to business success, they are difficult to interpret when judging a person from another culture. It is therefore better to judge the merits of the statement or behavior.[12] A brilliant individual from another culture may still be learning your language and thus make basic mistakes in speaking your language. Also, he or she might not yet have developed a sensitivity to dress style in your culture.

7. **Be attentive to individual differences in appearance.** A major cross-cultural insult is to confuse the identity of people because they are members of the same race or ethnic group. An older economics professor reared in China and teaching in the United States had difficulty communicating with students because he was unable to learn their names. The professor's defense was "So many of these Americans look alike to me." Recent research suggests that people have difficulty seeing individual differences among people of another race because they code race first, such as thinking "He has the nose of an African American." However, people can learn to search for more distinguishing features, such as a dimple or eye color.[13] In this way, individual differences are recognized.

BUSINESS IMPLICATIONS OF UNDERSTANDING CULTURAL DIFFERENCES

Top-level management at many companies emphasize cross-cultural understanding, ◀ Learning Objective 4 including overcoming communication barriers, because such activities improve profits. If you establish rapport with people from other cultures—and avoid antagonizing them—they will most likely become and remain your customers. Similarly, if you establish good rapport with valuable employees from other cultures, they are more likely to stay with the company.

Establishing a culturally and demographically diverse organization has a proven record of enhancing hiring and retention (keeping employees).[14] The enhanced recruiting and retention takes place primarily among members of minority groups who feel more comfortable when a reasonable number of other people from their group are part of the workforce.

A woman who joined a printing firm as the only woman supervisor in the plant quit after six months. The problem was that she felt uncomfortable being singled out as the only female member of management. The woman joined a larger competitor where she was among five other women supervisors. She said she enjoyed being in her new work environment because her sex was not an issue.

Following are three examples of how cross-cultural understanding has improved profits, reduced costs, or enhanced employee satisfaction:

- Xerox Corporation has a longstanding reputation of reaching out to minorities and appreciating the contributions of people from diverse cultures. As a result, Xerox has been able to recruit and retain talented people from many cultural groups. One of many examples is Ursula Burns, the president of the company's United States Business Operations. Burns is one of the highest placed black women in American business.

- Several large automobile dealerships across the United States and Canada have deliberately cultivated a culturally diverse sales force. This type of cultural diversity often leads to much improved sales to the diverse cultural groups. A Cadillac dealer in New York City reported that sales to Asiatic Indians have quadrupled since he hired a sales representative raised in India. The same dealer reports that more cultural diversity in the service end of the business has also boosted sales to diverse ethnic and racial groups.

- For almost 15 years, the United States Postal Service has been committed to hiring, promoting, and retraining an inclusive workforce. Surveys taken regularly indicate that such diversity has contributed to positive employee perceptions of such factors as fairness/cooperation, job/organization satisfaction, supervision, discrimination, and work conditions.[15]

Back to the Opening Case

One year after recruiting a more culturally diverse workforce for sales and service, the president and marketing director at Superior Motors believed that they had strengthened their business considerably. For example, a young Chinese American hired as a sales rep proved to have excellent contacts with wealthy Chinese families, and many of these contacts resulted in sales for Superior Motors.

TECHNIQUES FOR IMPROVING CROSS-CULTURAL RELATIONS

Learning Objective 5 ▶ Many training programs have been developed to improve cross-cultural relations and to help workers value diversity. All of the information presented so far in this chapter is likely to be included in such programs. In this section we describe programs for improving cross-cultural relations including cultural training, cultural intelligence training, language training, and diversity training. A skill-building exercise accompanies a description of three of the programs. We will also describe some precautions regarding how diversity training can sometimes backfire.

CULTURAL TRAINING

cultural training A
set of learning
experiences
designed to help
employees
understand the
customs, traditions,
and beliefs of
another culture.

For many years, companies and government agencies have prepared their workers for overseas assignments. The method most frequently chosen is cultural training, a set of learning experiences designed to help employees understand the customs, traditions, and beliefs of another culture. In today's diverse business environment and international marketplace, learning about individuals raised in different cultural backgrounds has become more important. Many industries therefore train employees in cross-cultural relations.

Cultural training is also important for helping people of one culture understand their customers from another culture in particular, such as Chinese people learning to deal more effectively with their American customers. For example, in one training program Chinese businesspeople are taught how to sprinkle their e-mail with English phrases like "How are you?" "It was great to hear from you" and "Can we work together?"[16]

The Job-Oriented Interpersonal Skills in Action box describes how cultural training can improve the effectiveness of establishing call centers overseas.

To practice improving your cross-cultural relations, do Skill-Building Exercise 4-3.

CULTURAL INTELLIGENCE TRAINING

A new development in assisting people work more effectively with workers in other cultures is *cultural intelligence training*, a program based on the principles of cultural intelligence described earlier in this chapter. A key part of the training is to learn the three contributors to CQ—head, heart, and body. Instead of learning a few simple guidelines for working effectively with people from another culture, the trainee is taught strategies for sizing up the environment to determine which course of action is best. The culturally intelligent overseas worker would learn how to determine how much humor to interject into meetings, what kind of handshake is most appropriate, and so forth. The following excerpt will give you a feel for what is involved in cultural intelligence training:

A Canadian manager is attempting to interpret a "Thai smile." First, she needs to observe the various cues provided in addition to the smile gesture

Job-Oriented Interpersonal Skills in Action

INDIAN CALL CENTER WORKERS LEARN TO THINK AND ACT LIKE AMERICANS

In a sleek new office building, two dozen young Indians are studying the customs of a place none of them have ever seen. One by one, the students present their conclusions about this fabled land. "Americans eat a lot of junk food. Table manners are very casual," says Ritu Khanna. "People are self-centered. The average American has 13 credit cards," says Nerissa Dcosata.

The Indians, who range in age from 20 to 27, have been hired to take calls from cranky or distraught Americans whose computers have gone haywire. To do this, they need to communicate in a language that is familiar but a culture that is foreign. "We're not saying India is better or America is better," says their trainer, Alefiya Rangsala. "We just want to be culturally sensitive so there's no disconnect when someone phones for tech support."

Call centers took root in India during the 2001 recession, when U.S. companies were struggling to reduce expenses. At first, training was simple. The centers gave employees names that were acceptable to American ears, with *Arjun* becoming *Aaron* and *Sangita* becoming *Susan*. The new hires were instructed to watch American television shows to get an idea of American folkways.

But whether Aaron and Susan were repairing computers, selling long-distance service, or fulfilling orders for diet tapes, problems immediately cropped up. The American callers often wanted a better deal or an impossibly swift resolution, and were aggressive and sometimes abrasive about saying so. The Indians responded according to their deepest natures: They were silent when they didn't understand, and they often committed to more than their employers could deliver. They would tell the Americans that someone would get back to them tomorrow to check on their problems, and no one would.

Customer satisfaction plummeted. The U.S. clients grew alarmed. Some even returned their business to U.S. call centers. Realizing that the multibillion-dollar industry with 150,000 employees was at risk, Indian call centers have recently embarked on more comprehensive training. New hires are taught how to express empathy, strategies to successfully open and close conversations, and above all how to be assertive, however unnatural it might feel.

Khanna, Dcosata, and their new colleagues work for Sutherland Global Services, an upstate New York firm that is one of the larger outsourcing companies in India. They've been put through a three-week training session where they research hot-button issues, and pretend they are American anchors reporting the latest news, and imitate celebrities.

On the students' last day of cultural and voice training, Rangsala warns them that at least half a dozen are still speaking incomprehensibly and might wash out. As they slip away one by one to make a short recording that will test their pronunciation skills, K. S. Kumar, Sutherland's director of operations for India, gives a little graduation speech. "You're shortchanging yourself if you don't stick with this." (The shift work and difficult work goals contribute to high turnover.)

Originally, the ever-agreeable Indian agents had a hard time getting people to pay bills that were six months overdue. Too often, says trainer Deepa Nagraj, the calls would go like this:

"Hi," the Indian would say. "I'd like to set up a payment to get your account current. Can I help you do that?"

"No," the American responds.

"OK, let me know if you change your mind," the Indian says and hangs up.

Now, says Nagraj, the agents take no excuses.

Like Sutherland, Mphasis is basing a lot of its hopes on training. Indrandiel Ghosh, an Mphasis trainer, gives refresher courses to reps who handle customer-service accounts for a big credit-card company. One rep says he recently was helping a customer change his card data because his wife left him. When the rep expressed sympathy, the man cut him short, saying he hadn't really liked his wife.

"In case you empathize and then you see they don't want your empathy, move on," Ghosh advises. "This is someone from another culture. That increases the complexity tenfold."

Questions

1. What do you see as a major cultural difference between Indians and Americans that make the call center job so challenging for Indians?

2. Some of the call center representatives in India are instructed to identify themselves as students in Salt Lake City, in addition to giving them American first names. What is your take on the ethics of these disguises?

Source: From David Streitfeld, "A Crash Course on Irate Calls," August 2, 2004. *Los Angeles Times.* Reprinted with permission.

SKILL-BUILDING EXERCISE 4-3

CROSS-CULTURAL RELATIONS ROLE-PLAY

One student plays the role of Ritu, a call center representative in Bombay, India. Her specialty is helping customers with cell phone problems. Another student plays the role of Todd, an irate American. His problem is that he cannot get his camera-equipped cell phone to transmit his photos over e-mail. He is scheduled to attend a party in two hours, and wants to take loads of photos with his cell phone. Todd is impatient, and in the eyes of Ritu, somewhat overbearing. Ritu is good natured and pleasant, but feels she must help Todd solve his problem without being bullied by him. Because Ritu is instructed to spend the minimum time necessary to resolve the problem, she spends about five minutes on this problem.

The observers should make note of how well Ritu has made the necessary cross-cultural adaptations.

itself (e.g., other facial or bodily gestures, significance of others who may be in proximity, the source of the original smile gesture) and to assemble them into a meaningful whole and make sense of what is really experienced by the Thai employee. Second, she must have the requisite motivation (directed effort and self-confidence) to persist in the face of confusion, challenge, or apparently mixed signals. Third, she must choose, generate, and execute the right actions to respond appropriately.

If any of these elements is deficient she is likely to be ineffective in dealing with the Thai employee. A high CQ manager has the capability with all three facets as they action in unison.[17]

As the example illustrates, to be culturally intelligent you need to apply cognitive skills, have the right motivation, and then put your knowledge and confidence into action. Armed with such skills you would know, for example, whether to greet a Mexican worker on a business trip to Texas with a handshake, a hug, or a kiss on both cheeks.

LANGUAGE TRAINING

Learning a foreign language is often part of cultural training, yet it can also be a separate activity. Knowledge of a second language is important because it builds better connections with people from other cultures than does relying on a translator. Building connections with people is still important even if English has become the international language of business. Many workers, aside from international business specialists, also choose to develop skills in a target language. Speaking another language can help build rapport with customers and employees who speak that language. As mentioned earlier, it is easier to sell to customers when using their native language.

Almost all language training has elements similar to taking a course in another language or self-study. Companies invest heavily in helping employees learn a target language because it facilitates conducting business in other countries. For this reason companies that offer language training and translation services are currently experiencing a boom. Medical specialists, police officers, and firefighters also find second language skills to be quite helpful because clients under stress, such as an injured person, are likely to revert to their native tongue. Learning a second language is particularly important when many of your customers and employees do not speak your country's official language. For example, Casa Rio, in San Antonio, Texas, found that its English-speaking managers were unable to communicate with Spanish-speaking employees regarding benefits and other issues.[18]

USING THE INTERNET TO HELP DEVELOP FOREIGN LANGUAGE SKILLS

A useful way of developing skills in another language, and learning more about another culture, is to create a computer "bookmark" or "favorite" written in your target language. In this way, each time you go to the Internet on your own computer, your cover page will contain fresh information in the language you want to develop.

Enter a search word such as "Italian newspaper" or "Spanish language newspaper" in the search probe. After you find a suitable choice, enter the edit function for "Favorites" or "Bookmarks" and insert that newspaper as your front page. For example, imagine that French is your target language and culture. The search engine might have brought you to the site *http://www.france2.fr*. This Web site keeps you abreast of French and international news, sports, and cultural events—written in French. Every time you access the Internet you can spend five minutes on your second language, thereby becoming multicultural. You can save a lot of travel costs and time using the Internet to help you become multicultural, including developing proficiency in another language.

As with any other skill training, investments in language training can pay off only if the trainee is willing to work hard at developing the new skill outside the training sessions. Allowing even 10 days to pass without practicing your target language will result in a sharp decline in your ability to use that language.

Skill-Building Exercise 4-4 presents a low-cost, pleasant method of enhancing your foreign language and cross-cultural skills.

DIVERSITY TRAINING

The general purpose of cultural training is to help workers understand people from other cultures. Understanding can lead to dealing more effectively with them as work associates or customers. Diversity training has a slightly different purpose. It attempts to bring about workplace harmony by teaching people how to get along better with diverse work associates. Quite often the program is aimed at minimizing open expressions of racism and sexism. Diversity training takes a number of forms. Nevertheless, all center on increasing awareness of and empathy for people who are different in some noticeable way from oneself.

diversity training Training that attempts to bring about workplace harmony by teaching people how to get along better with diverse work associates.

Training sessions in appreciating cultural diversity focus on the ways that men and women or people of different races reflect different values, attitudes, and cultural backgrounds. These sessions can vary from several hours to several days. Training sessions can also be held over a long period of time. Sometimes the program is confrontational, sometimes not.

An essential part of relating more effectively to diverse groups is to empathize with their points of view. To help training participants develop empathy, representatives of various groups explain their feelings related to workplace issues. A representative segment of a training program designed to enhance empathy took the following format. A minority group member was seated at the middle of a circle. First, the coworkers listened to a Vietnamese woman explain how she felt excluded from the in-group composed of whites and African Americans in her department. "I feel like you just tolerate me. You do not make me feel that I am somebody important." The next person to sit in the middle of the circle was a Muslim. He complained about people wishing him Merry Christmas. "I would much prefer that my coworkers stop to think that I do not celebrate Christian holidays. I respect your religion, but it is not my religion."

DEVELOPING EMPATHY FOR DIFFERENCES

Class members come up to the front of the room one by one and give a brief presentation (perhaps even three minutes) of any way in which they have been perceived as different, and how they felt about this perception. The difference can be of any kind, relating to characteristics such as ethnicity, race, choice of major, physical appearance, height, weight, hair color, or body piercing. After each member of the class (perhaps even the instructor) has presented, class members discuss what they learned from the exercise. It is also important to discuss how this exercise can improve relationships on the job.

A recent trend in diversity training is cross-generational diversity, or relating effectively to workers much older or younger than you. Wendy's International Inc., with the help of a consultant, has developed training programs that raise awareness of generational issues. Allen Larson, director of management resources, says "Since generational cohorts help form people's attitudes toward work, employees of different generations who must work together may find that their work styles conflict with those of coworkers."[19]

Cross-generational awareness training is one component in the corporate training program. The premise behind the program is that after acquiring cognitive knowledge, engaging in dialogue, and role-playing, employees will learn to accept people's differences, some of which are age driven. For example, younger employees might feel less guilty than would seniors when calling in sick just to have a day's vacation.

Skill-Building Exercise 4-5 provides you an opportunity to simulate an empathy-building experience in a diversity training program.

Diversity training has frequently improved cross-cultural relationships in the workplace. Yet such programs can also create ill will and waste time. One problem is that participants are sometimes encouraged to be too confrontational and express too much hostility. Companies have found that when employees are too blunt during these sessions, it may be difficult to patch up interpersonal relations in the work group later on.

A negative consequence of diversity training is that it sometimes results in perpetuating stereotypes about groups, such as people from Latin America not placing much value on promptness for meetings. A related problem is that diversity training might focus too much on differences instead of similarities.[20] For example, even if people are raised with different cultural values they must all work harmoniously together to accomplish work. Although a worker believes that relationships are more important than profits, he or she must still produce enough to be a good investment for the company.

SUMMARY

Today's workplace has become more culturally diverse, and business has become increasingly international. As a result, to succeed one must be able to relate effectively to people from different cultural groups from within and outside one's country. The true meaning of valuing diversity is to respect and enjoy a wide range of cultural and individual differences. The diversity umbrella continues to include more people as the workforce encompasses a greater variety of people.

The groundwork for developing effective cross-cultural relations is to understand cultural differences. Six key aspects of understanding cultural differences are

(1) cultural sensitivity, (2) cultural intelligence, (3) respect for all workers and all cultures, (4) cultural fluency—the ability to conduct business in a diverse, international environment, (5) differences in cultural values, and (6) avoidance of cultural bloopers. Cultural intelligence is based on cognitive, emotional/motivational, and physical (taking action) factors.

Countries differ in their national values, leading to differences in how most people from a given country will react to situations. The values studied here are (1) individualism versus collectivism, (2) acceptance of power and authority, (3) materialism versus concern for others, (4) formality versus informality, (5) urgent time orientation versus casual time orientation, and (6) high-context versus low-context cultures.

An effective way of being culturally sensitive is to minimize actions that are likely to offend people from another culture based on their values. These cultural bloopers can take place when working in another country or when dealing with foreigners in one's own country. Studying potential cultural bloopers is helpful, but recognize also that individual differences may be of significance.

Communication barriers created by cultural differences can often be overcome by the following: (1) be sensitive to the fact that these barriers exist; (2) show respect for all workers; (3) use straightforward language and speak slowly and clearly; (4) observe cultural differences in etiquette; (5) be sensitive to differences in nonverbal communication; (6) do not be diverted by style, accent, grammar, or personal appearance; and (7) be attentive to individual differences in appearance.

Improved cross-cultural understanding can improve profits through attracting and retaining diverse customers. Similarly, establishing good rapport with valuable employees from other cultures can improve employee recruitment and retention.

Cultural training is a set of learning experiences designed to help employees understand the customs, traditions, and beliefs of another culture. In today's diverse business environment and international marketplace, learning about individuals raised in different cultural backgrounds has become more important. Cultural intelligence training includes developing strategies for sizing up the environment to determine which course of action is best. Learning a foreign language is often part of cultural training, yet it can also be a separate activity.

Diversity training attempts to bring about workplace harmony by teaching people how to get along better with diverse work associates. Most forms of diversity training center on increasing awareness of and empathy for people who are different in some noticeable way from yourself.

QUESTIONS FOR DISCUSSION AND REVIEW

1. How can a person demonstrate to others on the job that he or she is culturally fluent (gets along well with people from other cultures)?

2. Several well-known companies conduct awareness weeks to celebrate selected diverse groups such as Hispanics or gays and lesbians. What is your opinion of the effectiveness of such activities for bringing about workplace harmony?

3. Some companies, such as Singapore Airlines, make a deliberate effort for customer-contact personnel to all be of the same ethnic group (Singapore natives). How justified is this practice in an era of cultural diversity and valuing differences?

4. A major purpose of diversity programs is to help people celebrate differences. Why should people celebrate a difference such as being a wheelchair user?

5. Provide an example of cultural insensitivity of any kind that you have seen, read about, or could imagine.

6. Why is knowing the language of the other person more important when selling to rather than buying from that person?

7. How could you use the information presented in Table 6-1, comparing U.S. values to those of other countries, to help you succeed in business?

8. If you were a supervisor, how would you deal with a group member who had a very low acceptance of power and authority?

9. The cultural bloopers presented in Skill-Building Exercise 6-2 all dealt with errors people make in regard to people who are not American. Give an example of a cultural blooper a person from another country might make in the United States.

10. Many people speak loudly to other people who are deaf, blind, and those who speak a different language. Based on the information presented in this chapter, what mistakes are these people making?

GO TO THE WEB

http://www.DiversityInc.com
(Extensive information about cultural diversity in organizations)

http://www.berlitz.com
(Information about language training and cultural training in countries throughout the world. Investigate in your second language to enhance the cross-cultural experience.)

AN INTERPERSONAL RELATIONS CASE PROBLEM

RALPH LAUREN SEEKS RACIAL HARMONY

Fashion magnate Ralph Lauren says he first became aware of racial tension within his company after an incident in 1997 at a Long Island sportswear boutique. A regional manager with Polo Ralph Lauren Corp. dropped by the new Polo Sport store in anticipation of an inspection by an important visitor: Jerome Lauren, Ralph's older brother and the executive overseeing Polo menswear. The mall where the boutique was located attracts a middle-class, racially integrated clientele. But the regional manager concluded that the store's ambiance was too "urban," meaning black, former Polo officials said.

The manager ordered two black and two Hispanic sales associates off the floor and back into the stock room, so they wouldn't be visible to Lauren. The sales associates followed orders, but they later hired a lawyer and threatened to sue Polo for discrimination. The company reached confidential settlements with the four.

Ralph Lauren says he learned about the incident several weeks after it happened and "was just sick" about it. The regional manager, Greg Ladley, was ordered to undergo racial-relations training but wasn't fired. A company spokesperson says that Ladley's recollection is that some sales associates working on inventory were asked to move to the stock room because they weren't "dressed appropriately."

After the episode, Ralph Lauren told subordinates, "We have to correct this. Let's make a change." But executives who worked at Polo at the time say their boss didn't make clear what changes they wanted.

AIR OF EXCLUSIVENESS
Polo, like some of its rivals, presents a multiracial face to the world, with black models in some of its ads, and a following of young black consumers wearing its familiar logo of a horse rider wielding a polo mallet. Yet internally, big fashion houses tend to exude an exclusiveness that is uninviting to many nonwhites. Few blacks or Hispanics have penetrated the upper ranks of major clothes manufacturers and retailers.

In response to complaints that have flared up at Polo, Lauren has met with lawyers, hired lieutenants to overhaul company personnel practices, and embraced diversity training. But he says he has left the details to others, as he is usually preoccupied with design work at his headquarters studio.

The Polo aura of Anglo-Saxon elitism is the elaborate creation of Polo's founder, Ralph Lauren, 62 years old, who remade himself as he rose from modest roots in the Bronx, to become the chair and CEO of a fashion powerhouse. Polo retail supervisors routinely tell salespeople to think Hollywood. "Ralph is the director," the instruction goes, "and you are the actors, and we are here to make a movie." But some black and Hispanic employees say the movie seems to lack parts for them.

COLOR-BLIND?

Lauren says he is color-blind when it comes to hiring talent. He frequently points out the wide visibility he has given Tyson Beckford, the striking shaven-headed black fashion model who has appeared in Polo ads since 1994. "Tyson is not just in jeans," Lauren says. "We put him in a pinstripe suit, in our best Purple Label brand. Tyson is in the annual report, in our advertisements on TV."

Lauren says Polo "is a leader to do the right things to bring in the people who are the best in the industry." Some of his subordinates complain, however, that it is difficult to find black and Hispanic applicants with the credentials for design jobs coming out of the New York fashion schools where Polo usually recruits.

A Polo staffer recommended in 1998 that Lauren meet Lacey Moore, a 20-year-old African American from Brooklyn, who had taken some college-level communications courses and had aspirations to be in the music business. Since high school, Moore had worn Polo Oxford shirts and knit tops with flashy gold chains and a hip-hop attitude: precisely the sort of hybrid image Lauren hoped would draw younger customers. "Lacy is edgy—he gets it," Lauren recalls thinking, snapping his fingers for effect. He hired the young man as a design assistant.

The new recruit's rap-influenced personal style and lingo confounded his coworkers. Moore felt isolated. He says he understood that in any competitive workplace "there are people who don't like you." But in Polo's cliquish and overwhelmingly white Madison Avenue headquarters, he says coworkers made it clear he wasn't welcome. "I kept getting this bad vibe," he says. He quit in 2000.

Shocked, Lauren telephoned Moore at home. "Lacey, I want you to come back," he recalls saying. After listening to Moore's complaints, Lauren says he made it clear to the young man's white coworkers, "I want you all to work this out." A couple of weeks later, Moore returned, but warily.

ADVICE AND PRESSURE

Polo has received advice and pressure on the race issue from a variety of outside counselors and advocates. A civil rights authority advised Lauren that achieving a truly diverse workforce requires hiring more than a few black employees. A black activist minister met with Polo officials and helped some minority workers reach confidential settlements with the company.

Today Moore (the young design assistant) says his colleagues seem friendlier. The human resource vice president has given Moore reassurance. "You feel there is someone looking out for you," says the young assistant, who helps prepare for fashion shows and consults on clothing design.

Lauren says he is paying more attention to what he sees at work. For example, he recalls that at a company Christmas party in 2000, he was surprised that a group of blacks and Hispanics had congregated in a separate room. "Why is this happening?" he wondered. "What's not welcoming to those employees?"

According to Lauren he didn't approach his workers to ask them, however, and is still wondering about the answers to those questions.

Case Questions

1. What advice can you offer Lauren to achieve fuller workplace diversity at Polo?

2. Is the Christmas (holiday) party incident a symptom of an organizational problem? Or were the black and Hispanic employees just behaving as they chose?

3. Does Ralph Lauren "get it" as a leader with respect to cultural diversity in the workplace?

Source: Adapted from Teri Agins, "Color Line: A Fashion House with an Elite Aura Wrestles with Race," *The Wall Street Journal,* August 19, 2002, pp. A1, A9.

INTERPERSONAL RELATIONS CASE PROBLEM

THE TRANSGENDER PHARMACIST

Kim Dower has held a pharmacist position at King Soopers in Denver for almost 10 years. Dower is biologically and physiologically male, yet is undergoing gender transformation and wants to wear women's clothes at work. According to Dower, management at King Soopers will not allow the cross-dressing. "I want to see King Soopers change their policy so other people like me can't be discriminated against," said Dower, 50, who is recently separated and has two children from a previous marriage. "I have struggled with this most of my life."

Dower hired a lawyer to represent him, and filed a complaint with the Equal Employment Opportunity Commission. "Our feeling is this is a very important case," said Dower's attorney, Betty Tsamis. King Soopers declined to comment on the charge, as is standard practice for a company facing a formal complaint.

Twelve months ago, Dower said, she informed a store manager that she was undergoing gender transformation. In March, she asked if she could begin to wear women's clothing while on the job. The manager took that request to a higher level of management, Dower said. The answer came back negative—no dressing as a woman while working as a pharmacist.

"There was no talking about it," Dower said. "They never contacted me. They never said, 'Let's talk about this.'"

Dower wants to eventually undergo sex reassignment surgery—a change of gender (sex) characteristics from male to female. However, her physician won't perform the surgery until she has lived as her target gender (female) around the clock for a year. Dower says she currently dresses as a man for only two occasions: work and visits with her father, who has Alzheimer's disease.

Editor's note: In cases of gender transition, the Denver Post respects preferred gender in pronoun use.

Case Questions

1. What would you recommend that management at King Soopers do about Dower's request to dress like a woman while on the job?

2. What business excuse might management at King Soopers offer for turning down Dower's request to wear women's clothing?

3. What compromise can you offer to satisfy the positions of both Kim Dower and management at the King Soopers?

4. What has this case got to do with cultural diversity in the workplace?

Source: Kelly Pate Dwyer, "Transsexual Charges Soopers Bias," July 7, 2004. The Denver Post. Reprinted with permission.

CHAPTER 5

Resolving Conflicts with Others

A Canadian company upgraded its desktop computers, including the installation of the latest version of a widely used operating system. Users of the systems were informed that the new software had a "help" function that would answer practically all their technical questions. Many workers were confused by the help function, so they needed to rely on the information technology (IT) department for assistance. Yet, many workers said they felt "like an idiot" when they called the IT help desk for assistance with desktop computing problems. One of the non-IT workers surveyed described the problem this way: "I don't need to call someone on the phone to ask a question, then have him come in and go zoom, zoom, zoom, zip, zip, zip, with a mouse and he's lost me so I've never learned anything."[1]

Learning Objectives

After reading and studying this chapter and doing the exercises you should be able to

1. Recognize your typical method of resolving conflict.
2. Specify why so much interpersonal conflict exists in organizations.
3. Identify the five styles of handling conflict.
4. Develop effective techniques for resolving conflict and negotiating.
5. Understand how to combat sexual harassment in the workplace.

Discussion Question

1. What might be done about this type of conflict between workers from outside the IT group, and IT support professionals?

The unfortunate incident between the worker from outside the IT department and the IT specialist illustrates two different meanings of conflict. A conflict is a situation in which two or more goals, values, or events are incompatible or mutually exclusive. The man with the problem wants his computer and software to run smoothly so he does not have to ask for help. Yet when he has to ask for help, he wants a deliberate, reassuring approach. The IT specialist is so busy that he wants to help people as quickly and efficiently as possible. Yet when he zips through the task, the person needing help is confused and has not learned much. A conflict is also a strife, quarrel, or battle. The worker needing help is angry that the help specialist moves so quickly through his process of giving assistance. In turn, the IT specialist wishes the person needing help were more computer savvy so he wouldn't receive an angry and confused look when he is trying to help.

This chapter will help you improve your ability to resolve conflicts with people at work. The same techniques are also useful in personal life. To improve your understanding of how to resolve conflict, this chapter will present specific techniques and also explain why so much conflict exists. To get you started relating the topic of conflict to yourself, take Self-Assessment Quiz 5-1.

Learning Objective 1 ▶

Learning Objective 2 ▶

SOURCES OF INTERPERSONAL CONFLICT IN ORGANIZATIONS

Conflict between and among people has many sources, or causes. In this section I describe six of the leading sources. If you understand the cause of a conflict, it can help you resolve the conflict and help prevent a similar recurrence. For example, if you learn that much conflict on the job is caused by people being uncivil toward each other, you might remind yourself to behave civilly. You can also learn how to deal with uncivil coworkers so they treat you less rudely. Although specific sources of conflict can be identified, keep in mind an important fact. All conflict includes the underlying theme of incompatibility between your goals, values, or events and those of another person.

COMPETITION FOR LIMITED RESOURCES

An underlying source of job conflict is that few people can get all the resources they want. These resources include money, material, and human resources. Conflicts arise when two or more people squabble over who should get the resources. Even in a prosperous organization, resources have to be divided in such a manner that not everybody gets what he or she wants.

Assume that you believe you need to have a photocopier immediately accessible the full workday. Yet the company has decided that three people must share one photocopier. As a result, you are likely to enter into conflict with the two others sharing the photocopier. The conflict will be intense if your two coworkers also think they need full-time access to a photocopier.

ROLE CONFLICT

A major source of conflict (and stress) on the job relates to being placed in a predicament. Role conflict stems from having to choose between two competing demands or expectations. If you comply with one aspect of a role, compliance with the other is difficult or impossible. An important example would be receiving contradictory orders from two people above you in your company. If you comply with the wishes of one person, you will antagonize the other.

A high-performing sales representative received a job offer from a manager in another division in her company. Her present manager told her she was not allowed

SELF-ASSESSMENT QUIZ 5–1

STYLES OF CONFLICT MANAGEMENT

Directions: Check the alternative that best fits your typical reaction to the situation described.

Part I: The Quiz

1. When someone is overly hostile toward me, I usually:
   _____ A. respond in kind
   _____ B. persuade him or her to cool down
   _____ C. hear the person out
   _____ D. walk away

2. When I walk in on a heated argument, I'm likely to:
   _____ A. jump in and take sides
   _____ B. mediate
   _____ C. keep quiet and observe
   _____ D. leave the scene

3. When I suspect that another person is taking advantage of me, I:
   _____ A. try to get the person to stop
   _____ B. rely on persuasion and facts
   _____ C. change how I relate to the person
   _____ D. accept the situation

4. When I don't see eye to eye with someone, I typically:
   _____ A. try to get him or her to see things my way
   _____ B. consider the problem logically
   _____ C. search for a workable compromise
   _____ D. let the problem work itself out

5. After a run-in with someone I care about a great deal, I:
   _____ A. try to make him or her see it my way
   _____ B. try to work out our differences
   _____ C. wait before renewing contact
   _____ D. let it lie

6. When I see conflict developing between two people I care about, I usually:
   _____ A. express disappointment
   _____ B. try to mediate
   _____ C. watch to see what develops
   _____ D. leave the scene

(Continued)

7. When I see conflict developing between two people who are relatively unimportant to me, I usually:

_____ A. express disappointment

_____ B. try to mediate

_____ C. watch to see what develops

_____ D. leave the scene

8. The feedback people give me indicates that I:

_____ A. push hard to get what I want

_____ B. try to work out differences

_____ C. take a conciliatory stance

_____ D. sidestep conflict

9. When having serious disagreements, I:

_____ A. talk until I've made my point

_____ B. talk a little more than I listen

_____ C. listen and make sure I understand

_____ D. listen passively

10. When someone does something that angers me, I generally:

_____ A. use strong, direct language

_____ B. try to persuade him or her to stop

_____ C. go easy, explaining how I feel

_____ D. say and do nothing

Part II: Score Analysis

When you've completed the questions, add all the As, Bs, Cs, and Ds to find where you collected the most responses. Then consider these profiles:

A. *Competitive.* If you picked mostly "A" responses, you feel best when you're able to direct and control others. Taken to extremes, you can be intimidating and judgmental. You are generally contemptuous of people who don't stand up for themselves, and you feel frustrated when you can't get through to someone.

B. *Collaborative.* If you scored high in this category, you may be from the "use your head to win" school of conflict management—strong-willed and ambitious, but not overbearing. You'll use persuasion, not intimidation, and are willing to compromise to end long-running conflicts.

C. *Sharing.* People who score high here don't get fired up. They listen to the opponent's point of view, analyze situations, and make a factual pitch for their case. But in the end, they will defer to opponents in the interest of harmony.

D. *Accommodative.* A high score suggests that you avoid conflict and confrontation at all costs and suppress your feelings—strong as they may be—to keep peace.

Observation: No one style of conflict management is better than another. Most people use all four, depending on the situation. But if you rely too much on one, start shifting your approach.

Source: Quiz on styles of Conflict Management, February 20, 1990, p. 6. *National Institute of Business Management.* Reprinted with permission.

to transfer and made her a counteroffer. The sales representative found herself in conflict with the two managers. Distraught over the conflict, she found employment with a competitive firm in a comparable position to the internal job offer she had received.

Role conflict can take various forms. You might be asked to accomplish two objectives that are in apparent conflict. If your boss asked you to hurry up and finish your work but also decrease your mistakes, you would experience the conflict of incompatible demands (plus perhaps a headache!). Another problem is when two or more people give you incompatible directions. Your immediate supervisor may want you to complete a crash project on time, but company policy temporarily prohibits authorizing overtime payments to clerical help or hiring office temporaries.

Role conflict also results when two different roles that you play are in conflict. Your company may expect you to travel 50 percent of the time, whereas your spouse threatens a divorce if you travel over 25 percent of the time. To complete the picture, *role–person conflict* takes place when the role(s) your organization expects you to occupy is in conflict with your basic values. Your company may ask you to fire substandard performers, but this could be in conflict with your humanistic values.

COMPETING WORK AND FAMILY DEMANDS

Balancing the demands of career and family life has become a major role conflict facing today's workforce. The challenge is particularly intense for employees who are part of a two-wage-earner family. Work–family conflict occurs when an individual's roles of worker and active participant in social and family life compete with one another. This type of conflict is frequent because the multiple roles are often incompatible. Imagine having planned to attend your child's solo recital and then being ordered at the last minute to be present at an after-hours meeting. Work–family conflict can lead to interpersonal conflict because your boss or coworkers might think that you are asking them to cover for you while you attend to personal matters.

Work–family conflict can be viewed from two perspectives, with both leading to conflict and stress. A person's work can interfere with family responsibilities, or family responsibilities can interfere with work. In the above example, the person might say, "This is terrible. The meeting called for at the last minute will block me from attending my child's solo recital." Or the same person might say, "This is terrible. My child's solo recital is going to block me from attending an important last-minute meeting."

Work–family conflict can be a major stressor and can lead to emotional disorders, as revealed by a study of 2,700 employed adults. Two types of work–family conflict were studied: family life creating problems at work, and work creating problems at home. Emotional problems were measured by diagnostic interviews. Both types of conflict were associated with having mood disorders, disturbing levels of anxiety, and substance abuse. Also, employees who reported work–family conflict were much more likely to have a clinically significant mental health problem.[2]

Many companies offer flexible working hours to a majority of their employees. In this way, a worker might be able to meet family demands that take place during typical working hours. An example would be taking off the morning to care for an ill parent, then working later that same evening. People who are exceptionally good at organizing their time and efforts will often experience less work–family conflict, by such behaviors as staying on top of work to minimize periods of time when they are completely work-centered.[3]

PERSONALITY CLASHES

Many workplace disagreements arise because people simply dislike each other. A personality clash is thus an antagonistic relationship between two people based on differences in personal attributes, preferences, interests, values, and styles. A personality clash reflects negative chemistry between two people, while personal differences are based more specifically on a value clash.

work–family conflict
A state that occurs when an individual's roles of worker and active participant in social and family life compete with each other.

personality clash
An antagonistic relationship between two people based on differences in personal attributes, preferences, interests, values, and styles.

People involved in a personality clash often have difficulty specifying why they dislike each other. The end result, however, is that they cannot maintain an amiable work relationship. A peculiarity about personality clashes is that people who get along well may begin to clash after working together for a number of years. A contributing factor is that as both people change and as the situation changes, the two people may no longer be compatible.

AGGRESSIVE PERSONALITIES, INCLUDING BULLIES

aggressive personality A person who verbally, and sometimes physically, attacks others frequently.

Coworkers naturally disagree about topics, issues, and ideas. Yet some people convert disagreement into an attack that puts down other people and damages their self-esteem. As a result, conflict surfaces. Aggressive personalities are people who verbally, and sometimes physically, attack others frequently. Verbal aggression takes the form of insults, teasing, ridicule, and profanity. The aggression may also be expressed as attacks on the victim's character, competence, background, and physical appearance.[4]

Aggressiveness can also take extreme forms, such as the shooting or knifing of a former boss or colleague by a mentally unstable worker recently dismissed from the company. Violence has become so widespread that homicide is the second leading cause of workplace deaths, with about 600 workers murdered each year in the United States. In July 2003 a worker at Lockheed Martin airplane parts plant stood up in the middle of a mandatory ethics training meeting, and left for his car. He returned with several guns, and then shot to death six coworkers and wounded eight others before committing suicide.[5]

Most workplace deaths result from a robbery or commercial crime. Many of these killings, however, are perpetrated by a disgruntled worker or former employee harboring an unresolved conflict. As companies have continued to reduce their workforce despite being profitable, these incidents have increased in frequency.

INCIVILITY AND RUDENESS

incivility In human relations, employees' lack of regard for each other.

A milder form of aggressiveness in the workplace is being rude or uncivil toward work associates. Incivility (or employees' lack of regard for one another) has gained attention as a cause of workplace conflict. What constitutes being uncivil or rude depends upon a person's perceptions and values.

Imagine two people having a business lunch together. One of them answers his cell phone during lunch, and while still eating engages the caller in conversation. To some people this everyday incident would be interpreted as double rudeness—interrupting lunch with a cell phone call and eating while talking. Another person might perceive the cell phone incident to be standard behavior in a multitasking world. Rudeness also includes swearing at coworkers, a cubicle dweller shouting loudly on the phone while making a personal call, and performing other work at a meeting. Typical forms of "other work" are sorting through paper mail or surfing the Internet on a notebook computer.

A study conducted by Lisa Penney found that 69 percent of 300 workers she surveyed reported experiencing condescending behavior and put-downs in the workplace. Also, those who reported incivility on the job were more likely to engage in counterproductive behaviors including bad-mouthing their company, missing deadlines, and being rude to customers or clients. "Even though civility may not seem like a very serious thing," says Penney, "it is related to behaviors that have more serious consequences" that can affect profits.[6] An investigation using many forms of data collection with 2,400 people found that being treated in an uncivil manner leads employees to decrease work effort, time on the job, and productivity. When incivility is not curtailed, job satisfaction and loyalty to the company also diminish.[7]

Job–Oriented Interpersonal Skills in Action

A CAREER PERSON'S GUIDE TO BULLY BUSTING

Cindy Champnella, executive director of human resources at Schoolcraft College in Michigan, has studied office bullies. She offers the following commentary and advice:

What can you do when the playground bully grows up and becomes your boss? The truth is some people still don't get that you can't lead by fear and intimidation. You can boss people using these tactics. You can berate them into compliance but you'll never be their leader.

I once had a colleague who was a bully. After she left the company her staff had a party. They ordered a big sheet cake with this inscription: "Ding, Dong the witch is dead." How's that for a legacy?

So what are the best tactics to use with the bully on the corporate playground? If he or she is your coworker:

- Be unfailingly nice. Friendly even. Send the bully a birthday card. Only those who live in fear of him are nice to him so he won't know what to make of your kindness. It will keep him off-guard.

- Refuse to be intimidated. Look the bully square in the eye when you see her. Don't evade her at social events. Smile when you see her even if you have to force yourself.

- Push back in a nice way. When the bully sends you a nasty e-mail, don't fire one back. Take a deep breath and wait for a while. When you respond, be polite, professional, detached, and firm.

- Don't buy into the bully's tactics. The bully will try to enlist you in her shame and blame game. Bullys love to look for ways to humiliate and punish others. Don't let her rope you into it, too. If she comes to you for assistance in these kinds of strategies, politely distance yourself from her. Your colleagues will have long memories.

- Don't even try to explain decisions from a values-based perspective.

The bully values two things—power and inflicting pain. He won't grasp any other motivation so don't even waste your breath.

- Encourage others not to kowtow to the bully, too. There is some power in numbers.

- Don't let the bully push you off the moral high ground. This is key. If you let go of your principles to make nice with a bully you'll kick yourself for your cowardice forever.

But what do you do if the bully is your boss? Now, the stakes are higher:

- Keep your head down. Avoid the bully whenever possible.

- Swallow your rage. You can't fight a bully-boss and win. He'll squash you like a bug.

- Refuse to become a junior bully. I've seen this happen to some formerly nice people. Juiced up by the bully's power and influence and working under the bully's protection, they begin to bully themselves. It's fun to push people around. See how much fun it is when the bully transfers to another division and you're left to work with those you pounced on.

- Never show fear. Bullies get this designation from the fact that they love to pick on the weak and powerless. If they see that they've scared you, you'll become their favorite victim.

Questions

1. After completing this chapter, explain which technique of conflict resolution seems well suited to dealing with office bullies.

2. What might the workers involved have done earlier so their Ding, Dong cake celebration would have been unnecessary?

Source: Adapted from Cindy Champnella, "Don't Let Corporate Bullies Ruin Your Job," *detnews.com,* February 13, 2004.

Learning Objective 3 ▶ # CONFLICT-MANAGEMENT STYLES

The information presented so far is designed to help you understand the nature of conflict. Such background information is useful for resolving conflict because it helps you understand what is happening in a conflict situation. The next two sections offer more specific information about managing and resolving conflict. Before describing specific methods of resolving conflict, it is useful to present more details about five general styles, or modes, of handling conflict. You received preliminary information on four of these five styles when you completed Self-Assessment Quiz 5-1.

As shown in Figure 5-1, Kenneth Thomas identified five major styles of conflict management. Each style is based on a combination of satisfying one's own concerns (assertiveness) and satisfying the concerns of others (cooperativeness).[8]

COMPETITIVE STYLE

The competitive style is a desire to win one's own concerns at the expense of the other party, or to dominate. A person with a competitive orientation is likely to engage in power struggles in which one side wins and the other loses (an approach referred to as win–lose). "My way or the highway" is a win–lose strategy. The competitive style works best when quick, decisive action is essential, such as in an emergency.

ACCOMMODATIVE STYLE

The accommodative style favors appeasement, or satisfying the other's concerns without taking care of one's own. People with this orientation may be generous or self-sacrificing just to maintain a relationship. An irate customer might be accommodated with a full refund, just to calm down the person. The intent of such accommodation might also be to retain the customer's loyalty. Accommodation sounds harmless, but, according to Sidney Simon, when it runs unchecked at the expense of what somebody really wants it can lead to debilitating resentment, sickness, or even violence.[9] The problem is that the suppressed feelings create inner conflict and stress.

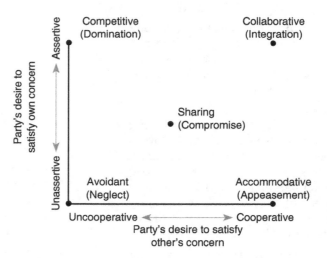

FIGURE 5-1 Conflict-Handling Styles According to Degree of Cooperation and Assertiveness

Source: Kenneth W. Thomas, "Organizational Conflict" in Steven Kerr, ed., *Organization, Behavior* (Columbus, OH: Grid Publishing, 1979), p. 156.

Accommodation works best when you are wrong, or when the issues are more important to the other side. For example, an automobile sales associate might say yes to a last-minute demand for another $25 concession, rather than continuing to haggle.

SHARING STYLE

The sharing style is halfway between domination and appeasement. Sharers prefer moderate but incomplete satisfaction for both parties, which results in a compromise. The phrase "splitting the difference" reflects this orientation and is commonly used in such activities as purchasing a house or car. The sharing (or compromising) style is well suited to a situation in which both sides have equal power, yet are committed to mutually exclusive goals such as the buyer and seller of the house wanting to maximize financial gain.

COLLABORATIVE STYLE

In contrast to the other styles, the collaborative style reflects a desire to fully satisfy the desires of both parties. It is based on an underlying philosophy of win–win, the belief that after conflict has been resolved, both sides should gain something of value. The use of a win–win approach is aimed at arriving at a settlement that meets the needs of both parties, or at least does not badly damage the welfare of the other side. The option chosen results in a mutual gain. When collaborative approaches to resolving conflict are used, the relationships among the parties are built on and improved. The following example uses a win–win approach to resolve conflict.

win–win The belief that after conflict has been resolved both sides should gain something of value.

> Bruce is an office assistant in a company that supplies food to restaurants, hospitals, and nursing homes. According to his budget analysis, Bruce needed a 5 percent salary increase to meet his monthly expenses. The company owner explained that there was no money in the budget for a salary increase. A cordial discussion about the issue led to an option for mutual gain. Bruce would receive the 5 percent salary increase as long as he increased his productivity enough to cover the increase. His target was to increase his productivity to the point that the company could decrease the hours worked by an office temporary. The amount of the decrease covered the 5 percent salary increase.

Wireless phone companies in search of antenna sites have led to win–win conflict resolution between companies and communities. Many of these companies have integrated antennas into church steeples, high-rise buildings, and other tall structures without defacing them. A wireless telephone company has sometimes constructed a new church steeple that harbors a giant antenna. The company wins by having an antenna to provide cell telephone service, and community groups do not object to the sight of a freestanding antenna. At the same time, the church wins by having a new steeple.

Collaborating is particularly important when both sides must be committed to the solution, such as the situation with the hidden cell antennae. Divorcing parents also need collaboration in their division of assets because they need to work together long term for the good of the children.

Finding win–win solutions to problems (or options for mutual gain) is one of the most important conflict-resolution skills. To obtain practice in this skill, do Skill-Building Exercise 5-1.

AVOIDANT STYLE

The avoider is a combination of a person who is uncooperative and unassertive. He or she is indifferent to the concerns of either party. The person may actually be withdrawing from the conflict to rely upon fate. Avoiding works well when an issue is trivial, or there are more pressing issues to worry about. For example, a supervisor

SKILL-BUILDING EXERCISE 5-1

WIN–WIN CONFLICT RESOLUTION

The class organizes into small problem-solving groups. Each group spends about 10 minutes finding a win–win solution to one of the following conflict situations.

1. Two coworkers want you to go to lunch with them more regularly, but you believe that you are too busy to go out to lunch regularly.
2. William, an accountant, wants workmates to call him "William." Yet several people in the office persist in calling him "Bill" or "Will."
3. You are offered a transfer within your company to an exciting job that you want strongly. Your manager says he cannot let you go because you are too valuable.

might not bother reprimanding workers who are a few minutes late because the supervisor is flooded with other work.

In the following description of specific techniques for resolving conflict, attempt to relate most of them to these five key styles. For example, you will observe that the confrontation and problem-solving technique reflects the collaborative style.

Learning Objective 4 ▶

GUIDELINES AND TECHNIQUES FOR RESOLVING CONFLICTS

Interpersonal conflict in organizations is inevitable. A career-minded person must therefore learn effective ways of resolving conflict. This section describes methods of conflict resolution that you can use on your own. All are based somewhat on the underlying model of win–win, or integrating the interests of both parties. Integrating both interests focuses on resolving the underlying concerns of the parties in conflict. By dealing with these concerns, it is more worthwhile for both sides to resolve the conflict than it is to have no agreement.

> Suppose a man named Bill Budweiser wanted to open a beer brewery and name his beer Budweiser. The company lawyers from Anheuser-Busch, which own the rights to the brand name Budweiser, would attempt to block him from using the same brand name—even if his family name is Budweiser. Bill Budweiser would hire his own lawyer to fight back. Two key concerns must be addressed. Mr. Budweiser's underlying concern is that he feels his civil liberties have been violated because he cannot name a business after himself. And Bill Budweiser must deal with Anheuser-Busch's concern about a smaller company capitalizing on its well-known name (brand equity).

Later in the chapter you will be asked to resolve the beer company conflict. The following paragraphs describe four methods of conflict resolution.

CONFRONTATION AND PROBLEM SOLVING

The ideal approach to resolving any conflict is to confront the real issue and then solve the problem. **Confrontation** means taking a problem-solving approach to differences and identifying the underlying facts, logic, or emotions that account for them. When conflicts are resolved through confronting and understanding their causes, people feel responsible for finding the soundest answer.[10]

Confrontation can proceed gently, in a way that preserves a good working relationship, as shown by this example. Assume that Mary, the person working at the desk next to you, loudly cracks chewing gum while she works. You find the gum chewing both distracting and nauseating. If you don't bring the problem to Mary's attention, it will probably grow in proportion with time. Yet you are hesitant to enter into an argument about something that a person might regard as a civil liberty (the right to chew gum in public places).

A psychologically sound alternative is for you to approach her directly in this manner:

You: Mary, there is something bothering me that I would like to discuss with you.

She: Go ahead, I don't mind listening to other people's problems.

You: My problem concerns something you are doing that makes it difficult for me to concentrate on my work. When you chew gum you make loud cracking noises that grate on my nerves. It may be my problem, but the noise does bother me.

She: I guess I could stop chewing gum when you're working next to me. It's probably just a nervous habit.

Back to the Opening Case

Perhaps the man who asked for help from the IT support group had a legitimate gripe about the IT specialist going through his routines too rapidly. But did the person requesting help make any attempt to confront and resolve the problem? Confrontation and problem solving might be effective in resolving this type of conflict.

CONSTRUCTIVE HANDLING OF CRITICISM

Learning to profit from criticism is an effective way of benefiting from conflict. People who benefit from criticism are able to stand outside themselves while being criticized. It is as if they are watching the criticism from a distance and looking for its possible merits. People who take criticism personally anguish when receiving negative feedback. Following are several specific suggestions for dealing with criticism, including two methods that will often get the other party on your side.[11]

1. **See yourself at a distance.** Place an imaginary Plexiglas shield between you and the person giving the criticism. Attempt to be a detached observer looking for useful information.

2. **Ask for clarification and specifics.** Ask politely for more details about the negative behavior in question so you can change if change is warranted. If your boss is criticizing you for being rude to customers, you might respond: "I certainly do not want to be rude. Can you give me a couple of examples of how I was rude? I need your help in working on this problem." After asking questions, you can better determine whether the criticism is valid.

3. **Decide on a response.** An important part of learning from criticism is to respond appropriately to the critic. Let the criticizer know what you agree with. Apologize for the undesirable behavior, such as saying, "I apologize for being rude to customers. I know what I can do differently now. I'll be more patient so as not to appear rude."

4. **Look for a pattern in terms of other criticism.** Is the criticism you are receiving something you have heard several times before from different people? The more times you have heard the same criticism, the more likely it is to be valid. If three different supervisors have told you that you do not follow through with your promises to get work done, the criticism is most likely valid.

5. **Disarm the opposition.** As an extension of the point just made, you will often decide to agree with the criticizer because the person has a legitimate complaint about you. If you deny the reality of that person's complaint, he or she will continue to harp on that point and the issue will remain unresolved. By agreeing with the criticism of you, you may set the stage for a true resolution of the problem.

Agreeing with criticism made by a person with formal authority over you is effective because by doing so you are then in a position to ask for his or her help in improving the situation. Rational managers realize that it is their responsibility to help group members overcome problems, not merely to criticize them. Imagine that you have been chronically late with reports during the last six months. It is time for a performance evaluation, and you know that you will be reprimanded for your tardiness. You also hope that your manager will not downgrade all other aspects of your performance because of your tardy reports. Here is how disarming the opposition would work in this situation:

Your manager: Have a seat. It's time for your performance evaluation, and we have a lot to talk about. I'm concerned about some things.

You: So am I. It appears that I'm having a difficult time getting my reports in on time. I wonder if I'm being a perfectionist. Do you have any suggestions?

Your manager: Well, I like your attitude. Maybe you are trying to make your reports too perfect before you turn them in. I think you can improve in getting your reports in on time. Try not to figure out everything to three decimal places. We need thoroughness around here, but we can't overdo it.

Disarming is effective because it takes the wind out of the other person's sails and has a calming effect. The other person is often waiting to clobber you if you deny guilt. If you admit guilt, you are more difficult to clobber. Skill-Building Exercise 5-2 gives you an opportunity to practice disarming the opposition.

SKILL-BUILDING EXERCISE 5-2

DISARMING THE OPPOSITION

In each of these two scenarios, one person plays the role of the person with more power in the situation. The other person plays the role of the individual attempting to disarm the criticizer.

1. A representative from a credit agency telephones you at work to inform you that you are 60 days behind schedule on your car payment. The agent wants a settlement as soon as possible. Unfortunately, the credit agent is correct. Run this happy scenario for about five minutes.

2. Your manager calls you into the office to discuss the 10-page report you just submitted. The boss says in a harsh tone, "Your report is a piece of trash. I counted 25 word-use mistakes such as writing *whether* for *weather* and *seen* for *scene*. (Your spell checker couldn't catch these errors.) Besides that I can't follow many of your sentences, and you left out the table of statistics. I'm wondering if you are qualified for this job."

COGNITIVE RESTRUCTURING

An indirect way of resolving interpersonal conflict is to lessen the conflicting elements in a situation by viewing them more positively. According to the technique of cognitive restructuring, you mentally convert negative aspects into positive ones by looking for the positive elements in a situation. How you frame or choose your thoughts can determine the outcome of a conflict situation. Your thoughts influence your actions. If you search for the beneficial elements in the situation, there will be less area for dispute. Although this technique might sound like a mind game to you, it can work effectively.

Imagine that a coworker of yours, Jeff, has been asking you repeated questions about how to carry out a work procedure. You are about ready to tell Jeff, "Go bother somebody else; I'm not paid to be a trainer." Instead, you look for the positive elements in the situation. You say to yourself, "Jeff has been asking me a lot of questions. This does take time, but answering these questions is valuable experience. If I want to become a manager, I will have to help group members with problems."

After having completed this cognitive restructuring, you can then deal with the conflict situation more positively. You might say to Jeff, "I welcome the opportunity to help you, but we need to find a mutually convenient time. In that way, I can better concentrate on my own work." To get started with cognitive restructuring, do Skill-Building Exercise 5-3.

cognitive restructuring Mentally converting negative aspects into positive ones by looking for the positive elements in a situation.

NEGOTIATING AND BARGAINING

Conflicts can be considered situations calling for negotiating, or conferring with another person to resolve a problem. When you are negotiating a fair salary for yourself, you are trying to resolve a conflict. At first the demands of the two parties may seem incompatible, but through negotiation, a salary figure may emerge that satisfies both.

negotiating Conferring with another person to resolve a problem.

SKILL-BUILDING EXERCISE 5-3

COGNITIVE RESTRUCTURING

The following are examples of negative statements about coworkers. In the space provided, cognitively restructure (reframe) each comment in a positive way.

Negative: Nancy is getting on my nerves. It takes her two weeks longer than anyone else on the team to complete her input.
Positive:

Negative: My boss is driving me crazy. He is forever telling me what I did wrong and making suggestions for improvement. He makes me feel like I'm in elementary school.
Positive:

Managers and staff specialists must negotiate both internally (e.g., with subordinates, managers, and team leaders) and externally (e.g., with suppliers and government agencies). Considerable negotiation also takes place among coworkers. Team members, for example, sometimes negotiate among themselves about work assignments. One might say to the other, "I'm willing to be notetaker this year if there is some way I can cut back on the amount of plant visits I make this year." Six useful negotiating tactics are presented here. Before studying them, do Self-Assessment Quiz 5-2.

SELF-ASSESSMENT QUIZ 5-2

THE NEGOTIATOR QUIZ

Directions: The following quiz is designed to give you tentative insight into your tendencies toward being an effective negotiator. Check whether each statement is mostly true or mostly false as it applies to you.

	Mostly true	Mostly false
1. Settling differences of opinion is a lot of fun.		
2. I try to avoid conflict and confrontation with others as much as possible.		
3. I am self-conscious asking people for favors they have not offered me spontaneously.		
4. I am generally unwilling to compromise.		
5. How the other side feels about the results of our negotiation is of little consequence to me.		
6. I think very well under pressure.		
7. People say that I am tactful and diplomatic.		
8. I have heard that I express my viewpoint clearly.		
9. Very few things in life are not negotiable.		
10. I always (or would always) accept whatever salary increase is offered me.		
11. A person's facial expression often reveals as much as what the person actually says.		
12. I wouldn't mind taking a few short-term losses to win a long-term battle.		
13. I'm willing to work long and hard to win a small advantage.		
14. I'm usually too busy talking to do much listening.		
15. It's fun to haggle over price when buying a car.		
16. I almost always prepare in advance for a negotiating session.		
17. When there is something I need from another person I usually get it.		
18. It would make me feel cheap if I offered somebody only two-thirds of his or her asking price.		
19. People are usually paid what they are worth, so there's no use haggling over starting salaries.		

20. I rarely take what people say at face value.   _____   _____

21. It's easy for me to smile when involved in a serious discussion.   _____   _____

22. For one side to win in negotiation, the other side has to lose.   _____   _____

23. Once you start making concessions, the other side is bound
to get more than you.   _____   _____

24. A good negotiating session gets my competitive urges flowing.   _____   _____

25. When negotiations are completed, both sides should walk
away with something valuable.   _____   _____

Total Score   _____   _____

Scoring and Interpretation: Score yourself 1 for each of your answers that agrees with the scoring key. The higher your score, the more likely it is that you currently have good negotiating skills, providing your self-assessment is accurate. It might prove useful to also have somebody who has observed you negotiate on several occasions to answer the Negotiator Quiz for you. Scores of 7 or lower and 20 or higher are probably the most indicative of weak or strong negotiating potential. Here is the scoring key:

1. Mostly true	8. Mostly true	15. Mostly true	22. Mostly false
2. Mostly false	9. Mostly true	16. Mostly true	23. Mostly false
3. Mostly false	10. Mostly false	17. Mostly true	24. Mostly true
4. Mostly false	11. Mostly true	18. Mostly false	25. Mostly true
5. Mostly false	12. Mostly true	19. Mostly false	
6. Mostly true	13. Mostly true	20. Mostly true	
7. Mostly true	14. Mostly false	21. Mostly true	

Focus on Interests, Not Positions

Rather than clinging to specific negotiating points, keep your overall interests in mind and try to satisfy them. Remember that the true object of negotiation is to satisfy the underlying interests on both sides, as in the case of Bill Budweiser. Part of focusing on interests is to carefully study the other side's comments for clues to the type of agreement that will satisfy both of you.

Careful listening will help you uncover the negotiating partner's specific interests and motivations. Here is how this strategy works:

You are considering accepting a job offer that will enable you to work on the type of problems you prefer and also develop your professional skills. You have a starting salary in mind that would make you very happy—10 percent higher than you are currently making. Your negotiating position is thus your present salary plus 10 percent. However, your true interests are probably to have more discretionary income than at present. (You want to make more purchases and invest more.) You will therefore be better off negotiating for a work situation that spreads your money further. You can now accept the offer by negotiating other points in addition to a 10 percent higher salary, including (1) working in a geographic area with a lower cost of living, (2) having a better opportunity for earning a bonus, or (3) receiving a generous expense account. During the negotiations you may discover that the other party is looking for a talented employee at a salary and benefits the company can afford.

Compromise

The most widely used negotiating tactic is compromise, settlement of differences by mutual concessions. One party agrees to do something if the other party agrees to do something else. Compromise is a realistic approach to resolving conflict. Most

compromise
Settlement of differences by mutual concessions.

labor–management disputes are settled by compromise. For instance, labor may agree to accept a smaller salary increase if management will subcontract less work to other countries.

Some people argue that compromise is not a win–win tactic. The problem is that the two parties may wind up with a solution that pacifies both but does not solve the problem. One example would be purchasing for two team leaders half the new equipment each one needs. As a result, neither department really shows a productivity gain. Nevertheless, compromise is both inevitable and useful.

Begin with a Plausible Demand or Offer, Yet Allow Room for Negotiation

The commonsense approach to negotiation suggests that you begin with an extreme, almost fanciful demand or offer. The final compromise will therefore be closer to your true demand or offer than if you opened the negotiations more realistically. However, a plausible demand is useful because it shows you are bargaining in good faith. Also, if a third party has to resolve a conflict, a plausible demand or offer will receive more sympathy than an implausible one will.

> *A judge listened to the cases of two people who claimed they were the victims of age discrimination by the same employer. The lawyer for the first alleged victim asked for $10 million in damages; the lawyer for the second victim asked for $200,000. The first person was awarded $50,000 in damages, and the second person $150,000. An inside source reported that the judge was so incensed by the first lawyer's demands that she decided to teach him a lesson.*

Although it is advisable to begin with a plausible demand, one must still allow room for negotiation. A basic strategy of negotiation is to begin with a demand that allows room for compromise and concession. If you think you need $5,000 in new software for your department, you might begin negotiations by asking for a $7,000 package. Your boss offers you $4,000 as a starting point. After negotiation, you may wind up with the $5,000 you need.

Make Small Concessions Gradually

Making steady concessions leads to more mutually satisfactory agreements in most situations. Gradually, you concede little things to the other side. The hard-line approach to bargaining is to make your concession early in the negotiation and then grant no further concession. The tactic of making small concessions is well suited to purchasing a new car. In order to reach a price you consider acceptable, you might grant concessions such as agreeing to finance the car through the dealer or purchasing a service contract.

Know Your Best Alternative to a Negotiated Agreement (BATNA)

The reason you would probably negotiate would be to produce something better than the result obtainable without negotiating. The goal of negotiating is thus not just to agree, but to obtain more valuable results than would otherwise have occurred. When you are aware of your best alternative to a negotiated agreement (BATNA), it sets a floor to the agreement you are willing to accept. Your BATNA becomes the standard that can protect both parties from accepting terms that are too unfavorable. It also keeps you from walking away from terms that would be beneficial for you to accept.

What might a BATNA look like in practice? Suppose you are negotiating a starting salary for a full-time, professional position. The figure you have in mind is $38,000 per year. Your BATNA is $32,500 because this is the salary your future in-laws will pay you to enter the family business. You will therefore walk away from any offer of less than $33,000—just taking salary into account.

Knowing the other side's BATNA is also important because it helps define the other participant's bargaining zone. Understanding each other's bargaining zones makes it possible to arrive at mutually profitable trade-offs. In the preceding salary negotiations, the company's BATNA might be to hire a less well-educated job candidate at $27,500 and then upgrade his or her knowledge on the job.

Use Anger to Your Advantage

Master negotiators make selective use of anger as a negotiating and bargaining tool. When a person becomes genuinely angry, the anger can energize him or her to be more resourceful and creative while bargaining. If you are angry about an issue or a negotiating point, the other side may be willing to submit to your demand rather than receive more of your anger. The director of a company wellness program might say with an angry look toward top management, "Why is there money in the budget for all kinds of frills like corporate jets, when a program that is preventing millions of dollars in lost productivity has to grovel for a decent budget?"

The downside of anger is that it can degenerate into incivility and personal insults. A touch of anger can be effective, but overdone it becomes self-defeating. You have to size up how far you can push people before damaging a work relationship— or being fired. To make effective use of anger during negotiation, it has to be used at the right time, with the right tone, and in the right amount.[12] A person who is always angry will often not be taken seriously.

Effective negotiation, as with any other form of conflict resolution, requires extensive practice and knowledge of basic principles and techniques. As a starting point you might take one of the negotiating tactics just described and practice it where the stakes are not so high. You might attempt to negotiate the price of a consumer electronics device, or negotiate for getting a particular Friday afternoon off from work.

A major theme running through the various approaches to conflict resolution, including negotiating and bargaining, is that cooperating with the other side is usually preferable to competing. A study with 61 self-managing teams with 489 employees supports this idea of the superiority of cooperation over competition in successful conflict resolution. The style of conflict resolution was measured through questionnaires. For example, a question geared toward cooperative behavior was "We seek a solution that will be good for the whole team." Conflict efficacy was measured by a questionnaire indicating that the extent to which team members believed that they could successfully measure different conflict situations. Group effectiveness was measured by the ratings of supervisor and team leaders on productivity, quality, and cost savings—central reasons why self-directed teams are formed.

The study found that the cooperative approach to conflict was positively related to conflict efficacy. In contrast, the competitive approach to conflict was negatively related to conflict efficacy. Equally important, conflict efficacy was strongly associated with supervisory and team leader ratings of team effectiveness.[13]

◀ Learning Objective 5

> *In ordinary life, we classify anger as an emotion—a catalytic and cathartic one that provokes comment, discussion and often backlash. At the bargaining table, however, anger is better viewed as nothing more than a tactic.*
> —Marc Diener, a speaker and attorney in Los Angeles

COMBATTING SEXUAL HARASSMENT: A SPECIAL TYPE OF CONFLICT

Many employees face conflict because a supervisor, coworker, or customer sexually harasses them. Sexual harassment is generally defined as unwanted sexually oriented behavior in the workplace that results in discomfort or interference with the job. It can include an action as violent as rape or as subtle as a sexually oriented comment about a person's body or appearance. Harassment creates conflict because the harassed person has to make a choice between two incompatible motives. One motive is to get ahead, keep the job, or have an unthreatening work environment. But to satisfy this motive, the person is forced to sacrifice the motive of holding on to his or her moral value or preferences. Here we will focus on the types and frequency of sexual harassment, recent legal rulings on the nature of harassment, the effects of harassment, and guidelines for dealing with the problem.

sexual harassment Unwanted sexually oriented behavior in the workplace that results in discomfort or interference with the job.

TYPES AND FREQUENCY OF HARASSMENT

The courts recognize two types of sexual harassment. In *quid pro quo* sexual harassment, the individual suffers job loss, or threatened loss of a job benefit, as a result of his or her responses to a request for sexual favors. The demands of a harasser can be explicit or implied. An example of quid pro quo harassment would be a manager promising an employee a promotion in exchange for sexual favors and then not promoting the employee because the employee refused.

The other form of sexual harassment is hostile *environment harassment.* It occurs when someone in the workplace creates an intimidating, hostile, or offensive working environment. An employee who is subjected to sexually suggestive comments, lewd jokes, or advances is a victim of hostile environment harassment. No tangible loss has to be suffered in this form of sexual harassment.

An analysis of many studies indicated that women perceive a broader range of social-sexual behaviors as harassing. The analysis also found that the female–male difference was larger for behaviors associated with hostile work environment harassment, derogatory attitudes toward women, dating pressure, or physical sexual contact. Men and women, however, agree closely that various types of sexual coercion, such as encounters that are made a condition of promotion, can be classified as quid pro quo harassment.[14]

Sexual harassment is also regarded as an expression of power by one individual over another because the harasser has more formal power than the harassed. The harasser, following this logic, is a power abuser as well as a legal offender. At the same time, sexual harassment is an aggressive act designed to achieve the aggressor's goals.[15] Carrying the power analysis of sexual attraction to the extreme, when a lower ranking male harasses a higher ranking female, he is attempting to momentarily gain power for himself. A combination of studies involving 86,000 respondents indicated that sexual harassment is more likely to take place in organizations where there is a relatively large power differential between organization levels, such as in a large bureaucracy.[16] (This is true, although large firms are more likely to have programs for preventing sexual harassment.)

Sexual harassment is widespread in the U.S. workplace and in other countries as well. According to the large-scale study just mentioned, when conclusions are based on more scientific studies, 58 percent of women report having experienced potential harassment behaviors, and 24 percent report having experienced sexual harassment on the job.[17] Furthermore, at least 10 percent have quit a job because of sexual harassment.[18] Women in nontraditional jobs (such as welder or pressroom supervisor) are especially likely to be harassed.

THE ADVERSE EFFECTS OF SEXUAL HARASSMENT

Aside from being unethical, immoral, and illegal, sexual harassment is widely thought to have adverse consequences. The harassed person may experience job stress, lowered morale, severe conflict, and lowered productivity. A study with business and university workers documents some of the problems associated with sexual harassment. It was found that even at low levels of frequency, harassment exerts a significant impact on women's psychological well-being, job attitudes, and work behaviors. For both business and university workers, women who had experienced high levels of harassment reported the worst job-related and psychological effects. The study also found that women who had experienced only a moderate level of harassment suffered from negative outcomes.[19]

A related study of the long-term effects of sexual harassment indicated that the negative effects remained two years after the incident. For example, 24 months after an incident of sexual harassment many women still experienced stress, a decrease in job satisfaction, and lowered productivity.[20]

GUIDELINES FOR PREVENTING AND DEALING WITH SEXUAL HARASSMENT

A starting point in dealing with sexual harassment is to develop an awareness of the types of behaviors that are considered sexual harassment. Often the difference is subtle. Suppose, for example, you placed copies of two nudes painted by Renoir, the French painter, on a coworker's desk. Your coworker might call that harassment. Yet if you took that coworker to a museum to see the originals of the same nude prints, your behavior usually would not be classified as harassment. Following is a sampling of behaviors that will often be interpreted as environmental harassment.[21] Awareness of these behaviors is important because many harassers have no desire to offend, or knowledge that they are offending others. Such individuals are insensitive, and often ill informed.[22] If people refrain from doing these acts, many instances of sexual harassment will be avoided.

1. Inappropriate remarks and sexual implications. Coworkers, subordinates, customers, and suppliers should not be referred to as sexual beings, and their appearance should not be referred to in a sexual manner. Telling a coworker she has gorgeous feet, or he has fabulous biceps, is out of place at work.

2. Terms of endearment. Refrain from calling others in the workplace by names such as "cutie," "sweetie pie," "honey," "dear," or "hunk." One might argue that these terms are simply sexist (different roles for men and women) and not sexual harassment. However, this argument is losing ground because any behavior that puts people down based on their gender can be interpreted as harassment from a legal perspective. Keep in mind also that some people find terms of endearment to have a sexual connotation. If you felt no physical attraction toward another adult would you call that person "cutie" or "hunk"?

3. Suggestive compliments. It is acceptable to tell another person he or she looks nice, but avoid sexually tinged comments such as mentioning that the person's clothing shows off his or her body to advantage.

4. Physical touching. To avoid any appearance of sexual harassment it is best to restrict physical touching to handshakes and an occasional sideways hug. Hugging a long-term work associate is much more acceptable than hugging a new hire. Minimize such behaviors as adjusting a coworker's earring, touching hair, and tweaking a person's chin.

5. Work-related kissing. It is best to avoid all kissing in a work context—except, perhaps, a light kiss at an office party. It is much more professional to greet a work associate with a warm, sincere handshake.

Company management also plays a major role in preventing and dealing with sexual harassment. Based on the observations of dozens of human resource specialists and employment law attorneys, several actions by management are critical.[23] The cornerstone of control of sexual harassment is creating and widely disseminating a policy about harassment. Dissemination includes stuffing copies of the sexual harassment policy in pay envelopes, distributing the policy to all employees by e-mail, and discussing the policy in department meetings.

The policy should carefully define harassment and state that the company has zero tolerance for such behavior. Company officials designated for hearing complaints should be specified. In addition, the company should have an *open-door policy* about harassment. Such a policy means that any employee with a concern about being harassed is able to go directly to a senior manager without worrying about his or her supervisor taking revenge.

Brief company training programs covering the type of information presented in this chapter are also part of a serious program to prevent and deal with sexual harassment. However, a one-time presentation of a 15-minute videotape about sexual harassment is not sufficient. Periodic discussion about the topic is recommended.

After sexual harassment has taken place, the victim will usually want to resolve the conflict. Two key strategies are either to use a formal complaint procedure or to resolve the conflict on your own. If you choose the latter course you will save yourself the time of going through a lengthy investigation procedure. Figure 5-2 presents details about the two key strategies for dealing with sexual harassment.

> The potential or actual victim of sexual harassment is advised to use the following methods and tactics to deal with the problem.
>
> **Formal Complaint Procedure.** Whenever an employee believes that he or she has encountered sexual harassment, or if an employee is suspected to be the perpetrator of sexual harassment, the complainant should report the incident to his or her immediate supervisor (if that person is not the harasser) or to the next higher level of management if the supervisor is the harasser. The supervisor contacted is responsible for contacting a designated company official immediately regarding each complaint. The officer will explain the investigative procedures to the complainant and any supervisor involved. All matters will be kept strictly confidential, including private conversations with all parties.
>
> **Dealing with the Problem on Your Own.** The easiest way to deal with sexual harassment is to speak up before it becomes serious. The first time it happens, respond with a statement such as: "I won't tolerate this kind of talk," "I dislike sexually oriented jokes," or "Keep your hands off me."

FIGURE 5–2 How to Deal with Sexual Harassment

SKILL-BUILDING EXERCISE 5-4

COMBATTING SEXUAL HARASSMENT

The two role-plays in this exercise provide practice in applying the recommended techniques for combatting sexual harassment. The activities have an implied sexual content, and they are for educational purposes only. Any students offended by these role-plays should exclude themselves from participating.

Scenario 1: The Offensive Jester. One student plays the role of Max, a man who delights in telling sexually-oriented jokes and anecdotes in the office. He often brings a tabloid newspaper to the office to read sexually-oriented passages to coworkers, both male and female. Another student assumes the role of Maxine, a woman in the office who takes offense to Max's humor. She wants to convince Max that he is committing sexual harassment with his sexually-oriented humor. Max does not see himself as committing sexual harassment.

Scenario 2: The Flirtatious Office Manager. One student assumes the role of Bertha, an office manager who is single. Another student plays the role of Bert, a married man who recently joined the company as an office assistant. Bert reports to Bertha, and she finds him physically attractive. Bertha visits Bert at his desk and makes such comments as "It looks like you have great quadriceps. I wonder what you look like in running shorts." Bert wants to be on good terms with Bertha, but he feels uncomfortable with her advances. He also wants to behave professionally in the office.

Run both role-plays in front of the class for about eight minutes. Other students in the class will observe the role-plays and then provide feedback about how well Maxine and Bert were able to prevent or stop sexual harassment.

Skill-Building Exercise 5-4 offers you an opportunity to simulate the control of sexual harassment.

A major recommendation for documenting acts of sexual harassment is to keep a running diary of incidents against you. A log of the incidents is impressive to company officials, lawyers, and judges (should a lawsuit ultimately be involved). Examples of log entries from a woman, and a man, follow:

- January 17, 2006: Jim Quattrone, the manager of accounts payable, asked me to have dinner with him for the sixth time, and I turned him down again. I said no, no, no.
- March 13, 2007: Meg Evans, my supervisor, said that I would receive a much better performance evaluation if I could come over to her house for dinner. She said her husband would be out of town, so I could stay overnight if I wanted to. I felt so uncomfortable and pressured. I made up an excuse about having an exclusive relationship.

SUMMARY

A conflict is a situation in which two or more goals, values, or events are incompatible or mutually exclusive. Interpersonal conflicts have many sources or causes. An underlying source of job conflict is that people compete for limited resources. Another leading cause of incompatibility is role conflict, having to choose between two competing demands or expectations. Competing work and family demands represent a major role conflict. Other key sources of conflict are personality clashes, aggressive personalities including bullies, and incivility and rudeness.

Five major styles of conflict management have been identified: competitive, accommodative, sharing, collaborative (win–win), and avoidant. Each style is based on a combination of satisfying one's own concerns (assertiveness) and satisfying the concerns of others (cooperativeness).

Confrontation and problem solving is the ideal method for resolving conflict. Learning to benefit from criticism is an effective way of benefiting from conflict. People who benefit from criticism are able to stand outside themselves while being criticized. Another way to deal with criticism is to disarm the opposition by agreeing with his or her criticism. Cognitive restructuring lessens conflict by the person looking for the positive elements in a situation.

Negotiating and bargaining is a major approach to resolving conflict. It includes focusing on interests rather than positions, compromising, beginning with a plausible demand or offer yet allowing room for negotiation, and making small concessions gradually. It is also important to know your BATNA (best alternative to a negotiated agreement). Using anger to your advantage can sometimes work.

Sexual harassment is a form of interpersonal conflict with legal implications. The two forms of sexual harassment are (1) demanding sex in exchange for favors and (2) creating a hostile environment. Sexual harassment is widespread in the workplace. Research has pinpointed adverse mental and physical consequences of sexual harassment.

A starting point in dealing with sexual harassment is to develop an awareness of the types of behaviors it encompasses. Company policies and complaint procedures about harassment are a major part of dealing with the problem. To deal directly with harassment, the harassed person can file a formal complaint or confront the harasser when the behavior first begins. Keeping a diary of harassing events is strongly recommended.

QUESTIONS FOR DISCUSSION AND REVIEW

1. Several large companies dismiss each year the 5 percent of their workforce receiving the lowest performance evaluations. What kind of conflicts do you think this practice leads to?
2. What good does it do for you to know a coworker's conflict style?

3. What are the disadvantages of having an accommodative style of handling conflict?

4. Remember the hypothetical conflict between Bill Budweiser and Anheuser-Busch? What solution do you propose to satisfy the underlying interests of both parties?

5. Several school systems in recent years have requested that teachers correct student work with a purple marker rather than a red one because the color red is associated with harsh criticism. What is your opinion of the merits of a shift from red markers to purple?

6. Have you ever attempted to disarm the opposition? How effective was the tactic?

7. How might a student use cognitive restructuring to get over the anger of having received a low grade in a course?

8. Visualize yourself buying a vehicle of your choice. Which negotiating technique (or techniques) would you be most likely to use?

9. Studies have shown that women working in male-dominated positions, such as a female construction supervisor or bulldozer operator, are more likely to experience sexual harassment than women in other fields. What explanation can you offer for this finding?

10. Is inviting a coworker to dinner a second time a form of sexual harassment if the coworker refused the first invitation?

GO TO THE WEB

http://www.bambooweb.com
(Provides guidelines for resolving conflict including conflict management tools)

http://www.mediate.com
(Resolving workplace conflict)

AN INTERPERSONAL RELATIONS CASE PROBLEM

A CONCERN ABOUT VIOLENCE

Vernon Bigsby is the CEO and owner of a large soft-drink bottling company in Fort Wayne, Indiana. The company periodically invests money in training to help the management and supervisory staff remain abreast of important new trends in technology and managing human resources. Bigsby recently became concerned about workplace violence. Although the company had not yet experienced an outbreak of violence, Bigsby was intent on preventing violence in the future. To accomplish this goal, Bigsby hired a human resources consultant, Sara Toomey, to conduct a seminar on preventing workplace violence.

The seminar was given twice, with one-half the managers and supervisors attending each session. Chad Ditmar, a night-shift supervisor, made the first wisecrack during the seminar. He said, "What are we here for? To prevent workers from squirting 'pop' at each other?" Toomey responded, "My job would be easy if I were here only to prevent horseplay. Unfortunately the reality is that there are thousands of lethal weapons going past your workers every day. Just think how much damage one angry worker could do to an innocent victim with one slash of a broken bottle." The laughter in the room quickly subsided.

About one hour into the seminar, Sara Toomey projected a PowerPoint slide outlining characteristics of a worker with potential for violence. She said, "Recognize that not every person who has many of these characteristics will become violent. However, they do constitute early warning signals. I would watch out for any worker with a large number of these traits and behaviors." (See Exhibit 1 for the computer slide in question.)

Ditmar supervises 45 workers directly involved in the bottling of three company brands of soft drinks. The workers in his department range in age from 18 to 57. The job usually can be learned within three days, so the workers are classified as semiskilled. After his initial wisecrack, Ditmar took the seminar quite seriously. He made extensive notes on what the consultant said, and took back to his office a printed copy of the PowerPoint slide.

EXHIBIT 1. PROFILE OF THE VIOLENT EMPLOYEE

- Socially isolated (a loner) white male, between the ages of 30 and 40.
- Fascination with the military and weapons.
- Interest in recently published violent events.
- Temper control problem with history of threats.
- Alcohol and/or drug abuser.
- Increased mood swings.
- Makes unwanted sexual advances toward other employees.
- Accepts criticism poorly and holds a grudge against the criticizer.
- Shows paranoid thinking and believes that management is out to get him (or her).
- Blames others for his or her problems.
- Makes violent statements such as spoken threats about beating up other employees.
- Damage or destruction of company property.
- Decreased productivity or inconsistent work performance.

The morning following the seminar, Ditmar sent an e-mail to Gary Bia, the vice-president of operations. Ditmar said, "I must see you today. I'm worried about a potentially explosive personnel problem." Bia made arrangements to see Ditmar at 5:45 in the afternoon, before Ditmar's shift began.

"What's up, Chad?" asked Bia.

"Here's what's up," said Ditmar. "After attending the seminar on violence, I think I've found our suspect. As you know, you do get some strange types working the night shift. Some of them don't have a normal life. I've got this one guy, Freddie Watkins. He's a loner. He wears his hair weird, with pink-colored spikes. He's got a tattoo and a huge gun collection that he brags about. I doubt the guy has any friends. He talks a lot about how he plays violent video games. Freddie told about how he once choked to death a dog that bit him.

"What really worries me is that Freddie once said he would punch out the next person who made a smart _____ comment about his hair.

"Do you agree or not that we might have a candidate for workplace violence right here in my department? I'm talking to you first, Gary, but maybe I should be speaking to the antiviolence consultant or to our security officer. What should we do next?"

Bia said, "I'm happy that you are bringing this potential problem to my attention, but I need some more facts. First of all, have you had any discipline problems yet with Freddie?"

Ditmar responded, "Not yet Gary, but we're talking about a potential killer right here on my shift. I think we have to do something."

Bia said, "Chad, I'm taking your concerns seriously, but I don't want to jump too fast. Let me think over your problem for at least a day."

Case Questions

1. What actions, if any, should Gary Bia take?
2. What type of conflict is Chad Ditmar facing?
3. What career advice can you offer Freddie Watkins?

AN INTERPERSONAL RELATIONS CASE PROBLEM

CAUGHT IN A SQUEEZE

Heather Lopez is a product development specialist at a telecommunications company. For the last seven months she has worked as a member of a product development team composed of people from five different departments within the company. Heather previously worked full time in the marketing department. Her primary responsibilities were to research the market potential of an idea for a new product. The product development team is now working on a product that will integrate a company's printers and copiers.

Heather's previous position in the marketing department was a satisfactory fit for her lifestyle. Heather thought that she was able to take care of her family responsibilities and her job without sacrificing one for the other. As Heather explains, "I worked about 45 predictable hours in my other job. My hours were essentially 8:30 A.M. to 4:30 P.M. with a little work at night and on Saturdays. But I could do the work at night and on Saturdays at home.

"Brad, my husband, and I had a smooth working arrangement for sharing the responsibility for getting our son Christopher off to school, and picking him up from the afterschool childcare center. Brad is a devoted accountant, so he understands the importance of giving high priority to a career yet still being a good family person."

In her new position as a member of the product development team, Heather is encountering some unanticipated demands. Three weeks ago, at 3 P.M. on a Tuesday, Tyler Watson, Heather's team leader, announced an emergency meeting to discuss a budget problem with the new product. The meeting would start at 4, and end at about 6:30. "Don't worry folks," said the team leader, "if it looks like we are going past 6:30 we will order in some Chinese food."

With a look of panic on her face, Heather responded to Tyler, "I can't make the meeting. Christopher will be expecting me at about 5 at the childcare center. My husband is out of town, and the center closes at 6 sharp. So count me out of today's meeting."

Tyler replied, "I said that this is an emergency meeting, and that we need input from all the members. You need to organize your personal life better to be a con-

tributing member to this team. But do what you have to do, at least this once."

Heather chose to leave the office at 4:30 so she could pick up Christopher. The next day, Tyler did not comment on her absence. However, he gave her a copy of the minutes and asked for her input. The budget problem surfaced again one week later. Top-level management asked the group to reduce the cost of the new product and its initial marketing costs by 15 percent.

Tyler said to the team on a Friday morning, "We have until Monday morning to arrive at a reduced cost structure on our product development. I am dividing up the project into segments. If we meet as a team Saturday morning at 8, we should get the job done by 6. Get a good night's rest, so we can start fresh tomorrow morning. Breakfast and lunch will be on the company."

Heather could feel stress overwhelming her body, as she thought to herself, "Christopher is playing in the finals of his little league soccer match tomorrow morning at 10. Brad has made dinner reservations for 6, so we can make it to the *Phantom of the Opera* at 8 P.M. Should I tell Tyler he is being unreasonable? Should I quit? Should I tell Christopher and Brad that our special occasions together are less important than a Saturday business meeting?"

Case Questions

1. What type of conflict is Heather facing?

2. What should Heather do to resolve her conflicts with respect to family and work responsibilities?

3. What should the company do to help deal with the type of conflict Heather is facing? Or, should the company not consider Heather's dilemma to be its problem?

INTERPERSONAL SKILLS ROLE-PLAY

Conflict Resolution Role-Play

Imagine that Heather, in the case just presented, decides that her job is taking too big a toll on her personal life. However, she still values her job and does not want to quit. She decides to discuss her problem with her team leader, Tyler. From Tyler's standpoint, a professional person must stand ready to meet unusual job demands, and cannot expect an entirely predictable work schedule. One person plays the role of Heather, another plays the role of Tyler, as they attempt to resolve this incident of work–family conflict.

CHAPTER 6

Enhancing Ethical Behavior

Learning Objectives

After reading and studying this chapter and doing the exercises you should be able to

1. Recognize the importance of ethical behavior for establishing good interpersonal relationships in organizations.
2. Identify several character traits associated with being an ethical person.
3. Identify job situations that often present ethical dilemmas.
4. Use a systematic method for making ethical decisions and behaving ethically.

As owner of a Mr. Handyman franchise in Los Angeles, T. L. Tenenbaum has rigid guidelines for the best approach to difficult drywall and plumbing problems. He also has ground rules for other home hazards his workers might encounter—say a misplaced pair of racy underwear or, as once happened, a butcher knife found under a bed. "Avert your eyes and pretend it doesn't exist," Tenenbaum instructs his techs on day one. "Pretend everything you see is perfectly normal."

Another common land mine: feuding spouses who involve technicians in personal matters—such as asking whether a married man should be friends with an ex-girlfriend.

"Agree with everyone, and don't take sides. We are doctors for their homes, and—people feel—for their relationships as well," Tenenbaum notes.

Trade professionals have long faced unique challenges when conducting business in the privacy of their customers' homes, but how they handled them was generally up to the individual. Now, a fast-growing industry of branded, home-maintenance franchises with such names as House Doctors and Mr. Handyman are trying to hone protocols for prickly on-the-job scenarios from scantily clad customers to overeager kids who want to play with tools.[1]

Discussion Question

1. What do you think the major home-maintenance franchises might be doing to improve the chances that the technicians will behave with good etiquette and good ethics?

The scenario just described illustrates that ethical issues in the workplace are not just about big business and corporate executives. People performing all types of work need a good sense of ethics (and etiquette) to be successful. *Ethics* refers to what is good and bad, right and wrong, just and unjust, and what people should do. Ethics is the vehicle for turning values into action. If you value fair play, you will do such things as giving honest performance evaluations to members of your group.

We study ethics here because a person's ethical code has a significant impact on his or her interpersonal relationships. This chapter's approach will emphasize the importance of ethics, common ethical problems, and guidelines for behaving ethically. Self-Assessment Quiz 6-1 gives you the opportunity to examine your ethical beliefs and attitudes.

SELF-ASSESSMENT QUIZ 6-1

THE ETHICAL REASONING INVENTORY

Directions: Describe how well you agree with each of the following statements, using the following scale: disagree strongly (DS); disagree (D); neutral (N); agree (A); agree strongly (AS). Circle the number in the appropriate column.

	DS	D	N	A	AS
1. When applying for a job, I would cover up the fact that I had been fired from my most recent job.	5	4	3	2	1
2. Cheating just a few dollars in one's favor on an expense account is okay if a person needs the money.	5	4	3	2	1
3. Employees should report on each other for wrongdoing.	1	2	3	4	5
4. It is acceptable to give approximate figures for expense account items when one does not have all the receipts.	5	4	3	2	1
5. I see no problem with conducting a little personal business on company time.	5	4	3	2	1
6. Just to make a sale, I would stretch the truth about a delivery date.	5	4	3	2	1
7. I would fix up a purchasing agent with a date just to close a sale.	5	4	3	2	1
8. I would flirt with my boss just to get a bigger salary increase.	5	4	3	2	1
9. If I received $400 for doing some odd jobs, I would report it on my income tax return.	1	2	3	4	5
10. I see no harm in taking home a few office supplies.	5	4	3	2	1
11. It is acceptable to read the e-mail messages and faxes of coworkers, even when not invited to do so.	5	4	3	2	1
12. It is unacceptable to call in sick to take a day off, even if only done once or twice a year.	1	2	3	4	5

13. I would accept a permanent, full-time job even if I knew I wanted the job for only six months.	5	4	3	2	1
14. I would first check company policy before accepting an expensive gift from a supplier.	1	2	3	4	5
15. To be successful in business, a person usually has to ignore ethics.	5	4	3	2	1
16. If I felt physically attracted toward a job candidate, I would hire that person over a more qualified candidate.	5	4	3	2	1
17. On the job, I tell the truth all the time.	1	2	3	4	5
18. If a student were very pressed for time, it would be acceptable to either have a friend write the paper or purchase one.	5	4	3	2	1
19. I would authorize accepting an office machine on a 30-day trial period, even if I knew we had no intention of buying it.	5	4	3	2	1
20. I would never accept credit for a coworker's ideas.	1	2	3	4	5

Total Score _____

Scoring and Interpretation: Add the numbers you have circled to obtain your total score.

90–100 You are a strongly ethical person who may take a little ribbing from coworkers for being too straitlaced.

60–89 You show an average degree of ethical awareness, and therefore should become more sensitive to ethical issues.

41–59 Your ethics are underdeveloped, but you at least have some awareness of ethical issues. You need to raise your level of awareness of ethical issues.

20–40 Your ethical values are far below contemporary standards in business. Begin a serious study of business ethics.

WHY BE CONCERNED ABOUT BUSINESS ETHICS?

When asked why ethics is important, most people would respond something to the effect that "Ethics is important because it's the right thing to do. You behave decently in the workplace because your family and religious values have taught you what is right and wrong." All this is true, but the justification for behaving ethically is more complex, as described next.[2]

A major justification for behaving ethically on the job is to recognize that people are motivated by both self-interest and moral commitments. Most people want to maximize gain for themselves (remember the expectancy theory of motivation?). At the same time, most people are motivated to do something morally right. As one of many examples, vast numbers of people donate money to charity, although keeping that amount of money for themselves would provide more personal gain.

Many business executives want employees to behave ethically because a good reputation can enhance business. A favorable corporate reputation may enable firms to charge premium prices and attract better job applicants. A favorable reputation also helps attract investors, such as mutual fund managers who purchase stock in companies. Certain mutual funds, for example, invest only in companies that are environmentally friendly. Managers want employees to behave ethically because unethical behavior—for example, employee theft, lost production time, and lawsuits—is costly.

Behaving ethically is also important because many unethical acts are illegal as well, which can lead to financial loss and imprisonment. According to one estimate, the cost of unethical and fraudulent acts committed by U.S. employees totals $400 billion per year. A company that knowingly allows workers to engage in unsafe practices might be fined and the executives may be held personally liable. Furthermore, unsafe practices can kill people. In recent history, two employees burned to death in a fire they could not escape in a chicken processing plant. Management had blocked the back doors to prevent employees from sneaking chicken parts out of the plant. Low ethics have also resulted in financial hardship for employees as company executives raid pension funds of other companies they purchase, sharply reducing or eliminating the retirement funds of many workers.

A subtle reason for behaving ethically is that high ethics increases the quality of work life. Ethics provides a set of guidelines that specify what makes for acceptable behavior. Being ethical will point you toward actions that make life more satisfying for work associates. A company code of ethics specifies what constitutes ethical versus unethical behavior. When employees follow this code, the quality of work life improves. Several sample clauses from ethical codes are as follows:

- Demonstrate courtesy, respect, honesty, and fairness.
- Do not use abusive language.
- Do not bring firearms or knives to work.
- Do not offer bribes.
- Maintain confidentiality of records.
- Do not harass (sexually, racially, ethnically, or physically) subordinates, superiors, coworkers, customers, or suppliers.

To the extent that all members of the organization abide by this ethical code, the quality of work life will improve. At the same time, interpersonal relations in organizations will be strengthened.

Learning Objective 2 ▶ ## COMMON ETHICAL PROBLEMS

moral intensity In ethical decision making, how deeply others might be affected by the decision.

To become more skilled at behaving ethically, it is important to familiarize yourself with common ethical problems in organizations. Whether or not a given situation presents an ethical problem for a person depends to some extent on its moral intensity, or how deeply others might be affected.[3] A worker might face a strong ethical conflict about dumping mercury into a water supply but would be less concerned about dumping cleaning fluid. Yet both acts would be considered unethical and illegal. Here we first look at why being ethical is not as easy as it sounds. We then look at some data about the frequency of ethical problems and an analysis of predictable ethical temptations, and also examine the subtle ethical dilemma of choosing between rights.

WHY BEING ETHICAL ISN'T EASY

As analyzed by Linda Klebe Treviño and Michael E. Brown, behaving ethically in business is more complex than it seems on the surface for a variety of reasons.[4] To begin with, ethical decisions are complex. For example, someone might argue that hiring children for factory jobs in overseas countries is unethical. Yet if these children lose their jobs, many would starve or turn to crime to survive. Second, people do not always recognize the moral issues involved in a decision. The home-maintenance worker who found a butcher knife under the bed might not think that he has a role to play in perhaps preventing murder. Sometimes language hides the moral issue involved, such as when the term "file sharing" music replaces "stealing" music.

Another complexity in making ethical decisions is that people have different levels of moral development. At one end of the scale some people behavior morally just to escape punishment. At the other end of the scale, some people are morally developed to the point that they are guided by principles of justice and want to help as many people as possible. The environment in which we work also influences whether we behave ethically. Suppose a restaurant owner encourages such practices as serving customers food that was accidentally dropped on the kitchen floor. An individual server is more likely to engage in such behavior to obey the demands of the owner.

A SURVEY OF THE EXTENT OF ETHICAL PROBLEMS

The ethical misdeeds of executives have received substantial publicity in recent years. However, recent surveys show that ethical violations by rank-and-file employees are widespread, particularly with respect to lying. According to two separate surveys, more than one-third of U.S. workers admit to having fabricated about their need for sick days. More employees are stretching the reasons for taking time off. Job applicants reporting false or embellished academic credentials have hit a three-year high. Here are the major findings of a composite of several surveys:[5]

- 36 percent of employees call in sick when they are well.
- 34 percent of employees keep quiet when they see coworker misconduct.
- 19 percent of employees see coworkers lie to customers, vendors, and the public.
- 12 percent of employees steal from customers or the company.
- 12 percent of résumés contain at least some false information.

Although these findings might suggest that unethical behavior is on the increase, another explanation is possible. Workers today might be more observant of ethical problems, and more willing to note them on a survey.

FREQUENT ETHICAL DILEMMAS

Certain ethical mistakes, including illegal actions, recur in the workplace. Familiarizing oneself can be helpful in monitoring one's own behavior. The next subsections describe a number of common ethical problems faced by business executives as well as workers at lower job levels.[6]

Illegally Copying Software
A rampant ethical problem is whether or not to illegally copy computer software. According to the Business Software Alliance, approximately 35 percent of applications used in business are illegal.[7] Figure 6-1 offers details about and insight into this widespread ethical dilemma.

Treating People Unfairly
Being fair to people means equity, reciprocity, and impartiality. Fairness revolves around the issue of giving people equal rewards for accomplishing equal amounts of work. The goal of human resource legislation is to make decisions about people based on their qualifications and performance—not on the basis of demographic factors such as gender, race, or age. A fair working environment is where performance is the only factor that counts (equity). Employer–employee expectations must be understood and met (reciprocity). Prejudice and bias must be eliminated (impartiality).

Treating people fairly—and therefore ethically—requires a de-emphasis on political factors, or favoritism. Yet this ethical doctrine is not always easy to implement. It is human nature to want to give bigger rewards (such as fatter raises or bigger orders) to people we like.

Follow the Platinum Rule: Treat people the way they wish to be treated.
—Eric Harvey and Scott Airitam, authors of Ethics 4 Everyone

A flagrant unethical and **illegal** job behavior is unauthorized copying of software. When confronted with software pirating, people are quick to rationalize their actions. Here are the top ten defenses of software pirates. (None of them are likely to hold up if you are caught.)

1. **I'm allowed to make a backup disk in case something happens to the original, so it must be okay to use it on another machine.** A backup is strictly a backup to be used on the same computer. The original should be safely locked away, and the copy should be stored away only as a backup.
2. **I didn't copy it—a friend gave it to me.** Technically you are right. You would not be guilty of illegally copying software in this case, although your friend would. However, since illegally copied software is regarded as stolen property, you are just as guilty as you would be for stealing it in the first place.
3. **My boss (or department head, or instructor) told me to. It's that person's problem.** The defense "I was just following orders" is a weak one. Complying with your boss's demands to commit an illegal act does not get you off the hook. You could be fired for obeying an order to commit a crime.
4. **I bought the software; shouldn't I be able to do what I want with it?** Software is seldom ever sold to individuals. What is sold is a license to use the software, not full rights to do what you want. When you break open the package, the law assumes that you have agreed to abide by those terms.
5. **It's not like I'm robbing somebody.** Software is intellectual property just like a song, a book, an article, or a trademark. You are taking bread from the table of software engineers when you copy their work.
6. **It's OK if you're using the software for educational purposes.** If education were a justification for theft, driving instructors would be able to steal cars with impunity. There is a doctrine of **fair use** that allows some limited use of written materials in classrooms without permission from the copyright holder.
7. **I needed it, but the price was unreasonably high. If I had to actually pay for it, there is no way I could ever afford it.** Software prices are high for the same reason the price of houses is high: both require a lot of highly skilled labor to create. You cannot steal a DVD player just because you cannot afford one.
8. **I didn't know it was illegal.** Unauthorized duplication of software is a felony in many states and provinces. State and federal laws provide for civil and criminal penalties if you are convicted. It would be difficult to convince a judge or jury that you had no idea that unauthorized copying was illegal.
9. **It's only illegal if you get caught.** Criminal behavior is illegal whether or not you are caught. If you do get caught illegally copying software, you could face fines, imprisonment, and/or civil penalties. Some educational institutions take disciplinary action against software pirates, including suspension.
10. **Oh, come on, everyone is doing it.** This excuse has been used to justify everything from speeding to lynching. The popularity of a criminal act does not make it legal.

FIGURE 6-1 The Top Ten Reasons for Illegally Copying Software (and Why None of Them Are Good Enough)

Source: The Top Ten Reasons for Illegally Copying Software (and Why None of Them Are Good Enough). Rochester Institute of Technology. Reprinted with permission.

Sexually Harassing Coworkers

In Chapter 5 we looked at sexual harassment as a source of conflict and an illegal act. Sexual harassment is also an ethical issue because it is morally wrong and unfair. All acts of sexual harassment flunk an ethics test. Before sexually harassing another person, the potential harasser should ask, "Would I want a loved one to be treated this way?"

Facing a Conflict of Interest

Part of being ethical is making business judgments only on the basis of the merits or facts in a situation. Imagine that you are a supervisor who is romantically involved with a worker within the group. When it comes time to assign raises, it will be difficult for you to be objective. A conflict of interest occurs when your judgment or objectivity is compromised. Conflicts of interest often take place in the sales end of

conflict of interest A situation that occurs when a person's judgment or objectivity is compromised.

business. If a company representative accepts a large gift from a sales representative, it may be difficult to make objective judgments about buying from the rep. Yet being taken to dinner by a vendor would not ordinarily cloud one's judgment. Another common example of a conflict of interest is making a hiring decision about a friend who badly needs a job, but is not well qualified for the position.

Conflicts of interest have been behind some of the major business scandals in recent times, such as Enron Corporation auditors giving the company a favorable rating. Many outsiders dealing with Enron—including auditors, bankers, and even regulators—were tempted by a piece of the equity action.[8] The conflict occurs when one party paid to make objective judgments about the financial health of a second party has a personal interest in how profitable the second party looks to the public. An auditor might be hesitant to give a negative evaluation of the financial condition of a company if the auditor's firm also provides consulting services to that company. Some financial research analysts give glowing public reports about the fiscal condition of a company when that company is a client of the analyst's own firm. The analyst's firm sells services for issuing new stock and assisting with corporate mergers and acquisitions.

Dealing with Confidential Information

An ethical person can be trusted by others not to divulge confidential information unless the welfare of others is at stake. Suppose a coworker tells you in confidence that she is upset with the company and is therefore looking for another job. Behaving ethically, you do not pass along this information to your supervisor even though it would help your supervisor plan for a replacement. Now suppose the scenario changes slightly. Your coworker tells you she is looking for another job because she is upset. She tells you she is so upset that she plans to destroy company computer files on her last day. If your friend does find another job, you might warn the company about her contemplated activities.

The challenge of dealing with confidential information arises in many areas of business, many of which affect interpersonal relations. If you learned that a coworker was indicted for a crime, charged with sexual harassment, or facing bankruptcy, there would be a temptation to gossip about the person. A highly ethical person would not pass along information about the personal difficulties of another person.

Presenting Employment History

As noted above, many people are tempted to distort in a positive direction information about their employment history on their job résumé, job application form, and during the interview. Distortion, or lying, of this type is considered to be unethical and can lead to immediate dismissal if discovered. A well-known case in point is George O'Leary, who was dismissed after five days on the job as head coach of the Notre Dame football team. After his résumé distortions were uncovered, O'Leary resigned and admitted he falsified his academic and athletic credentials for decades. He had falsely claimed to have a master's degree in education and to have played college football for three years.[9] Shortly thereafter, O'Leary made good use of his network of professional contacts and was hired by the Minnesota Vikings professional football team in a coaching position. Despite being disgraced nationally, O'Leary's political skills provided him with a safety net.

Using Corporate Resources

A corporate resource is anything the company owns, including its name and reputation. If Jake Petro worked for Ford Motor Company, for example, it would be unethical for him to establish a body shop and put on his letterhead and Web site, "Jake Petro, Manufacturing Technician, Ford Motor Company." (The card and Web site would imply that the Ford Motor Co. supports this venture.) Other uses of corporate resources fall more into the gray area. It might be quite ethical to borrow a laptop computer for the weekend from your employer to conduct work at home. But it would be less ethical to borrow the laptop computer to prepare income taxes. In the

> 1. Do not use a computer to harm other people. Avoid all obscene, defamatory, threatening, or otherwise harassing messages. Take precautions against others developing repetitive motion disorders.
> 2. Do not interfere with other people's computer work. (This includes intentionally spreading computer viruses.)
> 3. Do not snoop around in other people's files.
> 4. Do not use a computer to steal.
> 5. Do not use a computer to bear false witness.
> 6. Do not use or copy software for which you have not paid (see Figure 6-1).
> 7. Do not use other people's resources without authorization.
> 8. Do not appropriate other people's intellectual output.
> 9. Do not use the employer's computer for the personal promotion of commercial goods or services, unless granted permission by the employer.
> 10. Do think about the social consequences of the program you write.
> 11. Do use a computer in ways that show consideration and respect.

FIGURE 6-2 Eleven Commandments for Computer Ethics

Source: Adapted and updated from Arlene H. Rinaldi and Florida Atlantic University, rinaldi@acc.fau.edu; "Code of Conduct for Computer and Network Use," *http://www.rit.edu/computerconduct.*

latter case you might be accused of using corporate resources for personal purposes. Loading personal software on company computers so you can access your bank account and so forth, also can be considered an ethical violation.

Ethically Violating Computers and Information Technology

As computers dominate the workplace, many ethical issues have arisen in addition to pirating software. One ethical dilemma that surfaces frequently is the fairness of tracking the Web sites a person visits and those he or she buys from. Should this information be sold, like a mailing list? Another issue is the fairness of having an employee work at a keyboard for 60 hours in one week when such behavior frequently leads to repetitive motion disorder. Figure 6-2 lists some major ethical issues involved in computer use.

You may have observed that these common ethical problems are not always clear-cut. Aside from obvious matters such as prohibitions against stealing, lying, cheating, and intimidating, subjectivity enters into ethical decision making. Skill-Building Exercise 6-1 provides an opportunity to try out your ethical reasoning.

CHOOSING BETWEEN TWO RIGHTS: DEALING WITH DEFINING MOMENTS

defining moment
Choosing between
two or more ideals in
which one deeply
believes.

Ethical decision making usually involves choosing between two options: one we perceive to be right and one we perceive to be wrong. A challenging twist to ethical decision making is to sort through your values when you have to choose between two rights, or two morally sound choices. Joseph L. Badaracco, Jr., uses the term defining moment to describe choosing between two or more ideals in which we deeply believe.[10] If you can learn to work through defining moments, your ethical skills will be enhanced. Let's first take a nonwork example to illustrate a defining moment.

Imagine yourself as a basketball referee in a league for boys 10 years old and younger. Luis, the smallest boy on the team, has a self-confidence problem in general, and he has not scored a basket yet this season. This is the final game of the season. The other team is ahead by 10 points with one minute to go. Luis lets fly with a shot that goes into the basket, but his right heel is on the line. If the goal is allowed, Luis will experience one of the happiest moments in his life, and his self-confidence might increase. You strongly believe in helping people grow and develop. Yet you also strongly believe in following the rules of sports. What should you do?

SKILL-BUILDING EXERCISE 6-1

THE ETHICS GAME

Citicorp (now part of Citigroup) has developed an ethics game, The Work Ethic.[11] The game teaches ethics by asking small teams of employees to confront difficult scenarios such as those that follow. Discuss these ethical problems in teams. As you discuss the scenarios, identify the ethical issues involved.

Scenario 1:   One of your assignments is to find a contractor to conduct building maintenance for your company headquarters. You invite bids for the job. High-Performance cleaners, a firm staffed largely by teenagers from troubled families who have criminal records, bids on the job.

Many of these teenagers also have severe learning disabilities and cannot readily find employment. High-Performance Cleaners proves to be the second-highest bidder. You:

A. advise High-Performance Cleaners that its bid is too high for consideration and that your company is not a social agency.

B. award the bid to High-Performance Cleaners and justify your actions with a letter to top management talking about social responsibility.

C. falsify the other bids in your report to management, making High-Performance Cleaners the low bidder—and thus the contract winner.

D. explain to High-Performance Cleaners that it lost the bid, but you will award the company a piece of the contract because of its sterling work with teenagers in need.

Scenario 2:   You live in Texas and your company sends you on a three-day trip to New York City. Your business dealings in the Big Apple will keep you there Wednesday, Thursday, and Friday morning. You have several friends and relatives in New York, so you decide to stay there until Sunday afternoon. Besides, you want to engage in tourist activities such as taking a boat tour around Manhattan and visiting Radio City Music Hall. When preparing your expense report for your trip, you request payment for all your business-related costs up through Friday afternoon, plus

A. your return trip on Sunday.

B. the return trip and the room cost for Friday and Saturday nights.

C. the return trip, one-half of your weekend food expenses, and two extra nights in the hotel.

D. the return trip and your food costs for the weekend (which you justify because you ate at fast-food restaurants on Wednesday, Thursday, and Friday).

Scenario 3:   You are the leader of a self-managing work team in a financial services company. The work of your team has expanded to the point where you are authorized to hire another team member. The team busily interviews a number of candidates from inside and outside the company. The other team members agree that one of the candidates (Pat) has truly outstanding credentials. You agree that Pat is a strong candidate, yet you don't want Pat on the team because the two of you were emotionally involved for about a year. You think that working with Pat would disrupt your concentration and bring back hurtful memories. You decide to

A. tell the group that you have some negative information about Pat's past that would disqualify Pat for the job.

B. telephone Pat and beg that Pat find employment elsewhere.

C. tell the group that you agree Pat is qualified, but explain your concerns about the disruption in concentration and emotional hurt.

D. tell the group that you agree Pat is right for the position, and mention nothing about the past relationship.

Scoring and Observation: Scenario 1, about High-Performance Cleaners, raises dozens of ethical questions, including whether humanitarian considerations can outweigh profit concerns. Teams that chose "a" receive 0 points; "b", 20 points; "c", −10 points; "d", 10 points. (Answer "d" is best here because it would not be fair to give the bid to the second-highest bidder. However, you are still finding a way to reward the High-Performance Cleaners for its meritorious work in the community. Answer "c" is the worst because you would be outright lying.)

Scenario 2 raises ethical issues about using company resources. Teams that chose "a" receive 20 points; "b", −10 points; "c", −15 points; "d", 0 points. (Answer "a" is fairest because the company would expect to reimburse you for your roundtrip plus the expenses up through Friday afternoon. Answer "c" is the worst because it would be unjustified for you to be reimbursed for your vacation in New York.)

Scenario 3 raises issues about fairness in making selection decisions. Teams that chose "a" receive −20 points; "b", −10 points; "c", 15 points; "d", 0 points. (Answer "c" is the most ethical because you are being honest with the group about the reason you do not wish to hire Pat. Answer "a" is the most unethical because you are telling lies about Pat. Furthermore, you might be committing the illegal act of libel.)

You may have recognized that a defining moment is a role conflict in which you have to choose between competing values. A CEO might deeply believe that she has an obligation to the stockholders to make a profit, and also believe in being generous and fair toward employees. However, to make a profit this year she will be forced to lay off several good employees with long seniority. The CEO now faces a moment of truth. Badaracco suggests that the individual can work through a defining moment by discovering "Who am I?" You discover who you are by soul searching answers to three questions:

1. What feelings and intuitions are coming into conflict in this situation?
2. Which of the values that are in conflict are the most deeply rooted in my life?
3. What combinations of expediency and shrewdness, coupled with imagination and boldness, will help me implement my personal understanding of what is right?

Skill-Building Exercise 6-2 gives you an opportunity to deal with defining moments. The three questions just asked could help you find answers, but do not be constrained by these questions.

Learning Objective 3 ▶ ## GUIDELINES FOR BEHAVING ETHICALLY

Following guidelines for ethical behavior is the heart of being ethical. Although many people behave ethically without studying ethical guidelines, they are usually following guidelines programmed into their minds early in life. The Golden Rule exemplifies a guideline taught by parents, grandparents, and kindergarten teachers. In this section we approach ethical guidelines from five perspectives: (1) developing the right character traits; (2) following a guide to ethical decision making; (3) developing strong relationships with work associates; (4) using corporate ethics programs; and (5) following an applicable professional code of conduct.

DEVELOPING THE RIGHT CHARACTER TRAITS

Character trait An enduring characteristic of a person that is related to moral and ethical behavior.

Character traits develop early in life, yet with determination and self-discipline many people can modify old traits or develop new ones. A character trait is an enduring characteristic of a person that is related to moral and ethical behavior. For example, if a

SKILL-BUILDING EXERCISE 6-2

DEALING WITH DEFINING MOMENTS

The toughest ethical choices for many people occur when they have to choose between two rights. The result is a defining moment, because we are challenged to think in a deeper way by choosing between two or more ideals. Working individually or in teams, deal with the two following defining moments. Explain why these scenarios could require choosing between two rights, and explain the reasoning behind your decisions.

Scenario 1:   You are the manager of a department in a business firm that assigns each department a fixed amount of money for salary increases each year. An average-performing member of the department asks you in advance for an above-average increase. He explains that his mother has developed multiple sclerosis and requires the services of a paid helper from time to time. You are concerned that if you give this man an above-average increase, somebody else in the department will have to receive a below-average increase.

Scenario 2:   You are the team leader of an e-tailing (retail selling over the Internet) group. In recent months each team member has been working about 60 hours per week, with little prospect of the workload decreasing in the future. Since the e-tailing project is still losing money, higher management insists that one person be dropped from the team. One member of the team, Mildred, is willing to work only 45 hours per week because she spends considerable time volunteering with autistic children. Mildred's work is satisfactory, but her output is the lowest in the group because of her shorter number of working hours. You must make a decision about whether to recommend that Mildred be dismissed.

person has the character trait of untruthfulness, he or she will lie in many situations. Conversely, the character trait of honesty leads to behaving honestly in most situations.

The Character Counts Coalition is an organization formed to encourage young people to develop fairness, respect, trustworthiness, responsibility, caring, and good citizenship. The Coalition has developed a list of 10 key guidelines as a foundation for character development.[12] If you develop, or already have, these traits, it will be easy for you to behave ethically in business. As you read the following list, evaluate your own standing on each character trait. Remember, however, that extra effort is required to evaluate one's character traits because most people have an inflated view of their honesty and integrity.

1. **Be honest.** Tell the truth consistently, be sincere, avoid misleading or withholding information in relationships of trust, and do not steal.

2. **Show integrity.** Stand up for your beliefs about what you think is right and wrong, and resist pressures from others to do wrong.

3. **Follow through on promises.** Stick to your word and honor your commitments; pay your debts and return borrowed money or objects.

4. **Be loyal.** Support family, friends, employers, community, and country, and do not talk about people behind their backs.

5. **Be responsible.** Think before you act, consider the consequences of your actions, and be accountable for what you do.

6. **Pursue excellence.** Do your best with your talents, and persist in pursuing your goals.

7. **Be kind and caring.** Demonstrate that you care through generosity and compassion; avoid being selfish or mean.

8. **Treat all people with respect.** Be courteous and polite to everybody you meet. Judge all people on their merits rather than on superficial aspects of behavior. Be tolerant, appreciative, and accepting of individual differences.

9. **Be fair and just.** Treat all people fairly (how they deserve to be treated) and be open-minded. Listen attentively to others and try to understand what they are saying and feeling.

10. **Be a good citizen.** Obey the law and respect authority of appointed or elected officials, vote in local and national elections, do volunteer work, and protect the environment.

If you score high on all of the preceding character traits and behaviors, you are an outstanding member of your company, community, and school. Your ethical behavior is superior.

Learning Objective 4 ▶ ## FOLLOWING A GUIDE TO ETHICAL DECISION MAKING

A powerful strategy for behaving ethically is to follow a guide for ethical decision making. Such a guide for making contemplated decisions includes testing ethics. **Ethical screening** refers to running a contemplated decision or action through an ethics test. Such screening makes the most sense when the contemplated action or decision is not clearly ethical or unethical. If a sales representative were to take a favorite customer to Pizza Hut for lunch, an ethical screen would not be necessary. Nobody would interpret a "veggie super" to be a serious bribe. Assume, instead, that the sales rep offered to give the customer an under-the-table gift of $600 for placing a large offer with the rep's firm. The sales representative's behavior would be so blatantly unethical that conducting an ethical screen would be unnecessary.

ethical screening
Running a contemplated decision or action through an ethics test.

Several useful ethical screens, or guides to ethical decision making, have been developed. A guide developed by Treviño and Nelson is presented here because it incorporates the basic ideas in other ethical tests.[13] After studying this guide, you will be asked to ethically screen three different scenarios. The eight steps to sound ethical decision making follow.

1. **Gather the facts.** When making an important decision in business it is necessary to gather relevant facts. Ask yourself the following questions: "Are there any legal issues involved here?" "Is there precedent in our firm with respect to this type of decision?" "Do I have the authority to make this decision?" "Are there company rules and regulations governing such a decision?"

The manager of a child-care center needed to hire an additional child-care specialist. One of the applicants was a 55-year-old male with experience as a father and grandfather. The manager judged him to be qualified, yet she knew that many parents would not want their preschool children to be cared for by a middle-aged male. Many people perceive that a younger woman is better qualified for child care than an older man. The manager therefore had to gather considerable facts about the situation, including facts about job discrimination and precedents in hiring males as child-care specialists.

2. **Define the ethical issues.** The ethical issues in a given decision are often more complicated than a first glance suggests. When faced with a complex decision, it may be helpful to talk over the ethical issues with another person. The ethical issues might involve character traits such as being kind and caring and treating others with respect. Or the ethical issues might relate to some of the common ethical

problems described earlier in the chapter. Among them are facing conflict of interest, dealing with confidential information, and using corporate resources.

The manager of the child-care center is facing such ethical issues as fairness, job discrimination, and meeting the demands of customers at the expense of job applicants. The manager is also facing a diversity issue: Should the workforce in a child-care center be culturally diverse, or do we hire only young women?

3. **Identify the affected parties.** When faced with a complex ethical decision it is important to identify all the affected parties. Major corporate decisions can affect thousands of people. If a company decides to shut down a plant and outsource the manufacturing to a low-wage country, thousands of individuals and many different parties are affected. Workers lose their jobs, suppliers lose their customers, the local government loses out on tax revenues, and local merchants lose many of their customers. You may need to brainstorm with a few others to think of all the parties affected by a given decision.

The parties affected by the decision about hiring or not hiring the 55-year-old male include: the applicant himself, the children, the parents, and the board of directors of the child-care center. The government might also be involved if the man were rejected and filed charges of age and sex discrimination.

4. **Identify the consequences.** After you have identified the parties affected by a decision, the next step is to predict the consequences for each party. It may not be necessary to identify every consequence, yet it is important to identify the consequences with the highest probability of occurring and those with the most negative outcomes. The problem is that many people can be harmed by an unethical decision, such as not fully describing the possible side effects of a diet program.

Both short-term and long-term consequences should be specified. A company closing a plant might create considerable short-term turmoil, but in the long term the company might be healthier. People participating in a diet program might achieve their short-term objective of losing weight. Yet in the long term, their health might be adversely affected because the diet is not nutritionally balanced.

The *symbolic* consequences of an action are important. Every action and decision sends a message (the decision is a symbol of something). If a company moves manufacturing out of a community to save on labor costs, it means that the short-term welfare of domestic employees is less important than profit or perhaps the company surviving.

We return to the child-care manager and the job applicant. If the applicant does not get the job, his welfare will be adversely affected. He has been laid off by a large employer and cannot find work in his regular field. His family will also suffer because he will not be able to make a financial contribution to the family. Yet if the man is hired, the child-care center may suffer. Many traditionally minded parents will say, "Absolutely not. I do not want my child cared for by a middle-aged man. He could be a child molester." (It may be unethical for people to have vicious stereotypes, yet they still exist.) If the child-care center does hire the man, the act will symbolize the fact that the owners of the center value diversity.

5. **Identify the obligations.** Identify the obligations and the reasons for each obligation when making a complex decision. The manufacturer of automotive brakes has an obligation to produce and sell only brakes that meet high safety standards. The obligation is to the auto manufacturer who purchases the brakes and, more important, to the ultimate consumer whose safety depends on effective brakes. The reason for the obligation to make safe brakes is that lives are at stake. The child-care center owner has an obligation to provide for the safety and health of the children at the center. She must also provide for the peace of mind of the parents and be a good citizen of the community in which the center is located. The decision about hiring the candidate in question must be balanced against all these obligations.

6. **Consider your character and integrity.** A core consideration when faced with an ethical dilemma is how relevant people would judge your character and integrity.

What would your family, friends, significant others, teachers, and coworkers think of your actions? To refine this thinking even further, how would you feel if your actions were publicly disclosed in the local newspaper or over e-mail? Would you want the world to know that you gave an under-the-table kickback or that you sexually harassed a frightened teenager working for you? If you would be proud for others to know what decision you made when you faced an ethical dilemma, you are probably making the right decision.

The child-care center manager might ponder how she would feel if the following information were released in the local newspaper or on the Internet.

> The manager of Good Times Child Care recently rejected the application of a 55-year-old man for a child-care specialist position. She said that although Mr. _____ was well qualified from an experience and personality standpoint, she couldn't hire him. She said that Good Times would lose too much business because many parents would fear that Mr. _____ was a child molester or pedophile.

7. **Think creatively about potential actions.** When faced with an ethical dilemma, put yourself in a creative-thinking mode. Stretch your imagination to invent several options rather than thinking you have only two choices—to do or not do something. Creative thinking may point toward a third, and even fourth, alternative. Imagine this ethical dilemma: A purchasing agent is told that if her firm awards a contract to the sales representative's firm, she will find a leather jacket of her choice delivered to her door. The purchasing agent says to herself, "I think we should award the contract to the firm, but I cannot accept the gift. Yet if I turn down the gift, I will be forfeiting a valuable possession that the company simply regards as a cost of doing business."

The purchasing agent can search for another alternative. She may say to the sales rep, "We will give the contract to your firm because your products fit our requirements. I thank you for the offer of the leather jacket, but instead I would like you to give the jacket to the Salvation Army."

A creative alternative for the child-care manager might be to offer the applicant the next position that opened for an office manager or maintenance person in the center. In this way she would be offering a qualified applicant a job, but placing him in a position more acceptable to parents. Or do you feel this is a cop-out?

8. **Check your intuition.** So far we have emphasized the rational side of ethical decision making. Another effective way of conducting an ethical screen is to rely on your intuition. How does the contemplated decision feel? Would you be proud of yourself or would you hate yourself if you made the decision? Imagine how you would feel if you took money from the handbag of a woman sleeping in the park. Would you feel the same way if you took a kickback, sold somebody a defective product, or sold an 80-year-old man an insurance policy he didn't need? How will the manager of the child-care center feel if she turns down the man for the child-care specialist position?

You are encouraged to use the guide for ethical decision making when you next face an ethical dilemma of consequence. Skill-Building Exercise 6-3 gives you an opportunity to practice using the eight steps for ethical decision making.

DEVELOPING STRONG RELATIONSHIPS WITH WORK ASSOCIATES

A provocative explanation of the causes of unethical behavior emphasizes the strength of relationships among people.[14] Assume that two people have close professional ties to each other, such as having worked together for a long time or knowing each other both on and off the job. As a consequence they are likely to behave ethically toward one another on the job. In contrast, if a weak professional

ETHICAL DECISION MAKING

Working in small groups, take one or more of the following ethical dilemmas through the eight steps for screening contemplated decisions. If more than one group chooses the same scenario, compare your answers for the various steps.

Scenario 1: To Recycle or Not.   Your group is the top management team at a large insurance company. Despite the movement toward digitizing all records, your firm still generates tons of paper each month. Customer payments alone account for truckloads of envelopes each year. The paper recyclers in your area claim they can hardly find a market any longer for used paper, so they will be charging you just to accept your paper for recycling. Your group is wondering whether to recycle.

Scenario 2: The Hole in the Résumé.   Emily has been working for the family business as an office manager for five years. Because the family business is being sold, Emily has started a job hunt. She also welcomes the opportunity to work in a larger company so she could learn more about how a big company operates. As she begins preparing her job résumé, she ponders how to classify the year of unemployment prior to working at the family business. During that year she worked a total of 10 weeks in entry-level jobs at three fast-food restaurants. Otherwise she filled her time with such activities as walking in the park, watching daytime television shows, surfing the Internet, playing video games, and pursuing her hobby of visiting graveyards. Emily finally decides to tack that year onto the five years in the family business. She indicates on her résumé that she has been working *six* years at the family business. As Emily says, "It's a tight job market for office managers, and I don't want to raise any red flags." Evaluate the ethics of Emily's decision to fill in the year off from work, and perhaps offer her some advice.

Scenario 3: The High-Profit Toys.   You are a toy company executive starting to plan your holiday season line. You anticipate that the season's hottest item will be Robo-Woman, a battery-operated crime fighter and super-heroine. Robo-Woman should wholesale for $25 and retail for $45. Your company figures to earn $15 per unit. You receive a sales call from a manufacturing broker who says he can produce any toy you want for one-third of your present manufacturing cost. He admits that the manufacturer he represents uses prison labor in China, but insists that his business arrangement violates no law. You estimate you can earn $20 per unit if you do business with the manufacturing broker. Your decision is whether to do business with him.

relationship exists between two people, either party is more likely to engage in an unethical relationship. The owner of an auto service center is more likely to behave unethically toward a stranger passing through town than toward a long-time customer. The opportunity for unethical behavior between strangers is often minimized because individuals typically do not trust strangers with sensitive information or valuables.

The ethical skill-building consequence of information about personal relationships is that building stronger relationships with people is likely to enhance ethical behavior. If you build strong relationships with work associates, you are likely to behave more ethically toward them. Similarly, your work associates are likely to behave more ethically toward you. The work associates I refer to are all your contacts, both internal and external customers.

USING CORPORATE ETHICS PROGRAMS

Many organizations have various programs and procedures for promoting ethical behavior. Among them are committees that monitor ethical behavior, training programs in ethics, and vehicles for reporting ethical violations. The presence of these programs is designed to create an atmosphere in which unethical behavior is discouraged and reporting on unethical behavior is encouraged.

Ethics hotlines are one of the best established programs to help individuals avoid unethical behavior. Should a person be faced with an ethical dilemma, the person calls a toll-free line to speak to a counselor about the dilemma. Sometimes employees ask questions to help interpret a policy, such as "Is it okay to ask my boss for a date?" or "Are we supposed to give senior citizen discounts to customers who qualify but do not ask for one?" At other times, a more pressing ethical issue might be addressed, such as "Is it ethical to lay off a worker just five months short of his qualifying for a full pension?"

Sears, Roebuck and Co. has an ethics hotline the company refers to as an "Assist Line" because very few of the 15,000 calls it receives per year represent crises. Often the six full-time ethics specialists who handle the calls just listen; at other times they intervene to help resolve the problem. The Assist Line is designed to help with these kinds of calls: guidance about company policy; company code of conduct issues; workplace harassment and discrimination; selling practices; theft; and human resource issues. Employees and managers are able to access information and guidance without feeling they are facing a crisis. So the Assist Line is kind of a cross between "911" and "411" calls. At times an ethical problem of such high moral intensity is presented that employee confidentiality cannot be maintained. However, the Ethics Office handles the inquiries in as confidential a manner as practical and assigns them case identification numbers for follow-up.[15]

Wells Fargo & Co., a mammoth bank, emphasizes both a code of conduct and ethics training. Its Code of Ethics and Business Conduct specifies policies and standards for employees, covering a variety of topics from maintaining accurate records to participating in civic activities. Each year, employees also participate in ethics training. Any Wells Fargo employee may ask questions or report ethical breaches anonymously using an ethics hotline or dedicated e-mail address. The company will fire violators, dismissing about 100 people a year for misconduct ranging from conflicts of interest to cheating on incentive plans.

Patricia Callahan, executive vice president and director of human resources at the bank says, "I'm the biggest soft touch in the world. But when someone lies or cheats, you can't have people like that representing us to our customers, whose trust is all we have."[16]

The link between the programs just described and individual ethical skills is that these programs assist a worker's skill development. For example, if you become comfortable in asking about ethical issues, or turning in ethical violators, you have become more ethically skilled.

Back to the Opening Case

During their orientation at Handyman Matters (a major franchiser in the field) technicians must sit through a two-hour video about in-home conduct. The company also operates "secret shopper calls" where it gives customers scripts and asks them to monitor techs on certain protocols.

FOLLOWING AN APPLICABLE PROFESSIONAL CODE OF CONDUCT

Professional codes of conduct are prescribed for many occupational groups including physicians, nurses, lawyers, paralegals, purchasing managers and agents, and real estate salespeople. A useful ethical guide for members of these groups is to follow the code of conduct for their profession. If the profession or trade is licensed by the state or province, a worker can be punished for deviating from the code of conduct specified by the state. The code of conduct developed by the profession or trade is separate from the legal code, but usually supports the same principles and practices. Some of these codes of conduct developed by the professional associations are 50 and 60 pages long, yet all are guided by the kind of ethical principles implied in the ethical-decision-making guide described earlier. Figure 6-3 presents a sampling of provisions from these codes of conduct.

Professional Organization	Sample of Ethical Guidelines and Regulations
Institute of Management Accountants	1. Maintain an appropriate level of professional competence by ongoing development of their knowledge and skills.
	2. Refrain from disclosing confidential information acquired in the course of their work and monitor their activities to assure the maintenance of that confidentiality.
	3. Actual or apparent conflicts of interest and advise all appropriate parties of any potential conflict.
National Association of Legal Assistants	1. A legal assistant (paralegal) must not perform any of the duties that attorneys only may perform nor take any actions that attorneys may not take.
	2. A legal assistant may perform any task which is properly delegated and supervised by an attorney, as long as the attorney is ultimately responsible to the client, maintains a direct relationship with the client, and assumes professional responsibility for the work product.
	3. A legal assistant must protect the confidences of a client and must not violate any rule or statute now in effect or hereafter enacted controlling the doctrine of privileged communications between a client and an attorney.
National Association of Purchasing Management	1. Avoid the intent and appearance of unethical or compromising practice in relationships, actions, and communications.
	2. Refrain from any private business or professional activity that would create a conflict between personal interests and the interest of the employer.
	3. Refrain from soliciting or accepting money, loans, credits, or prejudicial discounts, and the acceptance of gifts, entertainment, favors, or services from present or potential suppliers which might influence, or appear to influence purchasing decisions.

FIGURE 6-3 Excerpts from Professional Codes of Conduct

Sources: Institute of Management Accountants Code of Ethics; National Association of Legal Assistants Professional Standards; National Association of Purchasing Management Principles and Standards of Purchasing Practice.

SUMMARY

Ethics refers to what is good and bad, right and wrong, just and unjust, and what people should do. Ethics turn values into action. A person's ethical code has a significant impact on his or her interpersonal relationships.

Understanding ethics is important for a variety of reasons. First, people are motivated by self-interest and a desire to be morally right. Second, good ethics can enhance business and avoid illegal acts. Third, having high ethics improves the quality of work life.

Being ethical isn't always easy for several reasons including the complexity of ethical decisions, lack of recognition of the moral issues, poor moral development, and pressures from the work environment. Ethical violations in the form of lying are widespread in the workplace.

Commonly faced ethical dilemmas include illegally copying software; treating people unfairly, sexually harassing coworkers, facing a conflict of interest, dealing with confidential information, presenting employment history, using corporate resources, and ethically violating computers and information technology.

A challenging twist to ethical decision making is to sort through your values when you have to choose between two morally sound choices. A defining moment is when you have to choose between two or more ideals in which you deeply believe.

One strategy for behaving ethically is to develop the right character traits, as specified by the Character Counts Coalition. Among these traits are honesty, integrity, promise keeping, loyalty, responsibility, pursuit of excellence, kindness, respect for others, fairness, and good citizenship. A key strategy for behaving ethically is to follow the eight steps in making a contemplated decision:

1. Gather the facts.
2. Define the ethical issues.
3. Identify the affected parties.
4. Identify the consequences.
5. Identify the obligations (such as to customers and society).
6. Consider your character and integrity.
7. Think creatively about potential actions.
8. Check your intuition.

Another way to raise the level of ethical behavior is to form strong professional relationships with work associates. This is true because people tend to behave more ethically toward people who are close to them. At times using a corporate program such as an ethics hotline can help a person resolve ethical dilemmas. Following an applicable code of professional conduct, such as that for accountants, paralegals, and purchasing specialists, is another guide to behaving ethically.

QUESTIONS FOR DISCUSSION AND REVIEW

1. How can behaving ethically improve a person's interpersonal relationships on the job?
2. What would most likely be some of the specific behaviors of a manager who scored 20 points on the ethical reasoning inventory?
3. A widespread practice is for top management to outsource (or "offshore") work such as call centers to low-wage countries such as India, the Philippines, and lately, Africa. What ethical problems do you see with outsourcing of this type?

4. The major business scandals in recent years have involved financial manipulations such as executives profiting from selling company stock while encouraging employees to buy the stock. In what ways do these financial scandals affect people?

5. Give an example from your own experiences or the media in which a business executive did something of significance that was morally right.

6. Provide an example of an action in business that might be unethical but not illegal.

7. Virtually all accountants have studied ethics as part of their education, yet many business scandals involve accountants. What's their problem?

8. What "commandment" about computer use would you like to add to the list in Figure 6-2?

9. Based on your knowledge of human behavior, why do professional codes of conduct—such as those for doctors, paralegals, and realtors—not prevent all unethical behavior on the part of members?

10. What decision of ethical consequence have you made in the last year that you would not mind having publicly disclosed?

GO TO THE WEB

http://www.ethics.org
(Ethics Resource Center)

http://www.businessethics.ca/codes
(Articles and a survey about business ethics)

AN INTERPERSONAL RELATIONS CASE PROBLEM

"HELP, I'M A VICTIM OF CLICK FRAUD"

Nathan McKelvey began to worry about foul play when Yahoo Inc. refunded him $69.28 early last year. He grew more suspicious when a $16.91 refund arrived from Google Inc. The refunds were for "unusual clicks" and "invalid click activity" and they suggested someone was sabotaging McKelvey's advertising strategy. He pitches his charter-jet brokerage the way companies increasingly do: contracting with Yahoo and Google to serve up small text ads to anyone searching the Web using certain words, such as "private jet" or "air charter." He pays the companies a fee every time someone clicks on his ads.

But Yahoo and Google determined someone was clicking on CharterAuction.com Inc.'s ads with no intention of doing business, thus unfairly driving up the company's advertising costs. McKelvey, turning detective, combed through lists of Internet Protocol (IP) addresses, the identifying codes supplied by computers when they access Web sites. He found several suspicious clicks from one address and about 100 more from one that was similar. They belonged to a New York-based rival, Blue Star Jets LLC, McKelvey says.

He had run into "click fraud," a term the industry uses to describe someone clicking on a search ad with ill intent. A fraudulent clicker can exploit the way Web ads work to rack up fees for a business rival, boost the placement of his or her own ads, or make money for himself or herself. Some people even employ software that automatically clicks on ads multiple times.

Some people believe that about 20 percent of clicks are from people not necessarily interested in the product advertised, and therefore in the industry's view, fraudulent; others say the problem is less severe. What's clear is that if left unchecked, click fraud could damage the credibility of Google, Yahoo, and the search-ad industry that spurred their meteoric growth. Click fraud is "the biggest threat to the Internet economy," Google's chief financial officer, George Reyes, said during an investor's conference.

During his sleuthing, McKelvey discovered that his industry was rife with click manipulation. He and others in the jet-charter brokerage fields say Yahoo and Google have been slow to help and vague on how they're tackling the problem. Meanwhile, McKelvey has cut his search-ad spending to $1,000 a month from $20,000. "I'm skeptical of the whole thing now," he says. He shifted the remaining $19,000 into other outlets, including magazines and events. "I feel like I've been snookered," he says. "Am I willing to take the risk and stick my neck out there at maybe $15 or $20 a click? Not now."

From the start of his business, McKelvey, now 35 years old, advertised through search engines. When a consumer search used words related to the charter-jet industry, his ad would pop up, often first on the list. Business rushed in, McKelvey says, and he bid on about 200 phrases including "jet charter," "business jet," "executive jet," and "charter flights." The advertiser who wins the bid gets his or her company's ad placed high in the search lists.

McKelvey's Web-hosting company traced dozens of clicks to an address belonging to an Internet service provider called BridgeCom International Inc. The company had assigned the IP address in question to Blue Star Jets. That was a lucky break for McKelvey because Internet service providers typically keep such information private.

Howard Moses, chief marketing office for Blue Star Jets, says some of Blue Star's staff and salespeople might have clicked on rivals' search ads looking for information. He denies the company engaged in any widespread, malicious clicking. "It's a little bit amusing to think that our staff is concentrating on driving their search-advertising spending up by $100 or something like that," Moses says.

McKelvey thinks the problem costs him more than the refunds he received. He believes there are more bad clicks he hasn't discovered. He says Yahoo and Google haven't helped. He contacted the Massachusetts attorney general's office, which he says decided not to take up the matter.

Case Questions

1. Is this case more about crime than ethics? Or is it more about ethics than crime? Explain your reasoning.

2. What would you recommend that McKelvey do about using the Internet searches as a source of leads for his business?

3. How might a code of ethics for companies that advertise on the Internet help resolve the issues raised in this case?

Source: From Kevin J. Delaney, "In 'Click Fraud,' Web Outfits Have a Costly Problem," *The Wall Street Journal,* April 6, 2005, pp. A1, A6. Reprinted with permission.

AN INTERPERSONAL RELATIONS CASE PROBLEM

THE HIGHLY RATED, BUT EXPENDABLE MARSHA

Department manager Nicholas had thought for a long time that Marsha, one of his financial analysts, created too many problems. Although Marsha performed her job in a satisfactory manner, she required a lot of supervisory time and attention. She frequently asked for time off when her presence was needed the most because of a heavy workload in the department. Marsha sent Nicholas many long and complicated e-mail messages that required substantial time to read and respond. When Nicholas responded to Marsha's e-mail message, she would typically send another e-mail back asking for clarification.

Marsha's behavior during department meetings irritated Nicholas. She would demand more time than any other participant to explain her point of view on a variety of issues. At a recent meeting she took ten minutes explaining how the company should be doing more to help the homeless and invest in the development of inner cities.

Nicholas coached Marsha frequently about the problems she was creating, but Marsha strongly disagreed with his criticism and concerns. At one time, Nicholas told Marsha that she was a high-maintenance employee. Yet Marsha perceived herself as a major contributor to the department. She commented once, "Could it be Nick, that you have a problem with an assertive woman working in your department?"

Nicholas developed a tactic to get Marsha out of the department. He would give her outstanding performance evaluations, emphasizing her creativity and persistence. Marsha would then be entered into the company database as an outstanding employee, thereby making her a strong candidate for transfer or promotion. Within six months, a manager in a new division of the company took the bait. She requested that Marsha be recruited into her department as a senior financial analyst. Nicholas said to the recruiting manager, "I hate to lose a valuable contributor like Marsha, but I do not want to block her career progress."

Two months later, Marsha's new manager telephoned Nicholas, and asked, "What's the problem with Marsha? She's kind of a pill to have working with us. I thought she was an outstanding employee."

Nicholas responded, "Give Marsha some time. She may be having a few problems adjusting to a new environment. Just give her a little constructive feedback. You'll find out what a dynamo she can be."

Case Questions

1. How ethical was Nicholas in giving Marsha a high performance evaluation for the purposes of attracting her to other departments?

2. What should the manager do who was hooked by Nicholas's bait of the high performance evaluation?

3. What might the company do to prevent more incidents of inflated performance evaluations for the purpose of transferring an unwanted employee?

INTERPERSONAL SKILLS ROLE-PLAY

Confronting the Ethical Deviant

One student plays the role of the manager who transferred Marsha into his or her department. The new manager has become suspicious that Nicholas might have manipulated Marsha's performance evaluations to make her appear like a strong candidate for transfer or promotion. In fact, the new manager thinks he may have caught an ethical deviant. Another student plays the role of Nicholas who wants to defend his reputation as an ethical manager. During the role play, pay some attention to ethical issues. As usual, other students will provide feedback on the effectiveness of the interaction they observed.

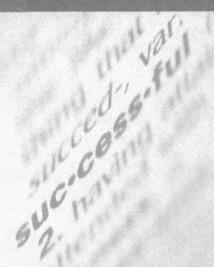

How This Book Can Help You

Who Can Use This Book

This book was written for you if you need to run meetings, either now or in the future—regardless of whether you are in business, training, nonprofit, health care, or any other professional context. Here are just a few reasons why meetings are more commonplace and important today than ever before.

- *Advances in technology*—such as videoconferencing and conference calls

- *More time spent in meetings*, 60 percent or more of some professional's time

- *High costs* to the organization

- *Increased reliance on collaborative work groups* and cross-functional work teams

- *More specialization*, which necessitates sharing diverse knowledge and expertise

This book is for you if you want specific tips to assure that your meetings will be:

- Necessary and not just a waste of time
- Marked by healthy discussion, not hostile confrontation
- Interesting, coherent, and well organized
- Based on new technology when appropriate
- A place for people to share, rather than show off, their ideas
- Constructive, thoughtful, and creative
- Inclusive, with full participation from all
- A forum for decisions that get acted upon
- Efficient and not a waste of energy

The book can also help you if you want general guidelines, rather than answers to specific questions. For example, you might want:

- A checklist for meeting preparation
- General guidelines for meeting facilitation
- A set of options for making decisions

Finally, if you are taking a professional course, a college course, or a workshop, you can use this book as a reference.

WHY THIS BOOK WAS WRITTEN

The thousands of participants in various communication courses and workshops we have taught—between the two of us, at Dartmouth's Tuck, Minnesota's Carlson, and Stanford business schools, as well as at hundreds of companies and organizations—tell us that they want a brief summary of meeting techniques. Such busy professionals have found other books on this subject too long or too remedial for their needs. That's why Prentice Hall is publishing this series, the Prentice Hall Guides to Advanced Communication—brief, practical, reader-friendly guides for people who communicate in professional contexts. (See the opening page in this book for more information on the series.)

- Brief: The book summarizes key ideas only. Culling from pages of text and research, we have omitted bulky examples, cases, footnotes, exercises, and discussion questions.
- Practical: This book offers clear, straightforward tools you can use. It includes only information you will find useful in a professional context.
- Reader-friendly: We have tried to provide an easy-to-skim format—using a direct, matter-of-fact, and nontheoretical tone. Those hoping to gain new ideas can read it as a text while those wanting to refresh their memory should be able to easily skim specific pages.

HOW THE BOOK IS ORGANIZED

The book is divided into two main sections: planning the meeting and conducting the meeting.

PART I: PLANNING THE MEETING (CHAPTERS 7–11)

Part I provides a detailed discussion of issues to consider before the meeting. Chapter 7 answers the question *Why Meet?* with tips on specifying a purpose for meeting, deciding on a channel of communication (e.g., meetings, presentations, writing, or an individual conversation), and analyzing your attitude toward meetings. Chapter 8 covers *Who to Include?* including how to select participants and gear your meeting toward their backgrounds, expectations, and emotions. In Chapter 9, we discuss *What to Discuss?*, that is, setting an agenda (scheduling, explanation, and format) and orchestrating roles (scribe, timer, etc.). *How to Record Ideas?* is the topic of Chapter 10 which covers equipment and planning techniques for graphic facilitation (that is, recording participants' comments publicly). Chapter 11 explains the final meeting planning issue, *Where to Meet?*—including the tradeoffs between face-to-face versus electronic meetings and the logistics for face-to-face meetings.

PART II: CONDUCTING THE MEETING (CHAPTERS 12–16)

Part II covers the specific skills and techniques needed to conduct the meeting. In Chapter 12, we discuss *Opening the Meeting* in terms of both task functions (making sure the job gets done) and process functions (making sure people participate). Chapter 13 covers *Verbal Facilitation*—things you can say to get people talking, stimulate discussion and debate, and avoid debilitating arguments and confrontations. In Chapter 14, we move to *Listening Facilitation* skills, mental and nonverbal techniques you can use to make sure you hear what participants say. *Graphic Facilitation* is the topic of Chapter 15, which covers techniques for recording participants' comments publicly during the meeting. Chapter 16 provides some guidelines for *Closing the Meeting*—various techniques for making decisions, ending meetings, and following up on meetings.

ACKNOWLEDGMENTS

We are grateful for all the help and support we have received while working on this project. This project would not have been possible without the love and support of our friends, colleagues, and family members. *MM:* My thanks to Paul Argenti, Marcia Diefendorf, Seth Daniel Munter, Lindsay Rahmun, Lynn Russell, Karen Weinstock, and JoAnne Yates; to my colleagues at MCA and ABC; and to the thousands of executives and students I've been privileged to teach. *MN:* I would like to thank Carolyn Boulger, Mary Munter, Jim O'Rourke, Pris Rogers, and JoAnn Syverson for their encouragement and unwavering support. I would also like to thank the entire staff of the Managerial Communication Center at the University of Minnesota's Carlson School of Management. Finally, I would like to thank Professors Marty Manor, Jack Rhodes, Ernest Bormann, and Robert L. Scott for opening my eyes to the exciting possibilities of communication studies and for supporting my curiosity and personal growth.

Finally, we would like to acknowledge our sources listed in the bibliography.

Mary Munter
Tuck School of Business
Dartmouth College

Michael Netzley
Carlson School of Management
University of Minnesota

Planning the Meeting

First, the good news: Meetings can draw from a wealth of intellects, information sources, talents, and energy; they can enhance our ability to discuss and evaluate issues, to make decisions, and to implement ideas. Now, the bad news: Most people do not manage meetings effectively. Why? Because most people put less thought into running a meeting that they put into writing a routine memo.

In the words of meeting authority Michael Begeman, "great meetings don't just happen—they're designed. Producing a great meeting is a lot like producing a great product. You don't just build it. You think about it, plan it, and design it: What people and processes do you need to make it successful? But first you have to have agreement among people that meetings are *work*—they are not an empty ritual to be suffered through before getting 'back to the office.' Meetings are events in which real work takes place."

To design a productive meeting, answer each of the five questions on the meeting planning checklist shown to the left. Each of the questions on this checklist is covered in the five chapters that follow: (1) why meet? (2) who to include? (3) what to discuss? (4) how to record ideas? and (5) where to meet?

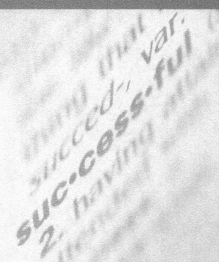

CHAPTER 7

Why Meet?
Define Your Purpose and Choose Your Channel

The first question to ask yourself in preparation for a meeting is "Why meet?" By answering this question, you can avoid one of the most prevalent complaints about meetings—that they are called unnecessarily. To avoid this pitfall, always (1) specify your purpose for meeting, (2) decide if a meeting is the best channel to use, and (3) analyze your attitude toward meetings.

Meeting Planning Checklist

1. Why meet? Define your purpose and choose your channel.
2. Who to include? Select and analyze the participants.
3. What to discuss? Orchestrate the roles and set the agenda.
4. How to record ideas? Plan for graphic facilitation.
5. Where to meet? Plan for technology and logistics.

Outline

1. Specify your purpose for meeting.
   General meeting goals
   Specific meeting purpose
2. Decide if a meeting is the best channel to use.
   Should you hold a meeting?
   Should you speak to one individual?
   Should you write?
   Should you make a presentation?
3. Analyze your attitudes toward meetings.
   Meetings are real work.
   Meetings are not easy.
   Meetings must balance competing needs.

SPECIFY YOUR PURPOSE FOR MEETING.

Many meetings are ill defined or unnecessary simply because no one has thought through the meeting purpose—sometimes called the meeting objective or outcome. Instead of just meeting because it's traditional or because it's already scheduled, always state your meeting purpose as specifically as possible—so that neither you nor the participants will have any doubt about why you are meeting. If the purpose or outcome is not important to all of the participants, then you probably don't need a meeting; instead, communicate only with the appropriate individuals.

Defining your meeting purpose specifically provides two important benefits. First, you will no longer waste time holding meetings unless you have a clear reason for doing so. Second, formulating your purpose precisely will help you communicate it more clearly to the participants.

To set a clear meeting purpose, think first about your general goal, then delineate your specific purpose or outcome.

GENERAL MEETING GOALS

General meeting goals are the broad-range reasons for calling a meeting. Typical examples of general meeting goals include: identifying or solving problems, brainstorming ideas, gathering or organizing information, decision making, and planning.

SPECIFIC MEETING PURPOSE

To establish a specific meeting purpose, delineate precisely what outcome you hope to accomplish, using this phrasing: "As a result of this meeting, we will _____." The table on the facing page shows some examples of general meeting goals followed by a specific meeting purpose.

TABLE 7-1 Examples of Meeting Goals and Purposes

General Meeting Goals	Specific Meeting Purposes
Identifying problems	As a result of this meeting, we will identify and discuss key problems we are having with the current process.
Solving problems	As a result of this meeting, our team will brainstorm solutions to this problem.
Brainstorming ideas	As a result of this meeting, our clients will brainstorm their ideas for new services that we should be offering.
Gathering information	As a result of this customer focus group, we will learn their preferences for our new services.
Organizing	As a result of this meeting, the team will agree on a timeline for this project.
Decision making	As a result of this meeting, the department will decide which software package to purchase.
Completing	As a result of this meeting, we will agree to contract modifications and Source: Adaptation of chart prepared by International Orientation Resources.
Planning for implementation	As a result of this meeting, we will work with the graphics department to develop our new promotion pieces.

DECIDE IF A MEETING IS THE BEST CHANNEL TO USE.

Once you have defined your purpose, decide whether that purpose would be best accomplished by a meeting—or another channel of communication instead.

SHOULD YOU HOLD A MEETING?

Hold a meeting if you need to: (1) gather information from a group—not if you already have enough information, (2) make a group decision—not if you have already made the decision, or (3) build group commitment, relationship, identity, or morale.

SHOULD YOU SPEAK TO ONE INDIVIDUAL?

Don't waste people's time in meetings in which they have no input or reason to be there. Instead, speak to an individual—not to a group—when you want to: (1) elicit individual feedback or response, (2) build an individual relationship or rapport, or (3) deal with a sensitive or negative issue—too sensitive or negative to discuss in a group. Remember, however, the disadvantages of speaking to one person only: (1) Speaking to only one person may make those with whom you do not speak feel excluded. (2) If you speak with more than one person separately, they will each hear slightly different information at different times.

SHOULD YOU WRITE?

Don't waste people's time in a meeting when you do not need interaction—such as for routine announcements, clarifications, or confirmation. People can read much faster than they can hear. Therefore, write when you (1) do not need interaction, (2) need precise wording (because you can edit), (3) have a great deal of detail (because readers can assimilate more detail than listeners can). If you write, however, you will have (1) no control over if or when the message is received, (2) a delayed response, if any, (3) no nonverbal communication, and (4) a possible lack of flexibility and too much rigidity.

SHOULD YOU MAKE A PRESENTATION?

To decide between a meeting and a presentation, think about which of two communication styles would be most effective to accomplish your purpose: "tell/sell" style or "consult/join" style. Choose to hold a meeting only for the consult/join style—that is, when you want to (1) gather information, (2) hear others' opinions, ideas, or input, or (3) discuss ideas or make a decision as a group. On the other hand, choose to make a presentation for the tell/sell style—that is, when you want to inform or persuade, when you (1) have sufficient information already, (2) do not need to hear others' opinions, ideas, or inputs, or (3) want to control the message content yourself, without discussion or a decision made by others.

The table following includes examples of some communication purposes best met by presentations versus meetings.

TABLE 7-2 Examples of Presentation vs. Meeting Purposes

Communication Purpose	*Presentation or Meeting?*
	Presentation *(Tell/Sell Style)*
As a result of this communication, senior management will learn what my department has accomplished this month. As a result of this communication, the customers will understand how to use our new product. As a result of this communication, the committee will approve my proposed budget.	The first set of examples are tell/sell style; therefore, do not hold a meeting. • You are informing, explaining, instructing, persuading, or advocating your own position. • You want to control the message content yourself, without input from others.
	Meeting *(Consult/Join Style)*
As a result of this communication, my team will decide among three options. As a result of this communication, we will learn which of the current products our customers prefer. As a result of this communication, the group will come up with a solution to this problem.	The second set of examples are consult/join style; therefore, call a meeting for group input, decision, or commitment. • You need information or input from others. • You want to interact or collaborate with others.

ANALYZE YOUR ATTITUDES TOWARD MEETINGS.

Imagine you have a clear purpose for your meeting and you have decided that a meeting is the most effective channel to accomplish that purpose. Before you move on to designing that meeting, take a moment to think about your attitude toward meetings.

MEETINGS ARE REAL WORK.

To make a meeting successful, in the words of meeting expert Michael Begeman, "first you have to have agreement among people that meetings are *work*—they are not an empty ritual to be suffered through before getting 'back to the office.' Meetings are events in which real work takes place. That's a big mind flip. . . As more and more of what people do takes place in teams, meetings become the setting in which most of the really important work gets done."

MEETINGS ARE NOT EASY.

Nobody expects most business projects—for example, designing a product or preparing a presentation—to be easy. You don't just start manufacturing a product or just start talking off the top of your head; instead, you think, plan, and design first. Similarly, great meetings don't just happen; they are designed. Once you consider meetings "real work," it is obvious that you need to plan as carefully as you would for other important business projects.

MEETINGS MUST BALANCE COMPETING NEEDS.

One thing that makes meetings particularly hard work is the constant need to balance two mutually exclusive needs—the need to maximize speed and get done on time, and the need to maximize input and take the time needed to be thoughtful and creative. This balance, as identified by conflict expert Lindsay Rahmun, is summarized in the table below.

TABLE 7-3 Balancing the Competing Needs of Meeting Management

Need to . . .		Need to . . .
Maximize speed	←→	Maximize input
End on time	←→	Take time needed to be thoughtful and creative
Prioritize task by emphasizing a fast decision	←→	Prioritize process by promoting discussion and inclusion
Be individually accountable; resist "groupthink"	←→	Be mutually accountable: move with the group
Work with limited perspective and resources	←→	Work with diverse perspectives and resources

CHAPTER 8

Who to Include?
Select and Analyze the Participants

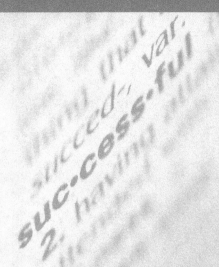

Once you have a clear idea about why you are meeting, your next task is to identify and analyze who should attend. Consider the optional number of and the nature of the participants. Then, to analyze those participants, think about their backgrounds, cultural characteristics, emotional and interest levels, and any timing issues.

Meeting Planning Checklist

1. Why meet? Define your purpose and choose your channel.
2. Who to include? Select and analyze the participants.
3. What to discuss? Orchestrate the roles and set the agenda.
4. How to record ideas? Plan for graphic facilitation.
5. Where to meet? Plan for technology and logistics.

Outline

1. Who to invite?
   How many participants?
   What type of a group do you want?
   Who needs to be there?
2. What are their backgrounds and expectations?
   What are their individual backgrounds?
   What are their cultural characteristics?
   How much information do they need?
3. What are they feeling?
   What emotions do they feel?
   How interested are they?
   How is the timing for them?
   Who needs a pre-meeting conversation?

WHO TO INVITE?

Deciding on the participants for a meeting is often not easy. You need to consider the most effective number to get the job done, the kind of group, and the important people who need to be there.

HOW MANY PARTICIPANTS?

As we discussed in the previous section, the tension between maximizing speed (task orientation) and maximizing input (process orientation) is tough to balance. Choices about the optimal number of participants reflect this dilemma.

- **Too many:** One common problem is inviting too many people to attend a meeting. Although it is important to gain input from multiple perspectives, too many participants can lead to superficial discussion if you want to hear from everyone. In addition, the larger the group size, the lower the percentage of people participating; some people may simply withhold their input.

- **Too few:** If, on the other hand, the group is too small, its problem-solving ability and group creativity may be handicapped.

- **Right number:** The appropriate size of the group depends on what you are trying to accomplish. For problem solving, around five people can attack a problem collectively yet all make visible contributions. For voting, an odd number of people is best. For consensus building, it's difficult to reach a consensus with more than about eight participants. For brainstorming, about ten people will be able to stir up the energy and creativity, yet all participate.

WHAT TYPE OF GROUP DO YOU WANT?

- **Heterogeneous vs. homogeneous:** For some projects, choose a homogeneous group (people with similar backgrounds, personalities, and values). Homogeneous groups build group relationships quickly and are less likely to have a lot of conflict. However, since they are more likely to produce unimaginative results, they are best used for well-defined, straightforward tasks. For other projects, choose a heterogeneous group. Such groups take more risks, are more critical of one another's ideas, and are generally better at novel or complex tasks; however, they often have trouble with building relationships.

- **Competitive vs. cooperative:** Cooperative groups demonstrate more effective interpersonal communication, higher levels of involvement, and better task performance. Homogeneous groups tend to be more cooperative; heterogeneous groups tend to be more competitive. Try to get competitive groups working toward a common goal; they will perform better, and group members will be more satisfied than groups whose members are striving to fulfill individual needs or pursuing competing goals.

- **Task vs. process:** Try to include some members who are efficiency/task-oriented and others who are effectiveness/process-oriented. (1) *Task-oriented members* focus on outcomes, not on other people's feelings or attitudes; if they dominate, meetings will be efficient, but members may be less satisfied. To these members, processes such as brainstorming or hot dot voting (explained on pages 149 and 189) may seem corny or a waste of time. (2) *Process-oriented members* frequently interject supportive comments such as "That's a great idea!" or "Let's hear what Jose has to say" or "I think we've made a lot of progress." If they dominate, meetings may go on too long without much getting accomplished.

WHO NEEDS TO BE THERE?

- **People with information:** Think about who needs to be there in terms of getting the task accomplished. Who has information or ideas to add? Who needs to contribute? What subgroups need to be represented?

- **People with power:** Who needs to be there because they have power or influence over the outcome of the meeting? How can you stop them from dominating the discussion? Who needs to be there because they are opinion leaders, those with significant informal influence?

- **People from different hierarchical levels:** What hierarchical levels will be included in the meeting participants? If you have people there from more than two levels of hierarchy, how will you avoid having people posturing and jockeying for position?

- **People who are indirectly involved:** Who needs to be there because they will approve, hear about, or be affected by the meeting? If you don't invite them to the meeting, how will you let them know what's going to happen or what happened? Are there any people who might sabotage the meeting outcome? Do you want to include them or deal with them outside the meeting?

WHAT ARE THEIR BACKGROUNDS AND EXPECTATIONS?

Once you have figured out who is or should attend the meeting, analyze them as carefully as possible.

WHAT ARE THEIR INDIVIDUAL BACKGROUNDS?

First, think about each participant individually. Think about their educational level, training, age, and interests. What are their opinions, interests, expectations, and attitudes? The more you can relate to the participants and make the meeting useful for them personally, the more successful you will be at attaining your communication objective.

WHAT ARE THEIR CULTURAL CHARACTERISTICS?

In addition, think about their cultural (or group) characteristics and expectations. What are their shared norms, traditions, standards, rules, and values? You may need to make adjustments based on these group or cultural norms. Think about possible adjustments, based on these cultural or group norms, such as:

- **Additional participants:** Some cultures may expect certain people to participate in the meeting, depending on cultural expectations about rank, authority, and group definition.

- **Different channel or time:** Different cultural groups—such as a technical department versus a marketing department, or a traditional organization versus a start-up venture—may have different norms for preferred channel and timing. These norms may range from standard face-to-face meetings held at a certain time weekly to email meetings held sporadically; or from formal, highly structured meetings to informal, free-form meetings.

- **Differences based on gender:** Sometimes it's useful to think about the cultural differences between men and women. Research shows, for example, that men tend to take arguments impersonally, women personally; that men seek quick authoritative decisions, whereas women use consensus building;

that men use stronger language even when they're not sure, but women use more qualified language even when they are sure; and that men use less active listening, and women use more.

HOW MUCH BACKGROUND OR NEW INFORMATION DO THEY NEED?

What do they already know about the topic? What new information do they need to know about the topic? How much jargon will they understand?

- **Low information needs:** If their information needs are low, don't waste time at the meeting giving unnecessary background, definitions, or new material.
- **High information needs:** If, to be able to discuss or decide intelligently, the participants need background information, consider including it in the agenda so they can read it in advance and be better prepared to discuss it during the meeting itself.
- **Mixed background needs:** With a mixed group, try summarizing background information with an opening such as "just to review," or referring people to the background information in the agenda.

WHAT ARE THEY FEELING?

Remember that the participants' emotional level is just as important as their knowledge level. Therefore, in addition to thinking about what they know, think about what they feel. Answering the following sets of questions will give you a sense of the emotions the participants may be bringing to the meeting.

WHAT EMOTIONS DO THEY FEEL?

What feelings may arise from their current situation or their emotional attitude? What objections or issues might they possibly raise?

- **What is their current personal situation?** Is there anything unusual that you should keep in mind about the individuals' or the group's morale, the time of day or year, or their economic situation?
- **What emotions might they bring to the meeting?** What, if any, feelings do they have about the topics to be discussed at the meeting? For example, do they feel positive emotions such as pride, excitement, and hope? If so, how can you capitalize on these feelings? Or do they bring negative feelings, such as anxiety, fear, or jealousy. If so, how can you defuse these negative feelings—either before or during the meeting?

HOW INTERESTED ARE THEY IN THE MEETING?

Is the meeting a high priority or low priority for them? How much do they care about the issue or its outcomes?

- **High interest level:** If their interest level is high, you can start the meeting without taking much time to arouse their interest.
- **Low interest level:** If, on the other hand, their interest level is low, you may need to arouse their interest before and during the meeting. For example, you might define a problem they don't know exists, establish a common

ground you all share, or point out the personal benefits they will derive from attending the meeting or from the outcomes of the meeting.

HOW IS THE TIMING FOR THEM?

You will not be able to reach your desired outcome if the timing is off for the participants. In addition to finding a time when the necessary people will be able to attend, think about other timing issues before you set your meeting. At what time of day are they (or at least the key decision makers) at their best? When is the meeting least likely to be interrupted? Do the participants have enough time to prepare before the meeting? What are any especially bad times for them, because they are under special pressure or deadlines?

WHO NEEDS A PRE-MEETING CONVERSATION?

Sometimes, it will be in your best interest to touch base with some, or even all, of the meeting participants before the meeting. For example, you might talk with key opinion leaders if a controversial issue will be covered, chat in advance with anyone who might feel surprised or blindsided by the topic, or mentor a subordinate who is presenting at the meeting.

CHAPTER 9

What to Discuss?
Orchestrate the Roles and Set the Agenda

The third item on your meeting checklist is to specify in more detail exactly what you are going to discuss during the meeting—by orchestrating roles and designing an agenda. These decisions should be driven by your meeting's purpose and the participants' needs, as analyzed in the previous two chapters.

Meeting Planning Checklist

1. Why meet? Define your purpose and choose your channel.
2. Who to include? Select and analyze the participants.
3. What to discuss? Orchestrate the roles and set the agenda.
4. How to record ideas? Plan for graphic facilitation.
5. Where to meet? Plan for technology and logistics.

Outline

1. Orchestrate the roles.
   Who will serve as facilitator?
   Who will serve as scribe?
   Who will serve as timer?
   Who will serve as minutes writer?

2. Set the agenda.
   Specify the purpose and the participants.
   Schedule agenda items.
   Explain each agenda item.
   Decide on the discussion format.
   Decide on a decision-making technique.
   Distribute the agenda in advance.

ORCHESTRATE THE ROLES.

Before you compose an agenda, decide what role(s) you are going to perform yourself and which you will delegate to someone else. Traditionally, the person who called the meeting performed all of the roles: facilitator, scribe, and timer. Unfortunately, it is very difficult, often impossible, to do a good job on all three of those roles at once. For example, you can get so involved in what is being said that you lose track of the time; or you can get so involved in writing down every good idea that the meeting begins to drag; or you can get so involved in problem solving yourself that you neglect to include others. For all these reasons, most meeting experts recommend separating the roles and not assigning the role of facilitator to the task-dominant person—who is usually the one who called the meeting.

If you choose to assign roles, remember that they can be flexible. The person serving as facilitator can pass that responsibility to another person for the next meeting. Or, if the team elects, certain role responsibilities can be assigned to one person for an extended period of time. Also, as you assign role responsibilities, be flexible in consideration of corporate cultural norms and participants' expectations.

WHO WILL SERVE AS FACILITATOR?

A good meeting facilitator runs the process without becoming involved in the task at hand; listens to, clarifies, and integrates information; keeps the group focused on the outcome or task; and creates an open environment in which everyone feels welcome to participate. Therefore, if you have strong feelings about the subject at hand, if you want to participate actively, if you are a particularly dominant personality, or if you are the leader or boss of the other participants, consider asking someone else to facilitate the discussion. For example, you might rotate the role of facilitator during a long meeting, hire an outside person to assume the role, or offer the task to someone with strong interpersonal skills.

If you do choose to facilitate the meeting yourself, you must refrain from dominating the discussion: it's difficult to listen to others' point of view when you are trying to convince them of your own. Antony Jay, in a classic *Harvard Business Review* article about meeting management, describes an effective meeting chair who "makes it a rule to restrict her interventions to a single sentence, or at most two. She forbids herself ever to contribute a paragraph to a meeting she is chairing."

WHO WILL SERVE AS SCRIBE?

Another increasingly popular technique is separating the roles of facilitator and scribe. It is very difficult to run the meeting and record ideas accurately at the same time. Using a scribe instead offers three benefits:

- **Enhances facilitation:** Managing the discussion is much easier and more effective, because the facilitator doesn't have to talk and write at the same time.
- **Improves legibility:** The scribe can write more carefully than can someone who is running the meeting at the same time.
- **Saves time:** Perhaps most importantly, using a scribe saves time during the meeting, because the facilitator can go on to discuss the next point while the scribe is still recording the previous point and confirming its accuracy.

WHO WILL SERVE AS TIMER?

You may wish to appoint someone else to serve as timekeeper, because it's hard to concentrate on the discussion and keep your mind on the time all at once. Going over the time limit, running off on tangents, and losing control of time can be big problems; conversely, controlling the flow too much and cutting people off can also be problems. Think about how you are going to deal with time issues, and, within reason, stick to your decision or group contract on timing.

WHO WILL SERVE AS MINUTES WRITER?

Meeting "minutes" summarize what was said and decided; allow participants to keep these ideas on file; and encourage follow-up action (action items, dates, and people), as explained on page 191. Because it is virtually impossible to facilitate a meeting and take notes at the same time, many meetings lack minutes and therefore lack follow-up. To avoid this prevalent problem, ask someone to perform the important function of taking notes during the meeting and writing up meeting minutes afterwards. In addition, if you use minutes, decide also who, if anyone, should check them over before they are distributed, how they should be distributed (email or hard copy), and who should receive a copy.

SET THE AGENDA.

Since the whole purpose of a meeting is to discuss ideas as a group, prepare your agenda carefully and in advance, so that participants can come fully prepared.

SPECIFY THE PURPOSE AND THE PARTICIPANTS.

Make it clear why you're meeting and who will be there.

- **Clarify your purpose.** What is your desired outcome from the meeting (e.g., a better understanding, additional information, or an agreement)? As we discussed on pages 137–139, you have already defined the meeting's purpose or outcome for yourself, using the phrasing "As a result of this meeting, we will . . ."

- **State the purpose on the agenda.** Now, state that purpose clearly on the agenda, so the participants will have no doubt about why they are meeting. Let them know what the desired meeting outcome is and how they are expected to participate (e.g., to generate ideas, narrow down ideas, or make a decision). In addition to stating it on the agenda, reiterate the purpose orally at the beginning of the meeting.

- **List the participants.** In addition, the agenda should include a list of all the participants and any roles they might be filling (e.g., scribe, as discussed on page 147) so the participants will know exactly who will be there and what, if any, duties they may have.

SCHEDULE AGENDA ITEMS.

Think also about the meeting length and order of items.

- **Meeting length:** Productivity tends to drop after about two hours or if you have too many topics to cover. Schedule a series of short meetings if the agenda requires more time. Deal with long reports by asking presenters to hand in a written report for the sake of the record, but to report verbally on only the most important items or the items on which they want group response.

- Sensitive topics: Decide where you want to schedule sensitive topics on the agenda. You can save sensitive topics for the end if you think opening with major disagreements might keep the meeting from proceeding effectively. Alternatively, you schedule the most important topic first, even if it is sensitive, to allow sufficient time to deal with it and to overcome the fear that people won't focus on the first items if they know a big controversy is coming up.

EXPLAIN EACH AGENDA ITEM.

Then, for each item on the agenda, make the following points clear to the participants:

- Purpose: What is the purpose of each agenda item? Clearly differentiate items that are "for your information," "for discussion," or "for a decision."
- Preparation and contribution: How, specifically, should they prepare? What should they read, look over, or think about? How, specifically, will they be expected to contribute? Instead of putting them on the spot during the meeting, let them know in advance what will be expected—for example, "Think about the pros and cons of this proposal" or "List five ideas before the meeting."
- Timing: What is your tentative timing for each topic? How rigid do you want to be about timing? How will you go about revising the agenda timing during the meeting if you wish to (e.g., by your decision or by group decision)?
- Presenter: Who is in charge of explaining or leading the discussion for each item? Will you have various presenters or will you run the whole meeting yourself?

DECIDE ON THE DISCUSSION FORMAT.

Instead of always using the same discussion format, think about the various formats from which to choose.

- Typical meeting format: Most meetings run by a free-flowing discussion ending with a decision. Because this format is so unstructured, however, discussions can drag on too long, overpowering personalities can dominate, participants are often swayed by social pressure, and few alternatives are generated.
- Brainstorming format: Most people have heard of brainstorming sessions but do not use such sessions as effectively as they might. Brainstorming can be enjoyable and effective, but only if the facilitator works hard to make sure that participants follow three ground rules: (1) before the meeting, prepare by thinking of as many diverse ideas as possible—the more unusual, creative, and at variance with current policy, the better; (2) during the meeting, follow up on other people's ideas ("Kenji's idea makes me think of . . ."), associate freely, and think of new ideas; and (3) do not criticize or evaluate any of the proposed ideas until after all the ideas have been generated. (See pages 175 and 186–187 for more on brainstorming.)
- Nominal group method: This method is a highly structured form of brainstorming that ensures that everyone participates and that no one dominates. Using this method, (1) participants list their ideas independently, in writing,

before the meeting starts; (2) the facilitator or scribe records everyone's ideas, in a round-robin fashion, on a flipchart or board; and (3) the group discusses any unclear items to make sure they understand them. Then, discussion and evaluation takes place.

- **Buzz groups:** If participants are not responding in the entire group, try breaking them into small "buzz groups." In a smaller group, people will almost always talk more freely and comfortably because the environment is less public and no one feels put on the spot. After the buzz groups meet, each group provides a written or oral summary to the entire group, which serves as the basis for group discussion.

DECIDE ON A DECISION-MAKING TECHNIQUE.

Let participants know in advance how decisions will be made at the meeting. In some situations, let them know the meeting is for discussion only, not for a decision—so they won't be frustrated because they expect to make a decision. In other situations, let the group know they will be serving as an advisory board and that you or someone else will be making the decision. As long as people know this in advance, they are usually glad to advise; if they go into the meeting expecting to be the decision maker and then are not, they are usually upset. In other meetings in which you want to decide as a group, let them know specifically how you plan to do so. On pages 189–190, we discuss various decision-making models. Choose one and explain it on your agenda.

DISTRIBUTE THE AGENDA IN ADVANCE.

If you want to elicit ideas from people, give them time to think about the agenda items before the meeting instead of distributing the agenda at the meeting itself. For a complicated financial or analytic agenda, distribute the agenda about a week in advance; for a less complex agenda, distribute it a couple of days in advance.

Sample Templates for Meeting Agendas

Sample Template #1

To:
From:
Date:
Subject:

Our next team meeting is scheduled for . . . *(to be followed by the date, time, place, and an explanation of the background or problem).*

Meeting Goal: To establish one consistent method for scheduling personnel to use throughout the company

Agenda: Our meeting will proceed according to the following agenda.

Agenda Item	Responsibility	Time
Introduction	Manager	5 minutes
Discussion of pros and cons of each method	Team	30 minutes
Decision about new method	Team	10 minutes
Next steps	Team	15 minutes

Preparation: Before the meeting, please:
- Read the attached document outlining the three scheduling methods currently being used.
- Be prepared to discuss the pros and cons of each of the three methods.

Sample Template #2

Agenda Item	Purpose	Tentative Timing	Presenter	Preparation
Review proposal	Information	5 minutes	Jane Manager	Familiarize yourself with the proposal and budget attached
Discuss pros & cons	Discussion	20 minutes	John Facilitator	Think of pros & cons for the attached proposal

---
Sample Template #3

Meeting Details
Date
Time
Place
Participants

Meeting Goal: Discuss the merits of the nine options we generated at our brainstorming session last week and achieve consensus on one of them: *(followed by a list of the nine options).*

Meeting Preparation: Consider each name option in terms of the following four criteria: *(followed by an explanation of the four criteria).*

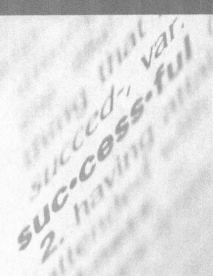

CHAPTER 10

How to Record Ideas?

Plan for Graphic Facilitation

One of the most important ways to enhance group discussion is to record participants' comments publicly. This technique is known as "graphic facilitation," because you use graphics—such as notes on flipcharts or boards—in addition to words (known as "verbal facilitation"). This section covers deciding (1) whether to record ideas, (2) what equipment to use, and (3) how to use frameworks and headings.

Meeting Planning Checklist

1. **Why meet?** Define your purpose and choose your channel.
2. **Who to include?** Select and analyze the participants.
3. **What to discuss?** Orchestrate the roles and set the agenda.
4. **How to record ideas?** Plan for graphic facilitation.
5. **Where to meet?** Plan for technology and logistics.

Outline

DECIDING WHETHER TO RECORD IDEAS

When most people think about meeting facilitation, they think of "verbal facilitation"—that is, what you say during the meeting to generate discussion (such as asking open questions, paraphrasing participant responses, etc.). These verbal facilitation skills are covered on pages 172–179.

We encourage you, however, to consider adding a second set of skills to your repertoire, known as "graphic facilitation"—that is, what you *write* during the meeting (such as notes taken on flipcharts or boards) to publicly record what participants say.

WHAT ARE THE BENEFITS?

Graphic facilitation is arguably one of the most underutilized aspects of effective meeting management. This is unfortunate, because it allows a group to achieve the competing goals of speed and inclusiveness (described on page 140)—in addition to the following benefits:

- **Accuracy:** Recording ideas publicly ensures an accurate record of what was said.
- **Morale:** Recording ideas makes people feel heard and appreciated, even if their ideas are rejected later on.
- **Links:** Recording ideas also encourages participants to see links between one another's comments and to build on or react to one another's ideas.
- **Timing control:** Recording people's points tends to discourage them from talking too long or repetitively.
- **Permanent record:** From your charts, you can later come up with a permanent record, either electronically if you have an electronic board or by minutes based on the charts.
- **Action plans:** The written display of ideas helps participants identify future action plans emerging out of those ideas.

WHY PREPARE IN ADVANCE?

Despite all of these benefits, meeting facilitators often wander into the meeting room having given no advance thought to graphic facilitation. In such cases, they may:

- **Find the wrong equipment,** or no equipment, available;
- **Waste time** preparing and writing as the participants sit and wait;
- **Squander opportunities** to make their meetings more successful.

Therefore, it's in your best interests to plan your "visual aids" for graphic facilitation in advance, just as you would plan your visual aids for a formal presentation in advance.

CHOOSING EQUIPMENT FOR GRAPHIC FACILITATION

Give some thought to what equipment would be most effective in your meeting. Before you decide on what equipment to use, (1) find out if a certain type of equipment is preferred or expected by the participants, their organization, or their culture; (2) think about the size of your group and your room, and be sure to choose something that can be read by all participants; and (3) consider the characteristics intrinsic in the various kinds of equipment, described below.

FLIPCHARTS

Flipcharts are a popular choice for recording group discussions in meetings. An advantage of flipcharts over boards is that you can take flipchart pages with you for a permanent record of the session. In addition, flipcharts tend to elicit a great deal of group discussion because they:

- Are "low tech"—therefore nonthreatening and unintimidating to low-tech participants and devoid of electronic problems;
- Allow for a brightly lit room;
- Make it easy to use color to increase visual interest;
- May be attached to the walls for easy viewing and further discussion—using tape, tacks, static-cling, or adhesive post-it paper.

TRADITIONAL BLACK OR WHITE BOARDS

Boards may encourage group discussion because, like flipcharts, they are low-tech, unintimidating, and allow for a brightly lit room. However, boards must be erased to regain free space, they do not provide hard copy, and they may appear "schoolish" and unprofessional to some participants.

ELECTRONIC BOARDS

Some electronic "copy boards" are used in face-to-face meetings; they look like traditional boards, with the added advantage that they can print hard copy of what you write on them, so you can keep a permanent record. Another kind of electronic board is used in electronic meetings; these can be annotated in one location and simultaneously viewed on computer screens in multiple locations. Such boards are capable of providing digitized hard copy of document computer files and two-dimensional objects.

ELECTRONIC "LIVE BOARDS"

In some electronic meetings, people participate not by talking, but by writing on electronic "live boards" from their computers. Unlike copy boards, they can be annotated from multiple locations and they may also have application-sharing capabilities.

PROJECTORS

You might also choose to use "still" projectors (either an overhead projector or a document camera) to record people's ideas. Projectors can be effective because of enhanced visibility, due to the large screen and to your ability to make the words larger by moving the projector closer to the screen. The problems with projectors include: (1) you must usually dim the lights, which may decrease audience interaction; (2) some participants may associate projectors with a formal presentation, which may decrease their participation; and (3) the projector sits in front of the screen with you next to it, possibly blocking someone's view.

The two kinds of projectors have different preparation requirements. If you use an overhead projector, be sure to bring special acetate sheets and special markers, which are not the same as regular marking pens. If you choose a document camera, you can use regular paper and pens; however, their resolution is not as high as that of an overhead projector.

HANDOUTS

Another option is to use handouts before, during, or after the meeting—either using email, which can be distributed faster and does not waste paper, or using hard copy, which has high resolution and can be more attractive in appearance and feel.

- **Handouts before the meeting:** Since you want to elicit participants' most thoughtful and informed thoughts, distribute any handouts or background information before the meeting, as a part of the agenda. These advance handouts provide an opportunity for participants to annotate them, thus combining their ideas with yours. You might want to bring extra copies along with you in case participants misplace theirs.

- **Handouts during the meeting:** If you have information that you do not want people to read in advance and that is too detailed or complex to show on a chart or board, use a handout. However, remember that people tend to read whatever is in front of them, so distribute new handouts only when you want them to be read. After you distribute them, either give the participants time to read them and/or direct their attention (referring to page numbers or exhibit numbers, if applicable) to the points you wish to discuss.

- **Summary handouts after the meeting:** On page 148, we discussed the importance of providing a summary handout, usually called meeting minutes, and of possibly delegating that task. This crucial summary reminds participants about what was said, allows them to keep these ideas on file, and encourages follow-up actions.

COMPUTER PROJECTORS

Another option is to use computer projection, together with computer graphics software, such as PowerPoint. Computer graphics allow you to create polished and dramatic images easily, but invite visual overload and overuse of animation bells and whistles. In general, such graphics are more effective in formal presentations, when you are doing most of the talking, than in meetings, when the participants are doing most of the talking—for the obvious reason that you cannot record on them in real time. You might, however, wish to use computer graphics to introduce or explain ideas before the discussion starts. On the other hand, if you can present the information just as effectively using a handout or chart, then choose the simple medium and leave the computer turned off. By turning the projector off, you can spend more time focusing on and interacting with the participants.

The table on the following page provides a quick reference to help you select the appropriate equipment for using graphics for meeting facilitation.

PLANNING DESIGN AND HEADINGS IN ADVANCE

Once you have selected your equipment, a little advance thought about design and headings can improve participation enormously.

USING A VISUAL FRAMEWORK TO FACILITATE DISCUSSION

One design issue to consider in advance is that of a visual framework. Visual frameworks enhance discussion because participants can see the relationship among ideas visually and are reminded of those relationships throughout the meeting. The chart on the following page illustrates several possible design options you might use to enhance group discussion. (See the Howell book in the bibliography, page 192, for much more on visual frameworks.)

Equipment for Graphic Facilitation

Equipment	Advantages	Disadvantages
Flipcharts	Unintimidating, no electronic problems, allow bright lights, may be attached to walls, provide hard copy	May seem too low-tech, clumsy to transport
Boards	Unintimidating, no electronic problems, allow bright lights	Must be erased to regain space, no hard copy, may appear "schoolish"
Electronic boards	Provide hard copy, some can be viewed in multiple locations	Must be erased to regain space
Live boards	Can be annotated from multiple locations	Must be erased to regain space
Overhead projectors	Good visibility, can make words bigger	Need dimmed lights, may be associated with formal presentations, projector may block view
Handouts	Can be distributed in advance, can be used for reference or note taking, can be used for summary	Can be lost, hard to control when people read them, can be distracting
Computer projectors	Allow for polished and dramatic images, may be used to introduce or explain ideas	Do not allow for real-time annotation of group ideas, may emphasize the graphics over the discussion

USING COLOR

Another design issue has to do with color. A little bit of color goes a long way toward making meetings more visually stimulating and graphically attractive for the participants. Color also allows you (or the scribe) to emphasize certain ideas—such as headings, summary phrases, or vote tallies. To use color effectively:

- **Plan your equipment.** Use either flipcharts, a white board, or an overhead projector. Be sure to have the correct kind of markers for the equipment and to check each marker in advance.
- **Choose dark, cool colors.** Usually, dark, cool colors—such as black, blue, and green—show up the best. Avoid warm, light colors—such as yellow and orange—because they often cannot be seen.
- **Use color consistently,** rather than randomly. For example, you might: (1) use one color to write up your main headings in advance, then another color to record participant ideas during the meeting; (2) use green to record ideas in an "Advantages" column and red to record ideas in the "Disadvantages" column; or (3) use one color to record various options, and a contrasting color to tally votes for each one.

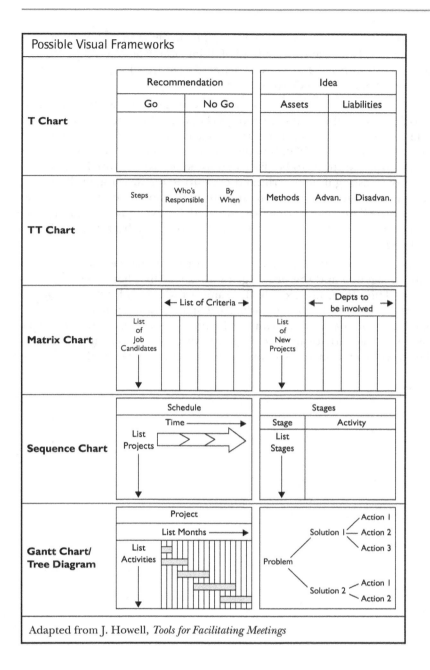

Possible Visual Frameworks

Adapted from J. Howell, *Tools for Facilitating Meetings*

COMPOSING CHART HEADINGS IN ADVANCE

A third way to enhance your ability to record ideas has to do with giving some advance thought to your headings. The headings you write on the board or charts are crucial to participant understanding and participation. Therefore, compose headings that:

- **Make the topic clear:** Since you want participants to offer ideas, each heading should keep them reminded of exactly what content they are discussing (e.g., what you are listing on a certain chart). Imagine a meeting participant whose attention wanders or who needs to leave the meeting momentarily or who joins the meeting late. Such participants should be able to tell the topic of discussion simply by looking at the heading.

- **Make the discussion process clear:** Those same imaginary participants should also be able to tell at a glance what kind of discussion process is underway; for example, "Brainstormed List of New Names," "Desired Project Outcomes," "To Do," or "What Are the Current Problems?"

- **Are written up in advance:** Once you decide in advance what your visual framework and main headings are going to be, write them up in advance. For example, provide a blank matrix chart with each criterion summarized across the top and each job candidate's name listed down the side, or outline a TT chart with various options to be discussed listed across the top. By doing so, you can avoid wasting time by writing them during the meeting itself and encourage people who arrive early to start thinking about the agenda items. Leave space to fill in ideas as they are generated; for example, you might write three different topics for brainstorming at the top of each of three different flipchart pages.

- **Tie to the agenda:** Participants should find it easy to glance back and forth between the agenda and the headings to track exactly where you are in the discussion. Therefore, use exactly the same wording and organization on your charts as you used in your agenda. Participants should also be able to see the meeting agenda at all times during the meeting. Either refer to their paper copy of the agenda or make the agenda visible (e.g., post it on an extra flipchart or project it on an extra overhead located at the side of the room).

CHAPTER 11

Where to Meet?
Plan for Technology and Logistics

*I*n the past, all meetings were face-to-face. Today's technology offers you many alternatives besides face-to-face meetings. This section covers the technology available for meetings as well as logistics to keep in mind as you plan your meeting.

Meeting Planning Checklist

1. Why meet? Define your purpose and choose your channel.
2. Who to include? Select and analyze the participants.
3. What to discuss? Orchestrate the roles and set the agenda.
4. How to record ideas? Plan for graphic facilitation.
5. Where to meet? Plan for technology and logistics.

Outline

1. Face-to-face versus electronic meetings
   When to meet face-to-face
   When to meet by videoconference
   When to meet by EMS
   When to meet by email
   When to meet by broadcasting or webcasting
   When to meet by conference call

2. Logistics for face-to-face meetings
   Choose a meeting site.
   Think about spatial relationships.
   Prepare with the scribe.
   Check the details.
   Check the equipment.

FACE-TO-FACE VERSUS ELECTRONIC MEETINGS

Electronic meetings utilize "groupware"—a broad term for related technologies that mediate group collaboration through technology. Groupware may include any combination of collaborative software or intraware, electronic- and voice-mail systems, electronic meeting systems, phone systems, video systems, electronic bulletin boards, and group document handling and annotation systems.

- **General advantages:** In general, electronic meetings are effective for reaching geographically dispersed participants and for speeding up follow-up, because ideas and action items are recorded and distributed electronically.
- **General disadvantages:** On the other hand, electronic meetings lack rich nonverbal cues of face-to-face interaction, are not as effective for establishing group rapport and relationships, and may present technical difficulties or crash. Many times, electronic meetings can be successful only if participants have spent face-to-face time together beforehand.
- **Other considerations:** (1) *Resources:* Think about what resources both you and your participants have available. (2) *Group expectations:* Some groups might find electronic meetings too slick, flashy, or technical; for other groups, not using the latest technology would be perceived as old-fashioned.

With these considerations in mind, think about the advantages and disadvantages of each of the six options discussed below.

WHEN TO MEET FACE-TO-FACE

- **Advantages:** Choose face-to-face meetings when (1) you need the richest nonverbal cues—including body, voice, proximity, and touch; (2) the issues are especially sensitive; (3) the people don't know one another; or (4) establishing group rapport and relationships is crucial.
- **Disadvantages:** Compared to videoconferences, face-to-face meetings (1) do not allow the possibility of simultaneous participation by people in multiple locations, and (2) can delay meeting follow-up activities because decisions and action items must be written up after the meeting. Compared to electronic meetings, face-to-face meetings may be dominated by overly vocal, quick-to-speak, and higher-status participants; they may involve high travel costs and time.

WHEN TO MEET BY VIDEOCONFERENCE

Videoconferences may take place on a large screen in a dedicated conference room, on television screens in several rooms, or on each participant's individual desktop computer with a small camera installed. Videoconference participants see and hear one another on the video; in addition, they may be able to view documents via document cameras and see notes taken on electronic "live boards."

- **Advantages:** Choose videoconferences when (1) the participants are in different places, but you want to communicate with them all at the same time; (2) you want to save on travel time and expenses; (3) you want to record the meeting for future use or distribution; or (4) you want to be able to see one another—as opposed to just audio or just words on a computer screen.
- **Disadvantages:** (1) They are usually not as effective as face-to-face meetings when you need to establish relationships; (2) they lack the richest nonverbal cues, such as proximity and touch; (3) fewer people tend to speak and they

speak in longer bursts than in face-to-face meetings; and (4) they may involve significant set-up time and costs.

WHEN TO MEET BY EMS

In electronic meeting systems (EMS), participants write to one another on their own separate computer screens. EMS are mediated (that is, they utilize a trained technical facilitator) and usually synchronous (that is, everyone participates at the same time).

- Advantages: Choose electronic meetings when you want to (1) generate more ideas and alternatives more quickly than with a traditional scribe; (2) allow the possibility of anonymous input, which may lead to more candid and truthful replies, equalize participants' status, and increase participation among hierarchical levels; (3) maximize audience participation and in-depth discussion because everyone can "speak" simultaneously, so shy members are more likely to participate and the "vocal few" are less likely to dominate the discussion; or (4) provide immediate documentation when the meeting is finished.

- Disadvantages: EMS (1) cannot replace face-to-face contact, especially when group efforts are just beginning and when you are trying to build group trust and emotional ties; (2) may exacerbate dysfunctional group dynamics and increased honesty may lead to increased conflict; (3) may make it harder to reach consensus, because more ideas are generated and because it may be harder to interpret the strength of other members' commitment to their proposals; and (4) may demand a good deal of facilitator preparation time and training.

WHEN TO MEET BY EMAIL

Email meetings differ from EMS in that they are *unmediated* (that is, messages go directly to other participants' computers) and *asynchronous* (that is, people respond at their convenience, at different times).

- Advantages: At their best, email meetings can (1) increase participation because people can respond when they wish and no scheduling is necessary; (2) speed up meeting follow-up activities because of electronic distribution; (3) decrease transmission time for circulating documents; (4) allow quick discussion and resolution of many small or obscure issues or problems; (5) decrease writing inhibitions with more conversational style than traditional writing; and (6) increase communication across hierarchical boundaries.

- Disadvantages: At their worst, email meetings can (1) decrease attention to the audience and to social context and regulation; (2) be inappropriately uninhibited or irresponsible, at worst destructive, known as "flaming"; (3) be inappropriately informal; (4) consist of "quick and dirty" messages, with typos and grammatical errors, and, more importantly, lack of logical frameworks for readers—such as headings and transitions; (5) result in a delayed response or no response; or (6) make it harder to gain commitment than with other kinds of meetings.

WHEN TO MEET BY BROADCASTING OR WEBCASTING

- Advantages: Can transmit to multiple audiences in multiple locations.
- Disadvantages: Usually one-way video, sometimes two-way audio.

WHEN TO MEET BY CONFERENCE CALL

- **Advantages:** Same as videoconferencing, plus conference calls allow for quicker response with less set-up time and use more easily accessible equipment than EMS or videoconferencing, and are therefore useful when vocal cues provide enough nonverbal feedback.
- **Disadvantages:** Same as videoconferencing, but lack of body language makes it harder to interact and to know who is going to speak next, and lack of text or visuals makes it harder to communicate a great deal of detailed information.

LOGISTICS FOR FACE-TO-FACE MEETINGS

Assuming you are meeting face-to-face rather than electronically, you need to think about various logistics. While you are doing so, keep in mind participant and cultural expectations; some cultures have very specific norms about where to meet or who should sit where.

CHOOSE A MEETING SITE.

Where you choose to meet can send a powerful signal. Think, for example, about the following questions.

- **Turf issues:** Do you want to meet on your own turf or in a more neutral site?
- **The room size:** How can you avoid an overly large and formal room or an overly small and cramped room?
- **Interruptions:** Where will participants be least likely to be interrupted?
- **The site:** Do you want to meet on-site for convenience or off-site to avoid distractions and signal importance?

THINK ABOUT SPATIAL RELATIONSHIPS.

An important way we communicate nonverbally during a meeting has to do with the way we choose to use the space around us. What you decide to do about the issues described below will send powerful, although often subconscious, messages to the participants.

- **Height:** The more similar your height is to that of the participants, the more informal and interactive an atmosphere you are establishing nonverbally. Therefore, sit down with the participants to increase interaction. In contrast, the higher you are in relation to the participants, the more authority and control you project nonverbally. Therefore, stand up to increase your authority and control.
- **Chairs:** The way you arrange the chairs communicates nonverbally what kind of interaction you want to have with the participants. To encourage interaction, place the chairs in a circle, horseshoe shape, or U shape. Straight lines of chairs are better for more formal, less interactive sessions.
- **Tables:** If you are all going to sit around a table and you have a choice about what kind of table to use, think about what the research shows. Use a round table if you want to encourage equality among participants. If the table is rectangular, you can choose to project more control by seating yourself at its head or less control by seating yourself on the side.

- **Your seating positions:** If you are all to be seated at your meeting, think about where you sit. We all associate the head of the table with dominance, in both work and social situations. Research supports this intuition. Dominant people or leaders do tend to sit at either end of the table. Therefore, choose to sit on the end of the table if you want to reinforce your dominance; choose the sides if you want to reinforce your equality with the participants.
- **Participants' seating positions:** More frequent talkers tend to sit at the head of the table or in the middle seats on the side of the table. Task-oriented people tend to sit at the ends of the table, process-oriented people in the middle side seat. In contrast, less frequent and nonparticipators tend to sit in the corner positions. You might want to think about ways to encourage them to participate more.

PREPARE WITH THE SCRIBE.

Because deciding what is recorded and when is a tool of control and influence, the most important advance preparation with your scribe has to do with empowerment—how the two of you will work together during the meeting.

- **Empowered scribe:** Do you want an "empowered scribe" who summarizes participant comments at his or her discretion?
- **Unempowered scribe:** Do you prefer an "unempowered scribe" who records only the specific wording you tell or signal to him or her to write?

Regardless of empowerment, prepare with the scribe in advance by answering these questions.

- **Readability?** Is the scribe's lettering legible and large enough for everyone to see? (See page 186.)
- **Participation?** Do you want the scribe to participate in the meeting or to observe and record only?
- **Confirmation?** Do you want the scribe to confirm with each participant that what got written is accurate (e.g., by taking pauses to confirm, by confirming quietly as you continue the discussion, or by questioning facial expression)? Or, do you want to confirm with the participant yourself, and then tell the scribe what to write?
- **Additional space?** What do you want the scribe to do when the flipchart sheet or the board becomes full? Do you want the scribe to post the full sheets? If so, where and how? Do you want the scribe to erase full boards? If so, how will you remember the information that was erased?
- **Color?** Do you want the scribe to use different colored markers or chalk? If so, what color-coding do you want to use? (See page 185.)
- **Double scribes?** If you think ideas will be flowing fast, do you want to use two scribes—each taking alternating turns recording an idea?

CHECK THE DETAILS.

Take responsibility for the details involved in logistical arrangements; such details can make or break an effective meeting. Plan to be there early enough to check logistics for:

- **Starting the meeting:** Make sure the room (including chairs and tables) is set up the way you want it—to encourage everyone to participate and make sure everyone can view the screen or wall.

- **Running the meeting:** Make any preparations necessary so you can proceed smoothly as the meeting progresses (e.g., attach charts to wall, use color-coding, or add more comments if you run out of room on the board).

CHECK THE EQUIPMENT.

Test your equipment to make sure it works.

- **For flipcharts:** Test the markers. Think about where to place the chart stands during the discussion, how to organize points you will write on the charts, where and how to post filled-in charts, and where to keep extra markers and paper.
- **For a board:** Check for chalk and erasers. Think about how to save material written on the board before it's erased.
- **For an overhead projector:** Think about where you should place the projector so that every single participant can read the screen. Be sure you have enough acetate sheets and special marking pens (which are not the same as flipchart markers) and you know where extra bulbs are kept.

Conducting the Meeting

Having planned your meeting, as discussed in Part I—defined your purpose, invited participants, set the agenda, and planned for facilitation and technology—you can now start thinking about how to facilitate the meeting, as described here in Part II. Chapter 12 covers the necessary skills for *opening the meeting*. The following three chapters discuss three skills to use during the meeting—*verbal facilitation skills* (getting them to talk) (Chapter 13), *listening facilitation* (mental and nonverbal) (Chapter 14), and *graphic facilitation skills* (recording what they say) (Chapter 15). Chapter 16 explains how to *close the meeting*.

The Meeting Implementation Checklist at left lists these five skills and the chapter in which each of them is covered.

CHAPTER 12

Opening the Meeting

The way you open the meeting will have an enormous impact on the meeting's effectiveness. The opening provides you with an opportunity to set the tone and begin to steer the participants down a productive path. During the opening, you need to accomplish two sets of functions. The first set is called "task functions"—how you go about accomplishing your work. The second is called "process functions"—how you get people to participate. Effective openings target both of these functions, orienting participants to the work at hand and encouraging them to get involved with the meeting.

Meeting Implementation Checklist

Outline

1. Task functions for opening the meeting
   Stress purpose and outcomes.
   Review the agenda.
   Deal with timing issues.
2. Process functions for opening the meeting
   Set the tone.
   Remind participants of their roles.
   Reach agreement on the ground rules.
   Involve people early.
   Use icebreakers with new groups.

TASK FUNCTIONS FOR OPENING THE MEETING

In terms of task functions, you should target three specific issues in your meeting opening.

STRESS PURPOSE AND OUTCOMES.

At the beginning of the meeting, always emphasize why you are meeting, based on your statement of purpose described on pages 137–139. By doing so, you will:

- **Keep the group focused:** Without a clear statement of purpose, the group is unlikely to stay focused and likely to waste valuable time. To motivate the participants, remember to frame the meeting purpose in terms of their benefits or interests.

- **Be able to see your progress:** Additionally, a clear statement of purpose or outcomes will make it possible for you to measure your progress as a team. Without desired outcomes, how can you tell whether you are progressing?

Here are some examples of clear statements of purpose, tied to participants' benefits:

"In this meeting, we hope to gather specific feedback about our latest ad campaign using a focus-group style."

"In this meeting, we are hoping to lay a foundation for designing new products that complement our existing line. Therefore, please think broadly and hold your critiques until our next meeting."

"In this meeting, we are hoping to narrow our supplier choice to two candidates. Afterwards, we will arrange individual interviews with each of you so that we may discuss your specific needs."

REVIEW THE AGENDA.

Make sure everyone understands and agrees on the meeting agenda and decision-making technique. This review will ensure that everyone understands the topics and reveal if there are any major disagreements about topics and procedures. You will find it much more effective to clarify these issues up front, rather than in the midst of a heated debate. It may also be useful to briefly mention the boundaries or constraints on the discussion. Discussing each of these points will quickly reveal if your agenda is set or if you need to make quick changes before proceeding.

DEAL WITH LATECOMERS.

Late arrivals are common in today's business environment. Professionals are increasingly faced with multiple demands on their time and delays caused by increased access through cell phones and pagers. When a participant walks into a meeting late, how will you react?

- **Consider the culture.** How are meetings generally run in the firm? Do meetings tend to start promptly or routinely start five to ten minutes late? It may be difficult to change cultural norms.

- **Think about the signal you are sending.** Deciding to start exactly on time can signal to participants that today's meeting is important or that you have enough respect for everyone's time to not waste ten minutes waiting for latecomers. On the other hand, waiting for everyone to arrive can signal that you value everyone's input and do not want to operate without all interested parties present. As a meeting facilitator, you must decide which you will value more: efficiency or inclusiveness.

- **Minimize late arrivals.** You may want to call a participant the morning of your meeting and politely confirm the time and place, especially if the person has a history of being late. You might also try the technique of having food and drink available before the meeting, or even cut off the refreshment supply when the meeting starts so participants have to arrive on time if they want to partake.

- **Handle late arrivals effectively.** While techniques for minimizing late arrivals can be helpful, they are not always 100 percent effective. What will you do when someone arrives late? Your options include: (1) *Saying nothing.* (2) *Warmly welcoming* the person and inviting him or her to pull up a chair. (3) *Politely singling out* the person with a subtle comment such as, "Ah! Here is Amit. Now we are complete." (4) *More forcefully singling out* the person by pausing the meeting and saying something such as, "Carol, thank you for coming. I hope you will talk with one of your colleagues and gather the information we have already discussed." Remember that singling a person out is a form of social punishment. If you want to set a positive, warm, and welcoming tone, it is not in your best interest to single out late arrivals. (5) *Talking to the person after the meeting* to encourage her or him to arrive promptly at future meetings. Talking to the person individually can be a very positive way to deal with the problem, especially if you are trying to encourage greater participation among the group.

PROCESS FUNCTIONS FOR OPENING THE MEETING

As we explained on pages 139–140, effective meeting management means more than just trying to get the task accomplished. It also means paying attention to the process by which you get that task done. Doing so will yield the following benefits:

- **Increase efficiency:** Research shows that discussing process functions (such as timing, ground rules, and decision making) will actually increase efficiency in your meetings. Poor meeting processes can have serious social consequences for the group that will inhibit otherwise effective work on the task. For this reason, you should resist jumping right into the task without first establishing process ground rules.

- **Increase collaboration:** Helping people understand ground rules and procedures before starting work on the task will help people contribute and prevent the inevitable embarrassment that comes from being corrected or breaking the rules. You will find it much easier to promote collaboration and accomplish your task-related goals if you take the time to first build a rewarding social environment.

In other words, the best way to waste time in your meetings is to completely ignore the process or social dimensions of your work and dive head first into the task. Here are several suggestions for managing process functions during the opening of your meeting.

SET THE TONE.

The tone of your meeting can be just as important as ideas or issues on your agenda. Meetings starting on a somber or critical tone can be inefficient. Such a negative tone raises barriers to collaboration and creativity—barriers that you must overcome if you wish to accomplish your goals. For example, calling an "emergency meeting" to "discuss last-minute and necessary changes to the software" may raise the defenses of those who have worked most closely (and probably overtime!) on the software. Instead, simply call an urgent meeting and then frame the necessary changes as "last-minute changes that will make a good customer even happier." Setting an appropriate social tone will help you avoid meetings that lack meaning for participants or are relatively unproductive. Happy participants make for more productive meetings.

REMIND PARTICIPANTS OF THEIR ROLES.

Meetings do not run smoothly by magic or by accident. On pages 147–148, we discussed the different roles you need to orchestrate a smooth and productive meeting. Take a moment at the beginning to remind everyone who is responsible for filling each role. Who will direct the discussion? Who will be the scribe? Who will distribute the minutes and by what date?

REACH AGREEMENT ON THE GROUND RULES.

Meetings will run more smoothly if everyone explicitly reaches agreement on the ground rules at the outset. If you wait until someone has erred before clarifying the rules, you risk humiliating that person in front of peers. If the rules are clarified at the start, however, a subtle reminder may be all that is necessary to keep the meeting moving. Ground rules may be either simple or elaborate. It does not matter. What does matter is that everyone understands and explicitly agrees to the rules. Once you have agreement, a brief and simple reminder at the outset will usually suffice. Here are some examples of ground rules.

We will start and stop on time.

We will not interrupt. Only one person will speak at a time.

We will show respect for one another and not engage in personal attacks.

We will treat all information as confidential.

We will not criticize ideas, either verbally or nonverbally, during brainstorming sessions.

INVOLVE PEOPLE EARLY.

Get people interested and enthused by involving them early. The earlier you get people involved, the more likely they are to participate throughout the meeting. Early involvement can be particularly important when establishing a new work group, if you have newcomers, or if your work group has a tendency to be quiet or reserved. You might consider using one of the icebreakers explained in the next section to encourage involvement. If people have been preassigned tasks, get their reports as early as possible to avoid having them think about the reports rather than being engaged in the task at hand. Another effective tool for encouraging involvement is to redirect a question to another group member. This technique clearly shows that you want to share responsibility and "stage time" with other people in the room.

USE ICEBREAKERS WITH NEW GROUPS OR IN CHALLENGING SITUATIONS.

You can increase everyone's initial comfort level by encouraging them to become acquainted and share a little information about themselves. Icebreakers are especially useful if (1) the participants don't know one another, (2) you expect emotions to rise and debate to become heated, or (3) you want to initiate a new or unusual procedure that requires especially high levels of participant interaction (such as the alternative approach to brainstorming, discussed on pages 186–187).

Icebreakers are designed to overcome the basic human tendency to remain quiet or reserved in unfamiliar situations or groups. Participants may feel less willing to ask questions if they don't understand where others are "coming from." Participants may also feel less likely to share their ideas if they don't know their own roles in or relationships within the group. Icebreaking activities help overcome these barriers to effective group interaction. Sample techniques include:

- Introducing yourself: One way to introduce yourself without wasting time is to tell your "elevator story." That is, if you were with someone on an elevator traveling up to the fourth floor together, what would you say to introduce yourself in that amount of time? Introducing yourself is especially important if you are the person visiting another group.

- Asking participants to introduce themselves: If the participants don't know one another, consider asking them to take one minute each to state their names, plus the information about themselves pertinent to the meeting topics (e.g., occupation, project role, or area of responsibility).

- Telling a relevant but short story: Is a unique opportunity or product about to be presented to the group? Has the client had a heart-to-heart conversation with you and requested changes? Did you stumble upon a creative solution while three-putting on the 16th green last weekend? Taking a minute or two to share your story can be a powerful way to capture everyone's attention and get them interested and involved in the topic. Before telling your story, however, make certain your story is relevant and that it points the audience down a productive path.

- Using an exercise: Specific icebreaker exercises can get participants out of routine patterns and prepare them for something new. You can probably find several books describing icebreaker exercises at your local bookstore; some may have participants work individually, while others may put people in pairs or in groups. Select an exercise that seems appropriate for the purpose of your meeting and seems likely to interest participants.

- Asking participants to move around, to enhance creativity. Sometimes, you can improve meeting productivity by inviting participants to physically move while engaged in creative processes such as brainstorming or problem solving. Robert and Michele Root-Bernstein state that "Body thinking in all its manifestations is often a fundamental part of creative expressions." Some experts recommend bringing toys—such as squeeze balls, Slinky toys, Rubik's Cubes, and other interesting gadgets—to team-building and creative meetings. By giving participants permission to "play" while working, you can take full advantage of a well-known connection between human movement and thinking.

Opening the Meeting

Setting the stage for control or collaboration

- When you need to maintain control of a meeting:
  1. Run the meeting yourself to signal "I'm in charge."
  2. Stand while others are sitting to signal "I have the floor."
  3. Sit at the head of the table to signal "I'm in charge."
- If you want a highly participative, collaborative meeting:
  1. Ask a team member or facilitator to run the meeting to signal "Let's share leadership."
  2. Sit while others are sitting to signal "I'm with you."
  3. Sit at one side of the table instead of at the head, to signal "I'm with you."

Increasing participation at a large meeting

- Use banquet seating.
- Ask participants to introduce themselves to each other.
- Get groups to generate ideas around their tables; then ask tables to report to the entire group.
- Make it easy for the meeting leader to move among the tables to create a sense of inclusion.

Dealing with confrontation

- Increase confrontation by standing or sitting directly across from the confrontational person.
- Decrease confrontation and seek to resolve your differences by sitting as close as you can to the person. This sends the signal that you want to resolve the conflict.

Adapted from M. Begeman

CHAPTER 13

Verbal Facilitation: Getting Them to Talk

Once you have opened the meeting, you need to ensure active involvement from the participants so you can tap into the group's diverse resources and perspectives. To do so, you need to use three sets of facilitation skills simultaneously. This chapter concentrates on the first of these: verbal facilitation skills. The following chapters cover the other two sets: listening skills and graphic recording skills.

"Verbal facilitation skills" are based on what you *say* during the meeting—specifically (1) facilitate; don't dominate; (2) stimulate discussion; (3) encourage healthy debate; and (4) avoid common problems.

Outline

1. Facilitate: don't dominate.
   Decide whether to participate.
   Be silent or talk infrequently.

2. Stimulate discussion.
   Ask open-ended questions.
   Use "door openers."
   Show support for every person's right to speak.
   Paraphrase what people say.
   Paraphrase feelings.
   Use brainstorming ground rules.

3. Encourage healthy debate.
   Why healthy debate is good
   How to encourage healthy debate
   How to discourage unhealthy debate

4. Avoid meeting facilitation problems.
   Avoid dominance by any one person or subgroup.
   Deal with disrupters.
   Avoid social loafing.
   Avoid groupthink.

FACILITATE: DON'T DOMINATE.

Few behaviors will bring an end to effective interaction more than a facilitator who dominates the discussion. Keep in mind the presentation versus meeting purposes, discussed on pages 138–139. Don't call a meeting if you want to present your own ideas; give a presentation. However, even if you truly want to elicit input from others, it can be difficult to avoid dominating a meeting you are running. After all, you called the meeting and probably care a good deal about its outcome. Therefore, give some thought to how much you are going to allow yourself to participate.

DECIDE WHETHER TO PARTICIPATE.

You must decide how much time and energy you need to manage the process. Some experts insist that a facilitator should facilitate only; others say that a facilitator can be a limited participant as well. In the end, the decision is yours.

- **Facilitate only:** One option is to choose to facilitate only, virtually never participating in the discussion, because most people cannot concentrate on running the meeting process and participating in the meeting discussion at the same time. Not allowing yourself to get caught up in the minutiae of the task will leave you free to better manage the process.

- **Participate only:** If you are so involved in the task at hand that you want to or need to play a large role in the discussion, consider asking someone else to facilitate the meeting, as discussed on page 147.

- **A little of each:** The most popular choice—although not always the most effective one—is to attempt to do both. If you decide to try this tricky combination, set strict rules for limiting your own input and stick to them.

BE SILENT OR TALK INFREQUENTLY.

No matter what you decide about participating, perhaps the single most important skill for effective meeting facilitation is the ability to stop talking and listen.

- **Use silence.** Learn to feel comfortable with your own silence. Find the self-discipline to let others express their ideas and ask questions. Silence gives others the opportunity to set the pace, feel like they have a fair chance to express their ideas, and articulate ideas that are important to them. Take the time to hear people out, even if their messages are unwelcome.

- **Explain your ideas quickly.** Unless you are giving a formal report during a meeting, avoid taking more than just a couple of minutes to explain your idea.

- **State your disagreements carefully by disagreeing with ideas, not people.** Say, for example, "That project may prove time consuming" instead of saying "Vijay's suggestion will simply take too much time." You might also say "I don't understand how you reached the conclusion reached on page 3" instead of "Carol, how can you justify your conclusion on page 3?"

STIMULATE DISCUSSION.

Not dominating the discussion yourself is one thing. Stimulating discussion among the participants is another. Try the following techniques to do so.

ASK OPEN-ENDED QUESTIONS.

Few things will get people talking more than open-ended questions. Open-ended questions are questions designed to elicit the most information from others—because they cannot be answered with a "yes" or a "no." In other words, open-ended questions are the opposite of "closed" or "leading" questions. The following examples show how closed questions can be rephrased in an open-ended style.

Closed questions	Open questions
Is the financial modeling project going well?	Tell us about the financial modeling project?
Can you meet the deadlines on this schedule?	What are your concerns about the deadlines on this schedule?
Do you like my solution?	What is your solution?

USE "DOOR OPENERS."

In addition to using open-ended questions, use "door openers"—nonjudgmental, reassuring ways of inviting other people to participate if they want to. Examples of door openers include: "All right, let's hear what the rest of the group has to say about this proposal" or "You look upset. Care to talk about it?" Conversely, avoid "door closers" that serve to end or discourage further conversation. For example, avoid the following:

- Criticizing: "No matter what I do, you aren't happy. Why do I even try?"
- Advising: "Well, if I were you, I would remember that . . ."
- Overusing logic: "I don't know why you are upset. The facts speak for themselves."
- Reassuring: "Don't worry, I am sure you will understand better after you have worked on the project a little longer."
- Stage-hogging: "I have a story just like that. Last year when we were working with the alpha team . . ." Keep in mind that even though your story may be relevant, people may feel one-upped.

SHOW SUPPORT FOR EVERY PERSON'S RIGHT TO SPEAK.

Support from a meeting facilitator can be a powerful form of social reward and encouragement. You can send very clear signals about the types of interaction you want during a meeting simply by expressing your interest in and support for the range of participants' ideas. Supporting the right to speak means that you want to hear and acknowledge different ideas. It does not mean that have to agree with each idea, only that you want to air the ideas.

Responses that show support include:
"Minimal encouragers" such as "I see," "Okay," or "Uh-huh"
"The idea shows a lot of thought. What do the rest of you think?"
"Let's consider what Kim has just recommended."

Responses that do not show support include:
"Now our next agenda item is . . . " (ignoring)
"That won't work, because . . ."
"That's wrong because . . ."
"I disagree because . . ."
"Where did you come up with *that* idea?"

PARAPHRASE WHAT PEOPLE SAY.

Another effective way to stimulate discussion is to paraphrase what participants say, restating their ideas accurately and concisely, to let them know you heard them. Paraphrasing is valuable because it (1) allows you to capture complete thoughts in a short phrase or sentence, and (2) gives the participant the chance to confirm your understanding or to elaborate further.

When paraphrasing another person's ideas, remember to employ the active listening skills we will discuss on pages 181–183. Listen for main ideas, patterns, and themes. Try to avoid judging or refuting while the other person is still speaking. Once the person has finished speaking, then briefly restate what he or she said and check to make sure your understanding is correct. For example, "So you have three objections to the plan," then list the objections; or "So what you're suggesting is . . ." then summarize the suggestion; or "Let me make sure I understand what you're saying. You think we ought to . . ."

PARAPHRASE FEELINGS.

In addition to listening to the ideas a person expresses in words, also pay attention to the messages the person expresses nonverbally. Attend to the speaker's facial expressions, gestures, tone of voice, and other body language. All of these nonverbal cues can give you insight into how a person is feeling. Examples of paraphrased feelings might include, "You sound upset about the policy's impact on your project team" or "You look pleased about those results."

USE BRAINSTORMING GROUND RULES.

Brainstorming can be enjoyable and effective, but only if the facilitator works hard to make sure that participants adhere to the following three ground rules:

- Before the meeting: Have participants prepare by thinking of as many diverse ideas as possible—the more unusual, creative, and at variance with current policy, the better.
- During the meeting: During the meeting encourage participants to (1) follow up on other people's ideas ("Fran's idea makes me think of . . ."), associate freely, and think of new ideas; and (2) avoid criticizing or evaluating any of the proposed ideas until after all the ideas have been generated.

ENCOURAGE HEALTHY DEBATE.

The previous section illustrated techniques for promoting active involvement and discussion. Once you have people involved, however, you need to turn your attention to keeping that discussion healthy. By "healthy debate," we mean discussion about the relative merit of ideas. "Unhealthy debate," in contrast, focuses on people rather than on ideas. Unhealthy disagreements are usually emotionally charged, and participants will often embrace a competitive mindset.

WHY HEALTHY DEBATE IS GOOD

A healthy debate over ideas is one of the best things that can happen during a meeting. Why? Because such debate allows you to:

- Leverage resources: Healthy debate allows us to do what we cannot do as an individual—tap into the wealth of resources available to a group, generate more creative solutions, and see more opportunities for improvement.

- **Make better decisions:** Groups are often able to generate better and more thoughtful decisions because they can draw on a wide range of experiences and perspectives and weigh and evaluate ideas thoroughly and thoughtfully. In fact, a strong body of research shows that a lack of healthy debate can lead to bad decisions with disastrous consequences.

HOW TO ENCOURAGE HEALTHY DEBATE

To achieve those benefits, your job is to help participants explore and consider a diverse range of ideas—by maintaining an equitable distribution of perspectives and participation.

- **Equitable perspectives:** If you hear one side of the debate dominating the conversation, it might be good to draw out other perspectives. One tool for eliciting other perspectives is to play devil's advocate and put an idea to the test by asking a question and drawing other people into the conversation.
- **Equitable participation:** You will also want to maintain an equitable distribution of participation. If just a couple of people are dominating the debate, it might be good to encourage participation and draw other meeting participants into the discussion.

AVOID PROBLEMS AND CONFRONTATIONS.

Encouraging participation, and especially creative thinking followed by healthy debate, necessitates that you learn how to avoid group facilitation problems. Avoiding such problems will keep group performance and participant satisfaction high. Here are some techniques you can use to overcome common facilitation problems.

DISCOURAGE UNHEALTHY DEBATE

Although discussion is positive, if the debate turns personal, or if emotions rise too high, then the disagreements have gone too far. You will need to relieve the tension so the meeting can get back on track. If you find your meeting developing into an unhealthy disagreement, try the following tactics to move the discussion away from personal attacks back into a more useful, socially rewarding arena of disagreements about ideas.

- **Take a break.** Sometimes, a short break will be all that is necessary to stop the personal disagreement. Give participants an opportunity to handle the situation professionally and on their own.
- **Change the participants' attitudes.** Disagreements that escalate too far can easily be understood as a product of one of the parties' mindset or emotional state. Escalating disagreements lack what negotiation experts Roger Fisher and William Ury call a "win/win" perspective. A win/win perspective is one in which both parties collaborate to find innovative solutions that meet everyone's needs. In contrast, escalating disagreements are usually marked by a "win" mentality (in which all that matters is getting what he or she wants, with no thought of others) or a "win/lose" mentality (in which winning is not enough; the other party must also lose). These mindsets often lead to escalating an argument and attacking other participants.
- **Address the emotions.** As a rule of thumb, handling unhealthy disagreements means that you must address the emotions involved. If you find yourself in a situation in which someone enters the room angry and then

directs that anger at one or more people, you may be well served to let that person express her or his frustration and to get the feelings out in the open. This strategy assumes, however, that the parties involved are able to maintain some degree of professionalism and respect. Once the emotions are on the table and the angry party has settled down a bit, you should find it much easier to work with that person and seek a solution that is good for everyone.

- **Caucus with the disagreeing parties.** Begin by taking a 15-minute break and encouraging the disputants to go in different directions. Once apart, pull each party into a private room and listen calmly. Talk with that person for several minutes while letting her or him calm down. Once the participant has calmed down, you may need only to point out that, "We are approaching some difficult territory, and maybe we should back off a little and focus on these specific ideas." A simple verbal warning may be enough. Once you have finished talking with the first disagreeing participant, locate the others and repeat the process. A quick and understanding conversation in a private room can be an extremely powerful tool for moving people back toward common ground and motives.

- **Use humor to relieve tension.** Another great technique for relieving tension is humor. Professional humor can be a great tool for helping people relax and feel more at ease with one another. The effective use of humor does not require you to become a stand-up comedian. Instead, you need only make people smile—such as with a bad pun or a personal story. Just remember that humor must be appropriate, lighthearted, and professional. Racist, ethnic, and sexist jokes are clearly inappropriate in today's business environment and may invite a lawsuit.

AVOID DOMINANCE BY ANY ONE PERSON OR SUBGROUP.

Try one of the following techniques if you want to avoid having certain people dominate the discussion:

- **Invoke the norm of "fairness"** to make sure everyone has a chance to speak. For example, "Jose, you have done a great job expressing your point of view on this matter. In all fairness, we should encourage others to express their views." This technique makes you appear reasonable and fair yourself.

- **Draw in each person,** giving him or her a chance to speak to the issue. You may want to take an active approach along the lines of "Let's hear from those who have not spoken yet." You may, however, want to avoid putting people on the spot by calling a name and singling someone out.

- **Evoke the ground rules.** This is where the ground rules, articulated at the start of your meeting, come in handy. Use a firm but tactful reminder, such as "Excuse me, Kris. Please remember we agreed only one person will speak at a time." Another example might be "Please wait, Karen. I just wanted to remind everyone we agreed to keep our comments brief."

- **Use nonverbal methods.** Try turning your body away from the interrupter and toward the person being interrupted. Or try raising your hand in a "wait a minute" gesture to signal that only one person should speak at a time. To stop two participants talking at each other simultaneously, try placing your hand on the table between them in a "wait a minute" gesture.

- **Move your position.** Position yourself next to disrupters, rather than across the table from them, so that they cannot easily make eye contact and interrupt you. This also allows you to lean over and nicely ask that person to "wait a moment."

DEAL WITH DISRUPTERS AND PEOPLE WITH PERSONAL AGENDAS.

An effective facilitator needs to keep the conversation centered on shared concerns without embarrassing or intimidating anyone.

- **Talk to disrupters off-line.** Talk with very verbal or high-status people privately, before or after the meeting instead of confronting them in front of the group. Try to understand their motives and enlist their aid in setting an example for the group.
- **Occupy the disrupter.** Give the disruptive person a job to do. Have this person keep the minutes or record ideas on the white board. Often, disruptive people are looking for status, and you can give them precisely that by offering them a job.
- **Use the following techniques.**

Disruptive Behavior	Facilitator's Response
Hostile: "That will never work" or "Is that the best we can do?"	"How does everyone else feel about this idea?" or "You may be right, but let's review the facts."
Loudmouth: constantly blurts out ideas	"Can you summarize your main point?" or "I appreciate your comments. Now, let's hear from others."
Interrupter: starts talking before others are finished	"Please wait a minute, Jane. Let's stick to the ground rules and let John finish."
Silent disrupter: reads newspaper, works on other projects, rolls eyes, shakes head, fidgets, etc.	Try to draw the person into the discussion, or talk to the person individually during a break.

AVOID SOCIAL LOAFING.

Yet another common problem to watch out for is called "social loafing." Social loafing occurs when one person contributes less work than the others. Research shows that the larger the group, the more likely people are to engage in social loafing. Possible causes of social loafing include a loss of personal accountability, loss of personal motivation (due to shared rewards), or lack of group coordination. To counter social loafing, make sure participants understand how their assigned task is important, hold everyone accountable for some aspect of the project, and express positive expectations that everyone in the group will be working hard.

AVOID GROUPTHINK.

"Groupthink" is a problem that may occur in groups that are too cohesive, in which discussion is cut off not because one person dominates, but because the entire group avoids healthy debate. Such groups try to avoid losing their harmonious environment by blocking out alternatives or different perspectives. Irving Janis, in his classic book on groupthink, identifies the following reasons why groupthink may occur.

- **Do-no-wrong mentality:** Some groups feel they are blessed or can do no wrong. As a result, they feel little incentive to engage in a healthy, diverse debate of ideas.

- Righteous cause: Sometimes a group will automatically assume they are doing "a good thing." Therefore, they will not debate whether what they are doing is right or not.

- Collective rationalization: Sometimes groups will simply ignore evidence that is contrary to the accepted position. Instead, they convince themselves that the accepted position is the right one.

- Self-censorship: To avoid causing waves, sometimes group members will censor themselves. Rather than raising an unpopular position and risking rejection or punishment, group members may sometimes say nothing at all.

- Illusion of unanimity: When team members assume the righteousness of their work, rationalize a position, and censor themselves, the next pitfall is the seemingly inevitable sense of unanimity. Nobody has disagreed; therefore we are unanimous.

- Direct pressure on dissenters: If all the above pressures have come to bear on group members and someone still speaks out, other group members may apply direct pressure (social punishment) on that person.

You can combat groupthink simply by valuing active discussion, healthy disagreement, and a diverse range of ideas and perspectives. In addition, specific techniques include (1) assigning a different person to the role of devil's advocate for each topic on the agenda, (2) breaking into subgroups and having each subgroup develop proposals independently, or (3) after a decision is made, holding a second-chance meeting and strongly encouraging members to express residual doubt.

CHAPTER 14

Listening Facilitation:

Hearing What They Say

Once you have gotten participants to speak, based on the skills discussed in the previous chapter, you need to be able to hear what they say by using effective listening skills. Various studies show that 45%–63% of your time at work is spent listening; yet, unfortunately, studies also show that as much as 75% of what gets said is ignored, misunderstood, or forgotten. Part of the reason for this is that most of us receive little or no training in listening.

The skills outlined in this chapter encourage you to become an "active listener"—in which you devote both mental and nonverbal energy toward understanding what is being said. These skills are essential to your ability to run a meeting in which you need to paraphrase and record participants' ideas.

Meeting Implementation Checklist

Outline

1. Mental listening skills
   Remove internal and external barriers.
   Show an active interest in understanding others.
   Hear the difference between issue and motives.
   Distinguish between logical and emotional content.
2. Nonverbal listening skills
   Body language
   Space around you

MENTAL LISTENING SKILLS

You cannot be an active listener unless you devote mental energy to the task of listening. Here are some ways to do so.

REMOVE INTERNAL AND EXTERNAL BARRIERS.

The easiest and most obvious way to make listening your primary focus at a given moment is to eliminate internal and external barriers to listening.

- Internal barriers are obstacles or distractions that you bring to the meeting. Are you worried about an important phone call you have to make after the meeting? Are you frustrated with your group's lack of progress? Do you find a side conversation more interesting than the speaker? These kinds of thoughts and emotions can all be internal distractions to active listening.
- External barriers are outside distractions that interfere with listening. Some you cannot control, such as the sound of a police siren passing by. Others, however, you can control, such as a room that is too hot or cold.

SHOW AN ACTIVE INTEREST IN UNDERSTANDING OTHERS.

Once you have minimized barriers, try to follow the advice of Stephen Covey, in his popular book *The 7 Habits of Highly Effective People:* "Seek first to understand, then to be understood." Poor listeners often reverse this advice and consequently miss out on opportunities to save time, improve meeting processes, or develop goodwill with co-workers. To avoid making the same mistake:

- Focus on people and their ideas. Avoid thinking about other issues that may be important to you, but relatively unrelated to the topic at hand. Make people and their ideas your first priority when listening.
- Act out of natural curiosity. Take an interest in people and their ideas. Find something in their message that is interesting. Seek to understand their assumptions, perspectives, and ways of seeing issues differently.

HEAR THE DIFFERENCE BETWEEN ISSUE AND MOTIVES.

How many times have you participated in a meeting in which two normally professional colleagues argue to the death over a seemingly trivial issue? Often, what appears to be an argument about a trivial issue is, in fact, an argument about an underlying motive. Roger Fisher and William Ury, in their book *Getting to Yes,* describe the difference between listening to issues and listening for underlying motives.

- Issue: The "issue" is the statement, recommendation, or request someone makes. For example, a participant may insist that the next meeting be rescheduled from 3:00 to 2:00.
- Motive: If the issue is the tip of the iceberg, the "motive" is the underlying reasons or needs that drive a person to take a particular position. For example, the participant may want the meeting moved up to 2:00 because she is the only person who has authority to sign for secure deliveries that typically arrive after 3:00.

Instead of arguing for or against a specific issue, active listeners work to identify underlying motives and then translate that motive into an alternative proposal that meets everyone's needs. Participants can often brainstorm solutions that deal with the underlying motives. In the example above, listening for the motive might allow you to brainstorm a solution that would allow someone else to sign for the deliveries, instead of arguing endlessly about when the meeting should start.

DISTINGUISH BETWEEN LOGICAL AND EMOTIONAL CONTENT.

Imagine that a meeting participant described all the research he had completed, how he had written a report including all the data for his boss, and how he was then told to go back and summarize the report in one page. A listener could respond in either of two ways.

- A logical response: A logical response assumes the speaker wants a logical solution or answer—such as explaining that his boss is a busy person and advising him to keep his reports short and concise.

- An emotional response: An emotional response assumes the speaker wants "a kind ear"—such as asking the participant about his frustration.

These are two very different responses. Effective listeners are keenly aware that there is a difference between logical and emotional content. They actively strive to identify which a colleague is seeking in order to respond appropriately.

NONVERBAL LISTENING SKILLS

The active listening skills we have discussed so far involve attitudes inside your own head. Nonverbal listening skills, on the other hand, involve demonstrating to the participants that you are listening through your use of (1) body language and (2) space around us.

BODY LANGUAGE

Body language is most effective as a listening skill when it sends a warm and inviting message to other meeting participants. Open and inviting body language helps us foster relationships and trust, encourage interaction and questioning, and make others feel comfortable around us.

- Posture: One important way to look open is through a relaxed yet alert posture with "an open center"—that is, facing the speaker squarely, with nothing blocking your torso, such as crossed arms. Avoid looking rigid and unmoving or moving randomly—such as rocking, slouching in your chair, or tapping your foot. When seated, you may want to lean forward slightly to signal your interest.

- Eye contact: Eye contact is one of the most important signals of interest and involvement. It makes possible what communication expert Lynn Russell calls the "listening/speaking connection": you connect with the speaker by reading his or her nonverbal reactions; the speaker connects with you because of your interest. Research shows eye contact to be the number one indicator of trustworthiness in Western cultures; people who do not maintain eye contact are often perceived as untrustworthy.

- Facial expressions and nodding: Facial expressions are another powerful tool for conveying your active engagement with the meeting participants. Instead of maintaining a deadpan face that shows no emotion or involvement, look interested, empathetic, and animated. Vary your facial expressions, depending on what you hear; for example, if appropriate, smile, or show concern, or look questioning. Finally, nod to show that you are listening to and understanding your colleagues.

- **Hand and arm gestures:** You should also avoid hand and arm behaviors that make you look nervous or defensive—such as keeping your arms crossed in front of your body, tapping your fingers, or playing with jewelry.

- **Awareness of others' body language:** In addition to "sending" effective messages nonverbally, an effective meeting facilitator "receives" nonverbal messages from participants as well. For example, if a participant is sitting with his arms crossed and looking sullen, you might want to find out if he is bored, defensive, or if that's just the way he sits.

SPACE AROUND YOU

Like body language, our use of space around us sends another set of messages that we can use to improve our meeting effectiveness. (See also page 162 for more on spatial aspects of meeting preparation.)

- **Space for yourself:** Since your height, relative to other meeting participants, sends a powerful message, think about whether you choose to sit or stand. Sitting will signal relative equality between you and other meeting participants, while standing will signal authority or control. Therefore, you might choose to sit during a brainstorming session in which you want everyone to be involved, or you might stand when you are trying to get the group moving toward making a decision.

- **Space between people:** By noting a participant's response to your closeness, you can gauge their comfort in the available space and adjust your position accordingly. For example, does a participant back up or close up nonverbally by crossing his or her arms when you lean forward? If so, you are probably getting too close for the person's comfort. Does the participant strain forward when listening? If so, he or she may be signaling that you are too far away.

- **Space at the table:** What should you do if you want everyone to feel equal in a meeting? The simplest solution may be to hold your meeting at a round table, which allows everyone to see one another and prevents individuals from singling themselves out by sitting at the head of a table. On the other hand, if you want greater control over the proceedings, consider using a rectangular table and sitting at the head.

- **Space based on culture:** Always keep in mind that the amount of space we leave between people depends on personal and cultural factors—so become aware of participants' spatial and seating expectations. For example, some cultures may maintain very close space to one another, while in other cultures people may keep greater distance between themselves. As another example, in Western culture, dominant or leading participants will tend to sit at the head of the meeting table, whereas in Japan, the highest-ranking people will tend to sit at the end of the table farthest away from the door.

CHAPTER 15

Graphic Facilitation:

Recording What They Say

The term "graphic facilitation" refers to recording ideas on visual aids, in full view of all participants, as the meeting progresses. Chapter 10 covered the benefits, equipment, and advance planning for graphic facilitation; this chapter covers how to implement those plans during the meeting itself.

Meeting Implementation Checklist

Outline

1. Recording discussions
   Plan your graphics.
   Record for accuracy.
   Record to move the discussion forward.
   Record to ensure inclusiveness.
   Record to be readable.
   Use your equipment credibly.
2. Recording brainstorming sessions
   Post individual ideas.
   Group ideas.
   Look for themes.
   Prepare final notes.

RECORDING DISCUSSIONS

To record a group discussion, consider using a scribe (as described on page 147) because it is difficult to write clearly at the same time as you are concentrating on understanding each person and trying to move the discussion along. With or without a scribe, however, use the following tips:

PLAN YOUR GRAPHICS.

As we explained on pages 153–158, plan your graphics to have:

- **Clear ties to agenda:** Participants should immediately see the relationship between the agenda items and the visual aids. For example, if the agenda lists three items for discussion, the same three items should serve as headings on your board or flipchart.

- **Effective headings:** Participants should always be able to see a heading that reminds them of the topic under discussion. (1) *Questions:* You might phrase your headings as questions (e.g., "Why has customer satisfaction dropped?" or "Can we develop a new system by June?"). (2) *Actions:* Another option is to phrase your headings as actions (e.g., "Brainstorm List of Solutions to Steel Shortage").

- **Color and graphic design if possible:** A little use of color goes a long way in meeting management. For example, you might use different colored markers to help participants distinguish between the heading versus the brainstormed list of ideas. Or, you might use a visual framework (as described on page 157) to show the relationship among the ideas to be generated.

RECORD FOR ACCURACY.

Try to accurately summarize each idea.

- **Record essential phrases only.** If the group is having a particularly dynamic moment, it may be useful to simply record a string of essential statements or phrases. Ideas expressed during a dynamic exchange can have great sticking power and may be used repeatedly by group members as the project moves forward.

- **Paraphrase ideas.** Work on capturing the essence of the idea in a short phrase. If you do paraphrase, it is usually a good idea to confirm your record before moving on to entirely new topics or ideas.

- **Confirm what you have written.** Briefly ask participants if they are happy with what you have recorded. Doing so will assure accuracy and reassure participants that you heard them.

RECORD TO MOVE THE DISCUSSION FORWARD.

- **Refer people back to what was recorded.** If a participant raises an issue that has already been discussed, you will find it easier to move that person away from a redundant conversation by referring to the list of discussed ideas and then redirecting the conversation.

- **Aim toward an action plan.** As we will explain on page 190, effective meetings end with an action plan. Recording ideas throughout the meeting provides a useful basis for forming that plan.

RECORD TO ENSURE INCLUSIVENESS.

Group members are far more likely to support the group's decision, even if their ideas are rejected, if they feel heard and believe that their input was valued during the process.

- **Record everyone's input.** Record everyone's ideas, no matter how irrelevant or tangential some may seem. Protecting feelings of inclusiveness and of being valued will serve your group's long-term interests when it is time to implement an idea or when you need everyone's buy-in.
- **Keep charts in full view.** Graphic facilitation is a visual support mechanism. Therefore, it is most effective when everyone can see the ideas being recorded.

RECORD TO BE READABLE.

Obviously, none of the benefits of recording ideas will occur unless all of the participants can read what is being recorded.

- **Use large and dark lettering.** Not only must your writing be large enough for everyone to see, the color of your ink must provide a stark contrast to the color of your paper. Try to use white or light-colored paper along with dark black, blue, green, and red markers.
- **Write neatly.** If you do not have neat handwriting, take the time to practice using markers and paper so that you can improve the readability of your record. If you don't, use a scribe.

USE YOUR EQUIPMENT CREDIBLY.

Make sure you or your scribe is familiar with how to use the equipment. For example, practice flipping the pages of a flipchart or putting up your transparencies straight. Decide in advance what you will do with filled-in flipchart pages (Attach them to the wall? How?) or when the board needs to be erased (How will the comments be permanently saved?).

RECORDING BRAINSTORMING SESSIONS

As explained on page 149, brainstorming is a highly effective method for generating creative ideas. Brainstorming involves having people think of diverse ideas, having participants follow up on others' ideas and think of new ideas, and making sure participants do not criticize or evaluate any ideas while they are being generated.

Traditional methods of graphic facilitation during a brainstorming session include (1) simply recording lists of ideas, usually on a flipchart or board, or (2) recording ideas on T charts or TT charts as described on page 157. These two visual diagrams will allow you to make lists, place important ideas side-by-side, and facilitate comparisons and discussions during the rest of the meeting.

These traditional methods are efficient and most appropriate for generating ideas. If your goal is to generate ideas and then regroup and organize them, you might want to try an approach developed by David Straker. His method also gets everyone involved, promotes feelings of inclusiveness, can break up a monotonous routine, and injects a dose of energy into a meeting. The method gets participants out of their chairs and engages them actively, using adhesive-backed or sticky notes, in the following four steps.

1. POST INDIVIDUAL IDEAS.

Either before or at the beginning of the meeting, ask the participants to write down their ideas on sticky notes, with only one idea per note. Participants then post their notes on a wall or board in any random or scattered order.

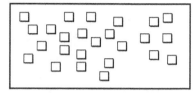

Step 1: Post Individual Ideas

2. GROUP IDEAS.

Once all the ideas are posted, ask the participants to "step back" and look for larger patterns. Which ideas can be "grouped" together? Everyone should feel free to move the notes and place similar items into groups. Discussion of where to place each idea is essential. If there are fewer than three notes in any group, the individual items should be moved to another group.

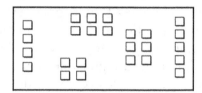

Step 2: Group Ideas

3. LOOK FOR COMMON THEMES.

After grouping similar ideas, participants should look for a common theme or topic that connects all the items in each particular group. Write the unifying idea or heading on a different color sticky note. From the board illustrated below, you can create a rough outline of options or solutions. You also have a complete set of notes for entering the groupings and ideas into the meeting minutes.

Step 3: Look for Common Themes

CHAPTER 16

Closing the Meeting

Meeting Implementation Checklist

Now that you have facilitated the meeting discussion—by what you say, how you listen, and how you record comments—the last step is to close the meeting effectively. Research indicates that people tend to remember what comes first and what comes last, something we call the "primacy-recency effect." Therefore, providing closure and follow-up at the end of a meeting will make everyone's time together more productive. Good closing skills will send participants off in a happy or satisfied mood and with a clear understanding of what they have accomplished. This chapter covers (1) making decisions, (2) ending the meeting, and (3) following up.

Outline

1. Making decisions
   Decision-making models
   Decision-making techniques
2. Ending the meeting
   Knowing when to end
   Summarizing the meeting
   Confirming the summary
   Ending on a positive note
3. Following up
   What minutes are
   Why minutes are important
   When to distribute

MAKING DECISIONS

Some meetings end with group decision making. In these cases, consider your options for decision-making models and decision-making techniques, as described in the following section. When considering these options, keep in mind the group norms (how are decisions usually made in this organization?) and your judgment of the group's needs (what is likely to be effective with this particular group of people?).

DECISION-MAKING MODELS

Different ways of making decisions may be appropriate in different situations. Make it clear to participants in advance what model you will be using.

- **Executive or expert decisions:** Sometimes, the person with final responsibility for the project makes an "executive decision"; other times, a person with expert knowledge makes an "expert decision." The advantage of this model is that it is the fastest way to make a decision; therefore, it is effective when the decision is not particularly important to everyone in the group or when there are severe time constraints. The disadvantage is that some people may feel angry and excluded—unless you make it clear to them in advance that they will be serving as an advisory board only.

- **Majority vote:** A common and simple method, this decision-making model has its positives and negatives. On the positive side, a majority vote can be quick and easy, and is best applied to routine or simple issues. On the negative side, however, those who "lose" the vote may not work very hard to support the final decision—especially in situations that evoke strong feelings or concerns.

- **Consensus:** Consensus means that all participants have agreed to a decision and can support it. The final decision may not always be each person's first choice, but the group still will have widespread agreement to move forward. The more complex or important the decision, the harder it may be to reach a consensus. Reaching a consensus takes longer but is likely to be implemented faster. Consensus does not mean unanimity, in which each participant has final veto power. Consensus means that each participant can live with the compromise.

    Consensus is often held up as an ideal approach. Making the additional time commitment up front can be a very wise investment if participant buy-in is essential and if the discussion allows you to overcome concerns or dissenting feelings that can later slow down task processes or even cause you to backtrack and reconsider your decisions.

DECISION-MAKING TECHNIQUES

Once you have decided on a decision-making model, consider your decision-making technique. Traditional techniques include a voice vote, a show of hands, and a secret ballot. Other possibilities include:

- **Hot dots:** This technique is a good way to narrow a list of options or identify the most important or valued items in a list while keeping the meeting active and lively. (1) Once you have generated a list, give each participant enough "hot dots" (colored adhesive-backed dots) to equal about one-third to one-half of the items on the list. For example, if you have 12 possible solutions on the list, give each participant four to six hot dots. (2) Ask participants to vote by sticking their hot dots directly onto the flipchart next to the list item they favor. For example, a participant may put three hot dots on the most desirable solution and one hot dot next to two other solutions that appear to have potential. (3) Tally the hot dots and see if participants have shown a clear preference for one or two solutions. (4) If you have a particularly long list of potential solutions or need to discuss finalists before selecting a single solution, then you can use the hot dots process multiple times and build stages into your decision-making process.

- **Color cards:** This technique allows participants to quickly demonstrate their opinion about a potential solution or suggestion. Each participant is given three cards—red (for a negative vote), yellow (for an "acceptable" vote), and green (for a "yes" vote). You can use the cards in either of two ways. (1) *Use at any point* during a meeting to indicate their current feelings regarding an idea. (2) *Use to reach a consensus.* When all cards display green or yellow, then a consensus has emerged. If red cards are showing, then you can discuss each person's concerns—one issue at a time. Continue the individual issue discussions until all cards are green or yellow.

- **Negative voting:** Negative voting provides dissenters with an opportunity to explain their thoughts and feelings so that the group can modify the solution to better suit everyone's needs. (1) For each item on your list of options, ask "What problems or concerns do we have with this idea?" Record any concerns on the flipchart or board. (2) Ask the participants to improve the original solution by brainstorming possible modifications or additions that will alleviate each stated concern. Record these modifications. (3) Next, ask the concerned party if she or he can live with the newly modified solution. If the answer is yes, ask the group if they can live with the modified solution. If everyone answers yes, you can move on to the next concern. If the answer is no, keep working to modify and improve the original solution.

ENDING THE MEETING

Not all meetings end with a decision. But all meetings should end using the "closing skills" described in this section.

KNOWING WHEN TO END

An effective meeting facilitator knows when to end the meeting, instead of letting it drag on beyond its usefulness. You'll know when it's time to end your meeting when any one of the following situations occurs: (1) discussion is complete and you have covered all the items on the agenda; (2) time has run out; (3) more information is needed before you can proceed further; or (4) ideas are being rehashed and nothing new is being presented.

SUMMARIZING THE MEETING.

Once you realize it is time to end your meeting, the first thing you should do is summarize what was decided and what must happen next. Not only does such a review help focus participants on outcomes of the current meeting, it also establishes a clear set of topics for the next meeting agenda. You can either summarize the meeting yourself or ask the person taking the minutes to do so. An effective summary will commonly include a list of:

- **Action items:** What actions have we agreed on?
- **Dates:** By what date will each action be completed?
- **People:** Who is responsible for taking the lead on each action item?

CONFIRMING THE SUMMARY

Before everyone leaves the meeting, be sure to confirm that everyone has agreed on these action items, dates, and people responsible. An exception might be if you know that someone is likely to disagree, then you might want to talk with him or her outside the meeting instead of in front of the entire group. The worst thing you can do, however, is to ignore the dissenting view. Always pay attention to your participants' emotional needs and keep them in mind when working through the process.

ENDING ON A POSITIVE NOTE

Take just a moment to recognize any accomplishments during the meeting. Not all meetings are going to end with profound problems or innovative solutions. Sometimes the gains are very small and incremental. Use the small gains as an opportunity to end on a positive note by complimenting the participants and thanking them for their input.

FOLLOWING UP

All of your group's time and effort in the meeting will be wasted unless you provide some kind of "follow-up" to ensure implementation of the ideas generated. Typically, this follow-up takes the form of some kind of permanent record of the meeting, usually known as the "minutes."

WHAT MINUTES ARE

Meeting minutes are a permanent record, distributed to all the participants.

- **Simple minutes:** Minutes do not need to be elaborate. They can be as simple as copying down the list of notes generated on a white board during a meeting. At the very least, minutes should summarize the decisions reached, action items, people, and dates.
- **Detailed minutes:** In some situations, you may need more elaborate minutes that also include an account of the discussion points and alternatives considered and brief report summaries, if reports or updates were given.

WHY MINUTES ARE IMPORTANT

Meeting minutes serve a very important role in managing work processes. Research shows that people tend to work most diligently on a task immediately after a meeting and just before the next meeting. A good set of meeting minutes can remind participants of the work they are responsible for and help people plan their schedules accordingly. Finally, good minutes can leave your audience with a positive impression of the meeting.

WHEN TO DISTRIBUTE

Have the meeting minutes typed and distributed, either by hard copy or email, to all attendees in a timely manner. Although the expectations for what is timely will vary from company to company, you are probably safe if you have the minutes distributed within 48 to 72 hours after the meeting. Distributing minutes in a timely manner sends the message that the work is important to you and that you consider everyone's time together to be worthwhile and successful.

We hope that the skills in this book will make your future meetings productive, inclusive, and even enjoyable. For your review, please refer to the two meeting checklists on the following two pages:

- Meeting Planning Checklist
- Meeting Implementation Checklist

Meeting Planning Checklist

7. Why meet? Define your purpose and choose your channel.
8. Who to include? Select and analyze the participants.
9. What to discuss? Orchestrate the roles and set the agenda.
10. How to record ideas? Plan for graphic facilitation.
11. Where to meet? Plan for technology and logistics.

Meeting Implementation Checklist

12. Opening the Meeting Task and process functions
    During the Meeting
13. Verbal Facilitation Getting them to talk
14. Listening Facilitation Hearing what they say
15. Graphic Facilitation Recording what they say
16. Closing the Meeting Decisions and follow-up

BIBLIOGRAPHY

This bibliography serves both to acknowledge our sources and to provide readers with references for additional reading.

3M Meeting Management Team and Jeannine Drew. *Mastering Meetings: Discovering the Hidden Potential of Effective Business Meetings.* New York: McGraw-Hill, 1994.

Begeman, Michael. Thirteen articles available online at www.3M.com/meetingnetwork/readingroom/meetingguides.html

Butler, Ava. "Negative Voting." *The Trainer's Guide to Running Effective Team Meetings.* New York: McGraw-Hill, 1996.

Covey, Stephen. *The 7 Habits of Highly Effective People: Powerful Lessons in Personal Change.* New York: Fireside, 1989.

Fisher, Roger and William Ury. *Getting to Yes: Negotiating Agreement Without Giving In.* New York: Penguin Books, 1991.

Howell, Johnna. *Tools for Facilitating Meetings.* Seattle: Integrity Publishing, 1995.

Imperato, Gina. "You Have to Start Meeting Like This!" *Fast Company,* April 1999.

Janis, Irving and Leon Mann. *Decision-Making: A Psychological Analysis of Conflict, Choice, and Commitment.* New York: Free Press, 1977.

Jay, Antony, "How to Run a Meeting." *Harvard Business Review,* March/April 1976.

Lancaster, Hal. "Learning Some Ways to Make Meetings Slightly Less Awful." *Wall Street Journal,* Managing Your Career column, May 26, 1998.

Munter, Mary. *Guide to Managerial Communication,* 5th ed. Upper Saddle River, NJ: Prentice Hall, 2000.

————. "Meeting Technology: From Low-Tech to High-Tech." *Business Communication Quarterly,* June 1998.

————. "Cross-Cultural Communication for Managers," *Business Horizons,* May 1993.

Root-Bernstein, Robert and Michele. *Sparks of Genius: The 13 Thinking Tools of the World's Most Creative People.* Boston: Houghton Mifflin, 1999.

Straker, David. *Rapid Problem-Solving with Post-it® Notes.* Burlington, VT: Ashgate, 1997.

Wolvin, Andrew and Carolyn Coakley. *Listening,* 5th ed. Madison, WI: Brown & Benchmark, 1996.

CHAPTER 17

Creating a Powerful First Impression

As the old saying goes, "You never have a second chance to make a good first impression." Regardless of where you are (whether a sales call, client meeting, reception, or interview), be prepared to present yourself in a positive light, creating a powerful and lasting impression every time you meet someone. These first impressions will establish the tenor of the relationship. According to Susan Bixler and Nancy Nix-Rice, "Books are judged by their covers, houses are appraised by their curb appeal, and people are initially evaluated on how they choose to dress and behave. In a perfect world, this is not fair, moral, or just. What's inside should count a great deal more. And, eventually, it usually does, but not right away. In the meantime, a lot of opportunities can be lost." Everything, from the way you dress to how you handle introductions, creates first and lasting impressions.

Even if you have been in these situations before, mentally rehearse what to do before you step on stage. The script has been written and the parts have been cast. Do you know the script? What should your actions and lines be?

Outline

1. Dressing to make a good impression
   Guidelines for everyone
   Guidelines for men
   Guidelines for women

2. Introducing yourself and others
   Introducing yourself
   Introducing others
   Getting through awkward moments
   Using business cards
   Designing business cards
   Exchanging business cards
   Using name tags
   Responding to an introduction
   Standing for an introduction
   Making small talk
   Connecting with people
   Disengaging yourself

3. Shaking hands
   How to shake hands
   When to shake hands
   When to extend your hand
   When not to extend your hand

4. Interviewing basics
   Preparing for an interview
   Dressing for the interview
   Making a good impression
   Writing thank-you notes

DRESSING TO MAKE A GOOD IMPRESSION

Whether you like it or not, you are judged by the way you look. Long before you utter a word or extend your hand, opinions have been formed. The most important thing to remember about how to dress is to always dress to make your customers, clients, coworkers, or guests feel respected and comfortable. Don't forget that your choice of wardrobe could have an impact on your career. In fact, a good rule of thumb is to let your wardrobe reflect the position to which you aspire, not the position you currently hold. Whatever you choose to wear, keep it clean and neat.

Correct attire for business may vary by the situation and the culture. Therefore, the question of how you should dress to make the best impression in a variety of business settings can create some troublesome dilemmas. The first things you need to know are several common terms often used to note the type of dress that is expected. To help you demystify these terms, take a look at the following definitions:

- Formal wear: Dinner jackets (tuxedos), evening gowns, or cocktail dresses.
- Business attire: Suits with collared shirt and conservative ties or tailored dresses and suits with conservative blouses.
- Business casual: Slacks with sports coat and button-up shirt or dresses and pant suits.
- Dress-down day: Slacks or skirts (no shorts or well-worn denim) and shirts with collars or blouses (no tee-shirts or tank tops). Colleagues don't need to see belly buttons and/or biceps.

Opinions about appropriate on-the-job or off-the-job attire often vary by parts in different regions of the country, so—when in doubt—it is always a good idea to ask what is appropriate for the situation. What is considered business attire in

California may not be viewed as such in New York City. In addition, most organizations have a dress code, whether published or not. When it involves your job, you should find out what it is and follow it. The following basics will let you play it safe when deciding what to wear and how to look:

GUIDELINES FOR EVERYONE:

- Strive for a tailored and professional look.
- Solid colored shirts and blouses are a safe bet in almost every setting; don't mix stripes and patterns.
- The proper length of your suit or sport jacket should be about 3/4 inch longer than your thumb (when your arms are straight down).
- Sleeve cuffs should be approximately five inches from the tip of your thumb and show about one-half inch of material below the coat sleeve.
- Don't wear anything that can be identified with educational, social, political, or religious organizations.
- Don't wear sunglasses inside a building.
- Wear clean, polished shoes; never sneakers.
- Remove any facial or body piercings (excluding earrings for women) and wear clothes that cover any tattoos.
- Be freshly bathed and wear clean, wrinkle-free clothes.
- Stand and sit up straight; walk with pride and purpose in all that you do.

GUIDELINES FOR MEN:

- Wear a suit with a long-sleeved, collared shirt, and a conservative tie.
- Never let any shirt show between the tie and the waist of the pants.
- Choose a belt to blend with or match your shoes.
- Wear mid-calf socks so that your bare leg does not show when you cross your legs.
- If you wear a double-breasted suit, be sure to keep it buttoned.
- If you wear a hat, remove it as soon as you enter a building.
- Remove change and keys out of your pockets to avoid unsightly bulges and jingling noises.
- Be freshly shaved or trim facial hair neatly.

GUIDELINES FOR WOMEN:

- Create a professional image. For example, choose a solid suit and a conservative blouse.
- Always wear hose with skirts or dresses. Carry an extra pair with you in case you develop a run.
- Select hemlines and necklines with modesty and professionalism in mind.
- Carry a small portfolio, a purse, or both.
- Don't wear backless or open-toed shoes.
- Practice moderation when applying fragrances and makeup so that it is you who gets noticed—not the "extras" that you have added to your appearance.

INTRODUCING YOURSELF AND OTHERS

Introducing yourself or others is a common business practice. Luckily, the rules of introductions are fairly simple. The first is to show respect for the most important person in the setting by mentioning that person's name first. The second is to try to include a brief comment about each person being introduced so that they have some basic knowledge of each other. These brief introductory statements provide opportunities to begin conversations as well as help associate names with faces, which improves name retention. It takes practice to remember names, but mastering this skill pays dividends as it builds meaningful relationships.

INTRODUCING YOURSELF:

Often, you will need to introduce yourself. In these situations, simply approach the person you don't know, extend your hand, smile, and say, "Hello, I am Tien Chen Wang," adding something appropriate given the circumstances, such as "I'm the host's assistant," or "I'm here representing the City of Seattle." Take notice of your setting before introducing yourself and don't intrude on someone who is in conversation with another person.

When you see someone you have met before, help them remember you. Say something such as "Hi, Micah, I'm Khoon Koh with Asian-American Imports. We met at this conference in Hong Kong last year." This simple gesture takes the pressure off the other person, who may be trying to remember your name and place your face. It also provides a conversation starter. A typical response would be something simple like "Oh, yes, weren't those Chinese meals great?"

INTRODUCING OTHERS:

Introductions of people you know or to whom you would like to show special respect (such as your company president or your manager) have a special twist. The rule is to introduce the "less respected" person (lesser authority, rank, or age) to the "more respected" person (higher authority, rank, or age). In other words, say the "most respected" person's name first. As a matter of courtesy, clients should always be granted the status of holding the "most respected" position.

In addition, use titles to show respect and convey information to those whom you are introducing. Here are a few examples to show how this introduction hierarchy works:

- "Ms. Senior Executive, let me present Mr. Junior Executive. Mr. Junior Executive, this is Ms. Senior Executive."
- "Ms. Gonzales, I would like to introduce Letitia Cosby, who will help you complete the paperwork for your loan. Letitia, this is Ms. Gonzales."
- "Dean Dolphin, I would like you to meet Nicholas and Helena Mithras. Their son Alex will be attending our school this fall. Mr. and Mrs. Mithras, Dean Dolphin is the dean of the business school."

GETTING THROUGH AWKWARD MOMENTS:

When it comes to introductions, there can be, and usually is, a little stress. What if you forget a name and get flustered? Do not worry. Your actions can alleviate the tension. If you forget someone's name, just say so. But help the other person by saying your name. This can be especially helpful if someone has forgotten or mispronounced your name. Your consideration may help them avoid a potentially embarrassing moment. In conversation, use the names of those around you. This will help those who may be meeting for the first time place names with faces.

USING BUSINESS CARDS:

These small, but powerful, pieces of paper serve as helpful tools to remember names and as information sources for follow-ups on professional and personal contacts. The wise use of business cards can be a great means of connecting you with others on a more personal basis.

DESIGNING BUSINESS CARDS:

- Chose a simple design. Have them printed on standard 3″ by 2″ card stock and be sure to include all of the following information: your name and title, company name, mailing address, fax number, email address, and phone number(s) (e.g., office, cell, and/or home phones).
- Don't get cute with your business cards. Remember that business cards are used for establishing contacts. Many people scan business cards into personal contact databases or file them in a card file for quick reference.

EXCHANGING BUSINESS CARDS:

- Keep your cards handy, neat, and clean. The tattered or crumpled card you pull out of your wallet or purse sends the wrong message.
- Take a moment to study a business card when you are handed one. This simple gesture indicates your interest in the person.
- Lay the card on the table or desk in front of you. This allows you to keep names straight, especially if there are several people in the setting.
- Be sure to give a person one of your business cards if you are offered one, unless you are trying to discourage further contact. If you don't have business cards, it's okay to write your contact information on a piece of paper or on the back of the other person's card if they offer you this solution.

USING NAME TAGS:

We wear name tags at business meetings and social events to make it easy to greet others and create conversations.

- Always be sure to place your name tag on your right shoulder, so that when you reach to shake hands, you can retain eye contact as you scan one another's name tags.
- Remember, the purpose of a name tag is to make greeting easier. Therefore, print your first and last name, making them big and bold.
- If the setting calls for it, print your title and the name of your organization.
- Refer to the name tag and use the person's name when you acknowledge an introduction.

RESPONDING TO AN INTRODUCTION:

When you are introduced, you are expected to respond in some way.

- Make it a practice to add the name of the person you just met to whatever pleasantry you use. This helps you remember the person's name. However, don't overdo it by constantly repeating names. So after being introduced, you might say, "How do you do, Ms. Trujillo?" or "I am pleased to meet you, Ms. Trujillo."

- Be sure to smile and make eye contact when you respond to an introduction.
- Whatever the setting, always remember to treat everyone you meet, from the janitor to the president, with the same respect.
- Speak clearly. Slurred names are hard to understand.

STANDING FOR AN INTRODUCTION:

Today, men and women stand when they are being introduced—regardless of whether the other person is a man or a woman. In a business situation, it is especially respectful to stand when a client enters your workspace. Well-mannered business men and women often come around their desk and shake hands with clients before getting down to business. However, if you work together or see each other often, there is no need to stand every time a colleague enters your work space.

MAKING SMALL TALK:

Small talk—that idle chit-chat that seems so easy with friends and colleagues—is often difficult with strangers.

- When it is time to strike up a conversation, making a comment about the weather may not be as "hokey" as it at first appears. Such simple comments serve as icebreakers, so stick to subjects that make it easy for everyone to comment on or to join the conversation.
- Stay current on a variety of topics, from late-breaking news and sports to the arts and best sellers. Then, no matter what the setting, you will be ready to start or join conversations.
- Another way to establish rapport is to find common interests or acquaintances with the people you meet. Be observant for cues in offices or other business settings, such as pictures, plaques, trophies, and other mementoes that might serve as conversation starters.
- One sure way to kill a conversation or turn off people is to bring up issues concerning politics or religion, because these may touch emotional nerves. The same holds true of personal health issues, marital problems, rumors, gossip, and money.

CONNECTING WITH PEOPLE:

Mastering the art of mingling is very important to most careers; you never know what doors may open because of your ability to mingle. Therefore, at business gatherings, make sure you talk with as many people as possible.

- When striking up conversations with people you don't know, take a discrete look at their name tags, look them in the eye, offer a firm handshake, and say, "Hello, I'm Miguel Cozamel" and follow up with a comment that tells something about you.
- Make sure that the person with whom you are speaking receives your full attention. Whether speaking with one person or a group, the rudest thing you can do is look around as if looking for someone "more important" with whom to speak.
- Finally, practice good listening skills. You'll soon learn that good listeners also make good conversationalists because they tune in to those around them. Even if you find the conversation boring, keep listening; you may be surprised at what you learn. Be enthusiastic and show your interest by

maintaining eye contact and asking questions. If you are having trouble involving people in conversations, ask questions that lead them to talk about themselves or ask for their opinions of appropriate matters. Then, your listening skills can come into play.

DISENGAGING YOURSELF:

At some point, conversations will come to a natural end. Look for cues when it is time to move on and make a graceful exit. Simple comments like the following will let you move on effortlessly:

- "Pardon me, I need to speak with Priscilla before she leaves."
- "Excuse me while I say hello to Lindsay."
- "Let me introduce you to Conrad."

Even if the conversation is spellbinding, you still need to keep moving and interacting with different people. When you find yourself in business-related conversations that need to be continued, offer your business card and say you will call later.

SHAKING HANDS

Handshakes are the norm in the western world, so be prepared to shake hands in business settings. In other cultures, however, handshakes may only be part of an introduction. Just as people size you up based on your appearance, they will make judgments about your handshake and when and how you use it. Because this gesture of connectivity is so common, knowing and practicing a little handshake etiquette will put you and others at ease.

HOW TO SHAKE HANDS:

- Extend your right hand with your thumb up.
- Shake firmly but considerately. Gauge your handshake to the strength of the person whose hand you are shaking.
- Pump the other person's hand once or twice.
- Break from the handshake quickly after a few seconds. Do not continue to hold the other person's hand during the entire introduction.
- Make eye contact with the person, but do not stare.
- Always keep your drink in your left hand. That way you never have to fumble around to shake hands or, even worse, extend a cold and clammy hand.

WHEN TO SHAKE HANDS:

In general, shake hands when you are:

- Meeting someone for the first time,
- Meeting someone you have not seen in a long time,
- Greeting your host or hostess,
- Greeting your guests, or
- Saying goodbye when you want to show extra respect.

WHEN TO EXTEND YOUR HAND:

- In almost any business setting, a handshake is always appropriate—whether it's man-to-man, woman-to-man, or woman-to-woman. (Until recently, it was considered impolite for a man to extend his hand to a woman, but that is no longer true in business.)
- However, if there are dignitaries or much higher-ranked executives present, you should wait for them to extend their hands.
- Always shake hands with anyone who extends his or her hand to you, no matter what the situation. It is extremely rude to ignore or refuse to shake hands when someone offers a hand to you.
- As you extend your hand, make eye contact, smile, and say "How do you do?" "Hello."
- If you extend your hand and the other person doesn't respond, simply withdraw your hand and continue talking.

WHEN NOT TO EXTEND YOUR HAND:

- If the other person's hands are full, simply nod your head and say something like "Hello," or "It's nice to see you again."
- If you approach a dignitary or someone of obviously higher rank, wait for that person to extend a hand first.
- If someone says he or she is sick and would prefer not to shake hands, it is okay to dispense with the formality.

INTERVIEWING BASICS

Nowhere are first impressions more important than in a job interview setting. You are on stage from the moment you enter the job search process. Whether unemployment rates are high or low, employers are always seeking to attract the best talent. Take the necessary steps to set yourself apart from others in the interviewing crowd and be recognized as the best. Remember, in the job search process, you are competing with other applicants as you attempt to sell your knowledge, skills, and abilities to a targeted and informed audience—a prospective employer.

You can conduct much of the initial job search process at a distance through employment agencies, networking, letter writing, emails, and telephone calls. Each of these contacts—from your cover letter and résumé to telephone calls and emails—creates an impression of your qualifications, as well as your level of interest and attention to detail, setting the stage for success. However, the most important hiring decision usually depends on a face-to-face encounter: the personal interview.

PREPARING FOR AN INTERVIEW:

As you prepare to sell yourself in the interview process,

- Read and learn all you can about your prospective employer and what they do. Show that you are informed.
- Think about your work-related achievements and how you can make them come to life with concrete examples.
- Take the time to practice answering questions before you arrive at an interview. Try to anticipate the questions an interviewer might ask. Ask a friend or

associate to conduct a mock interview with you. Remember, during the interview, you are on stage: the interview is show time—not the time for a dress rehearsal.

- Be prepared to answer thought-provoking questions (such as those listed here) to demonstrate your personal preparation and familiarity with the job and the organization: (1) What skills could you bring to our organization? (2) Why do you want to work for us? (3) What do you see yourself doing for our organization in five years? (4) Who was the most difficult person you ever worked with, and why was he or she difficult to work with? (5) What is your greatest weakness, and what have you done to overcome it? (6) How do you plan to achieve your career goals? (7) Which is more important to you, salary or the type of job? (8) What have you learned from your mistakes? (9) How has your education prepared you for your career? (10) Is there anything else I should know about you?

DRESSING FOR THE INTERVIEW:

Before going to an interview, find out how people dress where you will be interviewing. When the interview is being scheduled, ask how you should dress. Otherwise, when in doubt, you can never go wrong by slightly overdressing for an interview.

- In any case, unless the atmosphere is very relaxed, a business suit with a pressed white shirt and a tie is always safe for men.
- Women should wear a solid colored, knee-length skirt with a tailored blouse and pumps.
- If you are told not to dress up, a neatly pressed shirt or blouse and pants or skirt would be appropriate.
- Leave your briefcase at home. Instead, take a file folder or portfolio containing several copies of your résumé and some paper for notes. Your résumé may not have been given to everyone you will meet; this is a great tool for helping people remember your name and it serves as a conversation starter.

MAKING A GOOD IMPRESSION:

In the interview setting, first impressions are crucial. You may be the perfect person for the job, but research shows that if you don't create a powerful first impression on the interviewer, you may not get the job—regardless of your abilities. Remember, the organization at which you are interviewing is seeking the best employee from a qualified pool of applicants. In other words, they are attempting to eliminate candidates in their quest to fill the position. Don't be eliminated from consideration by your timing, dress, posture, or handshake.

- Demonstrate enthusiasm and respect by arriving a few minutes early. Show your respect for others by respecting their time. Plan to arrive before the scheduled appointment; however, if you arrive more than ten or fifteen minutes early, tell the receptionist that you do not want to disturb your host and will wait until the scheduled time. Be sure to leave extra time between appointments for unexpected delays.
- Introduce yourself to the first person you meet, tell them why you are there, and ask for directions to the person you are scheduled to meet. Don't forget that everyone is an interviewer. Even the receptionist who greets you may be forming an impression of you as you sit in the waiting area. Never be casual; always assume you are being observed.
- Show your interest in the job by reading company literature, trade publications, or professional journals—not the latest sports or glamour magazine.

- At the beginning and end of each interview, wait until the person in charge extends a hand and then follow the previously-discussed rules for shaking hands. Don't worry if your hand is a little damp. Nervousness can create sweaty palms and it only shows that you are truly excited about the job prospect. However, if your hand is really moist, discretely wipe it on your pants or skirt before shaking hands.

- Walk confidently as you move through the interview process from one person to the next. Sit up straight at all times, even when you are not being interviewed. Maintain eye contact with the person conducting the interview and provide brief but complete answers to all questions.

- Think before you answer questions. Once you have given an answer; there is no way to take back what you said.

- Simple "yes" or "no" answers to questions don't give any clues to the interviewer about your knowledge, skills, or abilities. When responding to questions, take the opportunity to explain how you can benefit your future employer.

- As you answer questions, take time to think about questions you want answered. This is your opportunity to learn more about the organization and the job for which you are applying.

As excited as you might be, relax, smile, and follow the interviewer's lead. Don't continue to talk after the interviewer has obtained all the needed information. To signal the end of the interview, interviewers will typically ask if you have any questions. Be prepared for what you will say and ask any questions you may have about the organization and/or the position. After dealing with your questions and concerns, interviewers typically rise, extend their hands, and tell you that they will be in touch.

WRITING THANK-YOU NOTES:

At the time of the interview, you should always thank your interviewer for their time and the opportunity of exploring how you might fit into their organization. However, a verbal "thank you" is not enough. When you begin the interview process, jot down the names and titles of everyone involved. Once you return from interviewing, write a short thank-you note to each of these individuals.

- Address your letter to the key person (include his or her title) who handled your visit.

- Begin by thanking them for their time and reminding them who you are and for what position you applied.

- Next, tell them why you want the job and how your skills and abilities will contribute to the organization's success. If you forgot to highlight anything important about your qualifications during the interview, do it now. Tell the person that you would like to become a member of their organization.

- Include a comment from your interview that personalizes your message.

- Finally, close by saying you are looking forward to hearing from them soon and, if appropriate, that you are enclosing any requested materials.

If you don't hear from a prospective employer after you send a thank-you letter, it's okay to follow up with one telephone call. It shows that you are persistent, interested, and enthusiastic about the opportunity. However, don't be impatient. Wait a couple of weeks and then call, but not on Monday, the most hectic day of the workweek.

CHAPTER 18

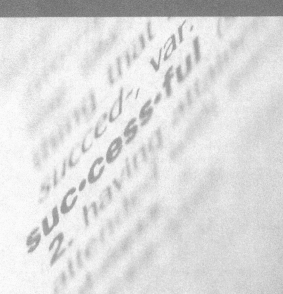

Communication Strategy

Managerial communication is different from other kinds of communication. Why? Because in a business or management setting, a brilliant message alone is not sufficient: you are successful only if your message results in your desired response from your audience. Therefore, instead of thinking of communication as a straight line from a sender to a receiver, visualize communication as a circle, as shown below, with your success based on achieving your desired response.

To get that desired audience response, you need to think strategically about your communication—before you start to write or speak. Strategic communication is based on five interactive variables: (1) communicator (the writer or speaker) strategy, (2) audience strategy, (3) the message strategy, (4) channel choice strategy, and (5) cultural context strategy. These variables may affect one another; for example, your audience analysis affects your communicator style, your channel choice may affect your message, and the cultural context may affect your channel choice.

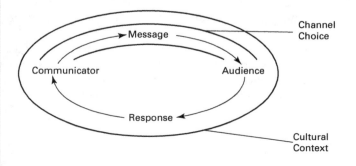

Outline

COMMUNICATOR STRATEGY

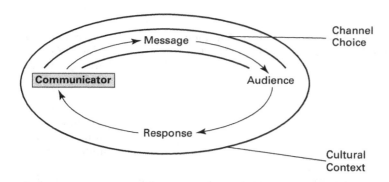

One element of your communication strategy has to do with a set of issues involving you, the communicator. Regardless of whether you are speaking or writing, your communicator strategy includes your objectives, style, and credibility.

WHAT IS YOUR OBJECTIVE?

It's easy to communicate and receive a random response from your audience—because their response might be to ignore, misunderstand, or disagree with you. However, effective strategic communicators are those who receive their desired response or desired outcome. To clarify this outcome, hone your thoughts from the general to the specific.

General objective This is your broad overall goal, toward which each separate communication will aim.

Action objectives Then, break down your general goal into a consciously planned series of action outcomes—specific, measurable, time-bound steps that will lead toward your general objectives. State your action objectives in this form: "To accomplish a specific result by a specific time."

Communication objective Your communication objective is even more specific. It is focused on the result you hope to achieve from a single communication effort (or episode)—such as a report, email, or presentation. To create a communication objective, start with the phrase: "As a result of this communication, my audience will . . ." Then complete the statement by identifying precisely what you want your audience to do, know, or think as a result of having read or heard your communication.

Examples of Objectives

General	Action	Communication
Update management on department performance.	Report two times each quarter.	As a result of this presentation, my boss will learn the results of two new HR programs.
Increase customer base.	Sign with 20 new clients each month.	As a result of this letter, the client will sign and return the contract.
Develop a sound financial position.	Maintain annual debt-to-equity ratio no greater than X.	As a result of this email, the accountant will give me the quarterly expense information for my report.
		As a result of this report, the board will approve my recommendations.
Increase the number of women hired.	Hire 15 women by March 31, 2007.	As a result of this meeting, we will come up with a strategy to accomplish our goal.
		As a result of this presentation, at least 10 women will sign up to interview with my firm.
Maintain market share.	Sell X amount by X date.	As a result of this memo, my boss will approve my my marketing plan.
		As a result of this presentation, the sales representatives will understand the three new product enhancements.

WHAT COMMUNICATION STYLE DO YOU CHOOSE?

As you define your communication objective, choose the appropriate style to reach that objective. The following framework, adapted from Tannenbaum and Schmidt, displays the range of communication styles used in virtually everyone's job at various times. Instead of trying to find one "right" style, use the appropriate style at the appropriate time and avoid using the same style all of the time.

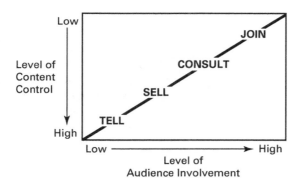

When to use the tell/sell style   Use the tell/sell style when you want your audience to learn from you. In the *tell* style, you are informing or explaining; you want your audience to understand something you already know. In the *sell* style, you are persuading or advocating; you want your audience to change their thinking or behavior. In tell/sell situations:

- You have sufficient information.
- You do not need to hear others' opinions, ideas, or input.
- You want to control the message content.

When to use the consult/join style   Use the consult/join style, sometimes called the "inquiry style," when you want to learn from the audience. The *consult* style is somewhat collaborative (like a questionnaire); the *join* style is even more collaborative (like a brainstorming session). In consult/join situations:

- You do not have sufficient information.
- You need to or want to understand others' opinions, ideas, or input.
- You need to or want to involve your audience, coming up with message content together.

When to use a combination of styles   In an ongoing communication project, you may need to use a combination of styles: for example, *join* to brainstorm ideas, *consult* to choose one of those ideas, *sell* to persuade your boss to adopt that idea, and *tell* to write up the idea once it becomes policy.

Examples of Objectives and Styles

Communication Objective	*Communication Style*
As a result of reading this memo, the employees will be able to compare and contrast the three benefits programs available in this company.	**TELL:** In these situations, you are instructing or explaining. You want your audience to learn, to understand. You do not need your audience's opinions.
As a result of this presentation, my boss will learn the seven major accomplishments of our department this month.	
As a result of reading this letter, my client will sign the enclosed contract.	**SELL:** In these situations, you are persuading or advocating. You want your audience to do something different. You need some audience involvement to get them to do so.
As a result of this presentation, the committee will approve my proposed budget.	

Examples of Objectives and Styles *(continued)*

Communication Objective	*Communication Style*
As a result of reading this cover letter, the employees will respond by answering the questionnaire.	**CONSULT:** In these situations, you are conferring. You need some give-and-take with your audience. You want to learn from them, yet control the interaction somewhat.
As a result of this question-and-answer session, my staff will voice and obtain replies to their concerns about the new vacation policy.	
As a result of reading this agenda memo, the group will come to the meeting prepared to offer their thoughts on this specific issue.	**JOIN:** In these situations, you are collaborating. You and your audience are working together to come up with the content.
As a result of this brainstorming session, the group will come up with a solution to this specific problem.	

WHAT IS YOUR CREDIBILITY?

Another aspect of communicator strategy involves analyzing your audience's perception of you. In other words, consider your own credibility: your audience's belief, confidence, and faith in you. Their perception of you has a tremendous impact on how you should communicate with them.

Five factors (based on social power theorists French, Raven, and Kotter) affect your credibility: (1) rank, (2) goodwill, (3) expertise, (4) image, and (5) common ground. Once you understand these factors, you can enhance your credibility by stressing your initial credibility and by increasing your acquired credibility.

Initial credibility   Initial credibility refers to your audience's perception of you before you even begin to communicate, before they ever read or hear what you have to say. Your initial credibility, then, may stem from their perception of who you are, what you represent, or how you have related to them previously.

As part of your communication strategy, you may want to stress or remind your audience of the grounds for your initial credibility. Also, in those lucky situations in which your initial credibility is high, you may use it as a "bank account." If people in your audience regard you highly, they may trust you even in unpopular or extreme decisions or recommendations. Just as drawing on a bank account reduces your bank balance, however, drawing on your initial credibility reduces your credibility balance; you must "deposit" more to your account, perhaps by goodwill gestures or further proof of your expertise.

Acquired credibility   In contrast, acquired credibility refers to your audience's perception of you after the communication has taken place, after they have read or heard what you have to say. Even if your audience knows nothing about you in advance, your good ideas and your persuasive writing or speaking will help earn you credibility. The obvious way to heighten your credibility, therefore, is to do a good job of communicating.

You might also want to associate yourself with a high-credibility person, acknowledge values you share with your audience, or use any of the other techniques listed on the chart on the facing page.

Factors and Techniques for Credibility

Factor	Based on . . .	*Stress initial credibility by . . .*	*Increase acquired credibility by . . .*
Rank	Hierarchical power	Emphasizing your title or rank	Associating yourself with or citing a high-ranking person (e.g., by his or her cover letter or introduction)
Goodwill	Personal relationship or "track record"	Referring to relationship or "track record"	Building your goodwill by emphasizing audience benefits, "what's in it for them"
	Trustworthiness	Offering balanced evaluation; acknowledging any conflict of interest	
Expertise	Knowledge, competence	Sharing your expert understanding	Associating yourself with or citing authoritative sources
		Explaining how you gained your expertise	
Image	Attractiveness, audience desire to be like you	Emphasizing attributes audience finds attractive	Building your image by identifying yourself with your audience's benefits; using nonverbals and language your audience considers dynamic
Common ground	Common values, ideas, problems, or needs	Establishing your shared values or ideas	
		Acknowledging similarities with audience	
		Tying the message to your common ground	

AUDIENCE STRATEGY

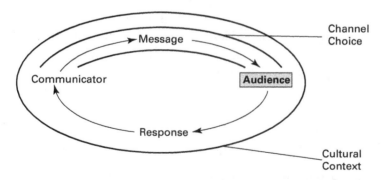

Audience strategy—that is, techniques for gearing your communication toward your audience's needs and interests—is possibly the most important aspect of your communication strategy, because it has the most effect on increasing your chances of being understood and of achieving your objective. Some communication experts recommend performing your audience analysis first; others recommend performing your communicator strategy first. All experts agree, however, that the two strategies interact with and affect one another. So, perhaps the best idea is to perform these analyses concurrently.

Audience strategy includes answering four sets of questions: (1) Who are they? (2) What do they know? (3) What do they feel? (4) How can you persuade them?

WHO ARE THEY?

"Who are they?" sounds like a fairly straightforward question, yet choosing the people to include and focus on is often subtle and complex. To decide whom to include and how to analyze them, answer the following four questions.

Who are the key influencers?   Who has the most direct power or influence over the outcome of the communication? Who has indirect influence (opinion leaders, potential allies, or "gatekeepers" from whom you need approval or routing)?

Who should be included in your audience?   Based on your analysis of the key influencers, decide who should be included in your audience.

- Primary audience will actually receive your message directly.
- Secondary audiences will receive your message indirectly—such as receiving a copy, approving in advance, or otherwise influencing the outcome. Sometimes your secondary audience may be more important than your primary audience.

What should you find out?   The more you can learn about your audience—both as individuals and as a group—the more likely you are to achieve your desired outcome from them. Find out about:

- Demographic issues, such as age range, education, occupation, socioeconomic status, ethnic origin, gender, culture, and language fluency
- Knowledge and beliefs, such as their backgrounds, opinions, and values
- Preferences, such as style, channel, and format

How can you find out about them?   Given your time constraints and relationship with the audience, learn as much about them as possible.

- Find any market research, Internet, or other public data that's available.
- Talk to audience members in advance or ask someone who knows them.
- Reflect on your past impressions or empathize with them.
- Keep collecting audience information throughout your communication project, based on their reactions and questions.

WHAT DO THEY KNOW?

Next, think about what the audience knows and what they need to know. More specifically, ask yourself these three questions.

How much background information do they need?   What do they already know about the topic? How much jargon will they understand?

- Low background needs: If their background information needs are low, don't waste their time with unnecessary background or definitions.

- High background needs: If their background information needs are high, be sure to define new terms or jargon, link new information to information they already know, and use an extremely clear structure.

- Mixed background needs: With mixed audiences, put background information in a separate appendix or handout, or gear the communication toward the key decision maker.

How much new information do they need?   What do they need to learn about the topic? How much detail and evidence do they need?

- High information needs: If they need it, provide sufficient evidence, statistics, data, and other material. Do they need the sources documented? If so, are the sources credible to them?

- Low information needs: On the other hand, many times they don't need a lot of new information: for example, they may trust your expert opinion or delegate the decision to you. Think in terms of how much information your audience needs, not how much information you can possibly provide.

- Mixed information needs: With mixed audiences, put additional detail in a separate appendix or handout, or gear the communication toward the key decision maker.

What are their expectations and preferences?   What do they expect or prefer in terms of style, channel, or format?

- Style preferences: What, if anything, do they expect in terms of cultural, organizational, or personal style—such as formal or informal, straightforward or indirect, interactive or noninteractive, stringent timing or flexible timing?

- Channel preferences: What, if anything, do they expect in terms of channel choice—such as hard copy versus email, group versus individual meetings, or handouts versus slides?

- Standard length and format preferences: What, if anything, do they expect in terms of standard document or presentation length or format—such as a standard format for one-page memos or standard half-hour weekly informal meetings?

WHAT DO THEY FEEL?

Remember, your audience's emotional level is just as important as their knowledge level. Therefore, in addition to thinking about what they know, think about what they feel. Answering the following questions will give you a sense of the emotions your audience may be bringing to the communication.

What emotions do they feel?   What feelings may arise from their current situation or their emotional attitude?

- What is their current situation? Is there anything about the economic situation, the timing, or their morale that you should keep in mind?

- What emotions might they feel about your message? Many communicators mistakenly think that all business audiences are driven by facts and rationality alone. In truth, they may also be driven by their feelings about your message: they may feel positive emotions (such as pride, excitement, and hope), or negative ones (such as anxiety, fear, or jealousy).

How interested are they in your message? Is your message a high priority or low priority for your audience? How likely are they to choose to read what you write or to listen carefully to what you say? How curious are they and how much do they care about the issue or its outcomes?

- High interest level: If their interest level is high, you can get right to the point without taking much time to arouse their interest. Build a good logical argument. Do not expect a change of opinion without continued effort over time; however, if you can persuade them, their change will be more permanent than changes in a low-interest audience.

- Low interest level: If, on the other hand, their interest level is low, think about using a consult/join style and ask them to participate: one of the strongest ways to build support is to share control. If, however, you are using a tell/sell style, use one or more of the techniques discussed on pages 213–214 to persuade them. In addition, keep your message as short as possible; long documents are intimidating and listeners tune out anything that seems like rambling. Finally, for low-interest audiences, act quickly on attitude changes because they may not be permanent.

What is their probable bias: positive or negative? What is their probable attitude toward your ideas or recommendations? Are they likely to favor them, be indifferent, or be opposed? What do they have to gain or lose from your ideas? Why might they say "no"?

- Positive or neutral: If they are positive or neutral, reinforce their existing attitude by stating the benefits that will accrue from your message.

- Negative: If they are negative, try one or more of these techniques: (1) Convince them that there is a problem, then solve the problem. (2) State points with which you think they will agree first; if audience members are sold on two or three key features of your proposal, they will tend to sell themselves on the other features as well. (3) Limit your request to the smallest one possible, such as a pilot program rather than a full program right away. (4) Respond to anticipated objections; you will be more persuasive by stating and rejecting alternatives yourself, instead of allowing them to devise their own, which they will be less likely to reject.

Is your desired action easy or hard for them? From their perspective, what will your communication objective entail in terms of their immediate task? Will it be time-consuming, complicated, or difficult for them?

- Easy or hard for them: Whether your desired action is easy or hard, always show how it supports the audience's beliefs or benefits them.

- Hard for them: If it is hard, try one of these techniques: (1) Break the action down into the smallest possible request, such as a signature approving an idea that someone else is lined up to implement. (2) Make the action as easy as you can, such as distributing a questionnaire that they can fill in easily or providing them with a checklist they can follow easily.

HOW CAN YOU PERSUADE THEM?

Of the following three sets of persuasion techniques, choose those that will work best for your particular audience.

Persuade by using audience benefits.   Stress "what's in it for them."

- Tangible benefits: Sometimes you will be able to highlight tangible benefits that you can offer your audience. Emphasize their value (for example, profits, savings, bonuses, or product discounts), significance as symbols (for example, offices, furnishings, or jewelry), or uniqueness and exclusiveness. Effective tangible benefits do not need to be elegant. Items such as T-shirts, mugs, or pens will work effectively—if they are valued by the audience.

- Career or task benefits: (1) Sometimes you can persuade by showing how your message will enhance your audience's job—by solving a current problem, saving them time, or making their job easier or more convenient. (2) Or you can appeal to the task itself. Some audiences may appreciate the chance to be challenged, or to participate in tough problem solving or decision making. (3) Other people respond to appeals to their career advancement or prestige. Let them know how they will win organizational recognition, enhance their reputation, or develop networking contacts.

- Ego benefits: For some audiences, persuade by enhancing their sense of self-worth, accomplishment, and achievement. For example, show them they are accepted and included by soliciting their suggestions or inviting them to participate. You can incorporate emotional support into your communication with informal verbal praise or with nonverbal smiles and nods with more formal statements.

- Personality benefits: Different personalities are persuaded differently. For example, persuade thinkers with lots of data, skeptics with lots of credibility, unemotional people with rationality, and emotional people with enthusiasm and energy.

- Group benefits: For group-oriented audiences, emphasize benefits to the group as a whole: appeal to any tangible group benefits, group task enhancements, group advancements, or sense of group worth. For audiences who value solidarity with the group, use statements of group consensus or coalition rather than expert testimony or your individual credibility. For people who are strongly influenced by the beliefs and actions of those around them, use the "bandwagon" technique. In the words of communication expert JoAnne Yates, "Although the fact that 'everyone is doing it' may not be a very good logical argument, it nevertheless influences some people."

Persuade by using credibility.   On pages 208–209, we discussed various factors that influence your credibility. Here are some techniques to apply your credibility as a persuasive tool. Remember, the less your audience is involved in the topic or issue, the more important your credibility is as a factor for persuasion.

- Shared values credibility and "common ground": Establishing a common ground with your audience is highly persuasive, especially when done at the beginning of your message. For example, refer to goals you share with your audience before focusing on your controversial recommendation to achieve them.

- Goodwill credibility and "reciprocity": A persuasive technique for applying goodwill credibilty is through "reciprocity" or "bargaining." People generally feel obliged to reciprocate gifts, favors, and concessions—even uninvited or unwanted ones. So, you might gain a favor by granting a favor; you might offer a concession to gain a concession.

- Goodwill credibility and "liking": People tend to be more persuaded by people they like. So, taking the time to meet your audience one-to-one, to establish a relationship, to uncover real similarities, and to offer genuine praise will make you more persuasive in the long run.

- **Image credibility and emotionality:** Another way to persuade is to connect emotionally with your audience. Show your emotional commitment and adjust your emotions to your audience's emotional state.

- **Rank and expertise credibility by association:** Sometimes, rank and expertise can be persuasive. So, either refer to your own rank or expertise, or else use rank or expertise by association (for example, have the CEO introduce you or cite credible experts).

- **Rank credibility and punishment:** The most extreme application of rank credibility is using threats and punishments, such as reprimands, pay cuts, demotions, or even dismissal. Researchers have found that threats produce tension, provoke counteraggression, increase fear and dislike, work only when you're on the spot to assure compliance, and may eliminate an undesired behavior without producing the desired behavior. Therefore, threats and punishments are inappropriate for most audiences and most situations.

Persuade by using message structure. Finally, in some situations, you might motivate your audience by the way you structure your message.

- **Opening and closing:** Emphasize audience benefits in your opening and closing.

- **The problem/solution structure:** If you can convince your audience that there is a problem, then according to "balance theory" (or the "consistency principle"), they will feel out of balance and want to come back to equilibrium by accepting your solution.

- **One-sided or two-sided structure:** Use a two-sided approach for a major or controversial subject, a sophisticated or negative audience, or an audience who will hear opposing arguments. This technique works because (1) they will hear your positive arguments more clearly after their concerns have been addressed, (2) they are more likely to reject alternatives explained to them than alternatives they bring up themselves, and (3) you will appear more reasonable and fair-minded. Use a one-sided argument for an uninformed or neutral audience.

- **Pro/con or con/pro:** List the "pros" first for a noncontroversial subject or if your credibility is high; list the "cons" first for a delicate, highly charged situation or if your credibility is low.

- **Ascending or descending order:** Use an ascending order (strongest arguments first) with an informed or interested audience; use a descending order for a less informed or engaged audience.

- **The "ask for less" (or "foot in door") technique:** If you break down your communication objective into the smallest possible request, one that you are likely to get (such as a pilot program), then later you will be more likely to get the larger request. Similarly, make it easy for the audience to respond: for example, provide a survey they can fill in easily, a checklist they can follow, or specific next steps or specific actions.

- **The "ask for more" (or "door in face") technique:** The opposite of "ask for less" is to ask for an extreme request that you fully expect to be rejected, followed by a more moderate request that is more likely to be honored.

You can also persuade by using the additional message strategies covered in the next section.

MESSAGE STRATEGY

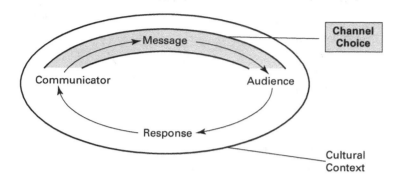

Structuring your message is a third variable in your communication strategy. Ineffective communicators simply state their ideas in the order they happen to occur to them; effective communicators use structure strategically. When you think, all kinds of ideas occur to you—some good, some bad, some complete, some fragmented; the end result of the thought process is your conclusion. But you don't want your audience to have to wade through all the false starts and disjointed ideas you went through during the thought process, so when you communicate strategically, you emphasize and organize your ideas clearly for your audience. The following illustration graphically demonstrates this difference:

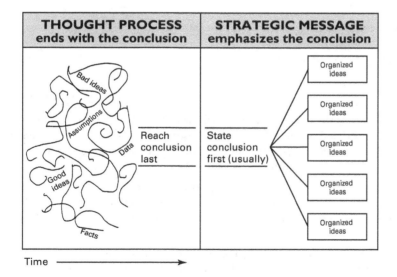

Instead of structuring your message as ideas happen to occur to you, ask the following questions: (1) How can you emphasize? (2) How can you organize?

HOW CAN YOU EMPHASIZE?

The Audience Memory Curve, illustrated here, summarizes research on what your audience is most likely to remember from your message.

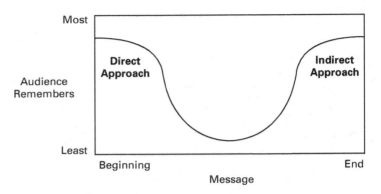

What does the Audience Memory Curve imply? First, that you should never bury important ideas in the middle of your message. Second, that you need to keep your audience's attention throughout by using the persuasion techniques described on pages 212–214. Third, that your opening or introduction is extremely important. Finally, that you should state your important ideas prominently—either at the beginning or at the end (or both).

Stating your main ideas first is called the direct approach; stating them last is called the indirect approach.

Using the direct approach The direct approach, stating your main ideas at the beginning of your message, is sometimes called "bottom-lining" your message, because you state the bottom line first. For example,

The committee recommends policy x for the following reasons:

> Reason 1
>
> Reason 2
>
> Reason 3

Advantages of the direct approach Using the direct approach has many advantages.

- Improves comprehension: People assimilate and comprehend content more easily when they know the conclusions first. Withholding your conclusion until the end is fine for a mystery story, but not for busy business audiences who may resent every minute they spend trying to figure out what you're attempting to communicate.

- Is audience-centered: The direct approach emphasizes the results of your analysis. In contrast, the indirect approach is communicator-centered because it mirrors the steps you went through to formulate your conclusions.

- Saves time: The direct approach saves your audience time. They can understand the message with little rereading or repetition, and they can decide immediately which sections they can skim, read carefully, or use as reference.

Why the direct approach is underutilized Why, then, do people often avoid the direct approach?

- Habit: For one thing, communicators find it is easier to write or speak the way they think, even though it is harder on their readers or listeners.

- Academic training: Many communicators have been reinforced in the use of indirect structure throughout years of schooling.
- Suspense: Some communicators think the indirect strategy will build suspense and keep their audience's attention. In fact, however, it merely befuddles them.
- Effort: Finally, some people want their audience to appreciate all the effort they went through, when, in fact, such an approach may lead to unnecessary confusion rather than understanding.

When to use the direct approach   Because the direct approach is easier and faster to follow, you should use it as much as possible in Anglo-American business situations, probably about 90% of the time. (See pages 223–224 for more on cultural differences.) Specifically, use the direct approach for:

- All nonsensitive messages, that is, those with no emotional overtones
- Sensitive messages if the audience's bias is positive
- Sensitive messages if the audience is results-oriented
- Sensitive messages if your credibility is particularly high

Using the indirect approach   An indirect approach, saving your main idea until the end of your message, involves spelling out your support first, then finishing with your generalization or conclusion. Indirect structure is sometimes called the "mystery story approach." For example,

Reason 1

Reason 2

Reason 3

Therefore, the committee recommends policy x.

When to use the indirect approach   Because this approach is hard to follow, takes longer for your audience to understand, and does not take advantage of the audience's attentiveness at the beginning of the message, use it only when the following conditions apply:

- Cultural norms so dictate
- Your message is sensitive (with emotional overtones)
- Your audience's bias is negative
- Your audience is analysis-oriented
- Your credibility is low

Advantages of the indirect approach   When these conditions apply, the indirect strategy may soften your audience's resistance, arouse their interest, and increase their tendency to see you as fair-minded. Also, the indirect approach gives you the chance to let your audience "buy into" ideas they agree with or a problem they need to solve, before you present your solution.

HOW CAN YOU ORGANIZE?

Once you have emphasized your main idea by placing it first (direct approach) or last (indirect approach), organize your supporting points accordingly.

Examples of Strategic Messages

Communication objective	If it is a . . .	Then, use this approach . . .	And organize by . . .
Staff will follow procedure.	Routine procedure	Direct	Listing the steps in the procedure
	New procedure, hostile audience	Indirect	Discussing the benefits of procedure, followed by steps in procedure
Boss will approve plan.	Busy audience, or your credibility high	Direct	Explaining the plan, then the reasons why
	Audience is analysis-oriented, and your credibility low	Indirect	Listing the supporting reasons, then the plan
Customer will purchase our service.	Audience is results-oriented, or bias is indifferent	Direct	Recommending your service, followed by audience benefits from service
	Audience bias is negative	Indirect	Listing the benefits from your service and/or problems with competitor's service, then recommend your service

CHANNEL CHOICE STRATEGY

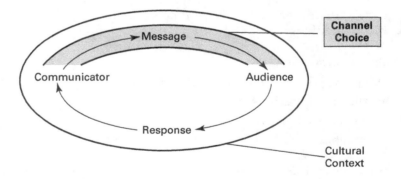

Channel choice refers to the choice of medium through which you send your message. In the past, this strategic choice was basically between two channels: writing and speaking. Today, many more channels exist—including fax, email, voicemail, electronic meetings, and videoteleconferencing. These new channels have changed how we think about channel choice. For example, traditional writing is usually fairly reserved and controlled; email, however, may be informal and spontaneous. Before you choose a channel from among this expanded set of alternatives, think about these general questions. Do you need to:

- Be formal or informal? Both writing and speaking can be either formal or informal—for example, formal reports or informal emails, formal presentations or informal meetings.

- Receive an immediate response and have control over whether your message is received or not?

- Elicit high audience participation or not? Face-to-face or not?

- Have a "rich" communication or not? Text only is the least rich channel; text plus pictures plus voice plus body language is the most rich channel.

- Have a permanent record or not? Retransmit easily or not?

- Use a channel preferred by your audience or their culture?

Once you have considered these general issues, choose from among the following options, weighing the advantages and disadvantages of each. If you do not have your choice of channels, think about how you can utilize the advantages of, and overcome the disadvantages of, the channel you need to use.

WRITING

Writing channels include traditional writing, fax, email, and web page.

Traditional writing

- Advantages of traditional writing: Choose writing when you want to (1) use precise wording and grammar, because you can edit; (2) include a great deal of detail, because readers can assimilate more detail than listeners; (3) save time for your audience, because reading is faster than listening; (4) enable your reader to focus on certain sections of interest; (5) have a private communication; (6) reach a geographically dispersed audience; (7) have a permanent and accessible record.

- Disadvantages of traditional writing: If you write, you will have (1) delayed transmission time, (2) no control over if or when the message is received or who else might read it, (3) a delayed response, if any, (4) no nonverbal communication, (5) possible lack of flexibility and too much rigidity.

Facsimile (fax)

- Advantages: Same as traditional writing, but with faster transmission time; can "blast fax" to multiple audiences simultaneously.

- Disadvantages: Same as traditional writing, but usually less private; may not reproduce graphics precisely.

Electronic mail (email)

- Advantages: Same as traditional writing, plus (1) less likely to be inhibited and reserved, at best, more likely to be spontaneous and creative; (2) less likely to take much preparation time; (3) more likely to contact people in all levels of an organization; (4) more likely to include written nonverbal cues by using "emoticons," such as :-) :-(; (5) easy for audience to respond quickly; (6) can "blast email" to multiple audiences simultaneously.

- Disadvantages: (1) May be inappropriately uninhibited or irresponsible, at worst, destructive (known as "flaming"); (2) may be hard to read because less likely to edit, full of typos and mistakes, and, more importantly, lack of logical frameworks for the reader—such as headings and transitions; (3) may be useful for short messages only; (4) cannot ever be erased or shredded, becomes property of the company, may be used in lawsuits; (5) may be sent to the wrong person by mistake and irretrievably, forwarded without your permission, sent to too many people unnecessarily; (6) may be a way to avoid confrontation or to avoid consensus building; (7) may be responded to too quickly or mistaken for formal text or formal commitment.

Web page

- Advantages: (1) Provides easy access to document at all times, (2) can reach audiences you don't know, (3) allows for self-selected audiences.
- Disadvantages: (1) Least personal and private written channel, (2) usually one-way communication, (3) not addressed to specific audience; readers have to look for it.

SPEAKING TO A GROUP (FACE-TO-FACE)

You can speak to a group in a tell/sell or a consult/join style.

Tell/sell presentations

- Advantages: *Compared to writing,* choose presentations when you want to (1) control if and when the message is received and have your audience hear the same information at the same time, (2) receive an immediate and interactive response, (3) include nonverbal communication, (4) build group identity and group relationships. *Compared to meetings,* choose presentations when you want to (1) use the tell or sell styles, (2) do most of the speaking yourself.
- Disadvantages: Presentations (1) are less private and confidential than writing, (2) do not provide a permanent and accessible record, (3) require that the audience must be in the same place, (4) do not allow as much detail as writing, because listeners cannot assimilate as much detail as readers, (5) are less precise than writing, because you cannot edit what you say, (6) may be intimidating and speaker-dominated.

Consult/join meetings

- Advantages: *Compared to presentations,* choose meetings when you want to (1) elicit ideas from others, (2) foster group participation and discussion, (3) resolve group issues, (4) receive input from various people or groups, (5) reach a consensus and establish action steps, (6) use consult or join styles. *Compared to electronic meetings,* choose face-to-face meetings when (1) you need the richest nonverbal cues, including body, voice, proximity, and touch; (2) the issues are especially sensitive; (3) the people don't know one another; (4) establishing group rapport and relationships is crucial.
- Disadvantages: *Compared to videoconferences,* face-to-face meetings (1) do not allow the possibility of simultaneous participation in multiple locations, (2) can delay meeting follow-up activities because decisions and action items must be written up after the meeting. *Compared to electronic meetings,* face-to-face meetings (1) may be dominated by overly vocal higher-status participants, (2) may involve high travel costs and time.

SPEAKING TO A GROUP (ELECTRONICALLY)

Unlike the face-to-face speaking channels discussed previously, the following three channels use different kinds of *groupware*—a broad term for a group of related technologies that mediate group collaboration through technology—that may include any combination of collaborative software or intraware, electronic and voicemail systems, electronic meeting systems, phone systems, video systems, electronic bulletin boards, and group document handling and annotation systems.

Videoconferences

- Advantages: Choose videoconferences when (1) the participants are in different places, but you want to communicate with them all at the same time; (2) you want to save on travel time and expenses; (3) you want to inform, explain, or train—as opposed to persuade or sell; (4) you want to collaborate via document sharing.

- Disadvantages: (1) They are usually not as effective as face-to-face meetings when you need to persuade or to establish personal relationships; (2) they lack the richest nonverbal cues, such as proximity and touch; (3) fewer people tend to speak and they speak in longer bursts than in other kinds of meetings; (4) they may involve significant set-up time and costs.

Audioconferences   Audioconferences are usually called telephone conference calls.

- Advantages: Have most of the advantages of videoconferencing, but are (1) cheaper, (2) based on more readily available equipment, (3) less time-consuming and trouble to set up, and (4) less prone to technical glitches.

- Disadvantages: Have most of the disadvantages of videoconferencing plus (1) lack of body language makes it harder to interact and to know who is going to speak next, and (2) lack of text or visuals makes it harder to communicate a great deal of detailed information.

Broadcasting or webcasting

- Advantages: Can transmit to multiple audiences in multiple locations.
- Disadvantages: Usually one-way video, sometimes two-way audio.

Electronic meetings   Electronic meeting systems (EMS)—with participants writing on their computers—are *mediated* (that is, they utilize a trained technical facilitator) and usually *synchronous* (that is, everyone participates at the same time).

- Advantages of EMS: Choose electronic meetings when you want to (1) generate more ideas and alternatives more quickly than with a traditional note-taker; (2) allow the possibility of anonymous input, which may lead to more candid and truthful replies, equalize participants' status, and increase participation among hierarchical levels; (3) maximize audience participation and in-depth discussion because everyone can "speak" simultaneously, so shy members are more likely to participate and the "vocal few" are less likely to dominate the discussion; (4) provide immediate documentation when meeting is finished.

- Disadvantages of EMS: EMS (1) cannot replace face-to-face contact, especially when group efforts are just beginning and when you are trying to build group values, trust, and emotional ties; (2) may exacerbate dysfunctional group dynamics, and increased honesty may lead to increased conflict; (3) may make it harder to reach consensus, because more ideas are generated and because it may be harder to interpret the strength of other members' commitment to their proposals; (4) may demand a good deal of facilitator preparation time and training.

Email meetings   Email meetings are *unmediated* (that is, messages go directly to other participants' computers) and *asynchronous* (that is, people respond at their convenience, at different times).

- **Advantages:** At their best, email meetings can (1) increase participation because people can respond when they wish and no scheduling is necessary, (2) speed up meeting follow-up activities because of electronic distribution, (3) decrease transmission time for circulating documents, (4) allow quick discussion and resolution of many small or obscure issues or problems, (5) decrease writing inhibitions with more conversational style than traditional writing, (6) increase communication across hierarchical boundaries.

- **Disadvantages:** At their worst, email meetings can (1) decrease attention to the audience and to social context and regulation; (2) be inappropriately uninhibited or irresponsible, at worst destructive (known as "flaming"); (3) be inappropriately informal; (4) consist of "quick and dirty" messages, with typos and grammatical errors, and, more importantly, lack of logical frameworks for readers—such as headings and transitions; (5) result in a delayed response, or no response; (6) make it harder to gain commitment than with other kinds of meetings.

SPEAKING TO AN INDIVIDUAL

Speak to an individual—not to a group—when you want (1) a private, confidential communication, (2) individual feedback or response, (3) less preparation time, or (4) a fast, simple answer.

Conversation (face-to-face)

- **Advantages:** Compared to email or voicemail, talk with someone face-to-face when (1) you want to build your individual relationship or rapport; (2) the message is especially sensitive or negative; (3) you want a candid, low-risk, fast reply.

- **Disadvantages:** Lacks most of the advantages of writing and speaking to a group plus (1) the person must be located in the same place as you are; (2) if you speak with more than one person, they will hear different information at different times; (3) may be easily misunderstood with no permanent record; (4) may make some people feel excluded.

Telephone

- **Advantages:** (1) Good for candid, low-risk, fast replies; (2) better than face-to-face for reaching people in different places, saves time and travel costs; (3) better than voicemail for establishing rapport.

- **Disadvantages:** (1) Harder to build a personal relationship because fewer nonverbal cues than face-to-face; (2) if you telephone more than one person, they will hear different information at different times.

Voicemail

- **Advantages:** Use voicemail when you want (1) to handle small items quickly; (2) faster distribution than with paper; (3) more emotional content than email, because of nonverbal vocal cues; (4) messages more easily retrieved than email, no computer required; (5) to "blast voicemail" to multiple audiences simultaneously; (6) less likelihood of a permanent record being made; (7) to forward others' vocal messages with your comments.

- **Disadvantages:** (1) Like writing, when you use voicemail, you will have a delayed response, no control over if and when message is received, and no immediate interactivity; (2) like email, voicemail may be forwarded on and distributed widely without your permission; (3) lacks a record; (4) is usually effective for brief messages only; (5) may carry less weight than a document: people may listen to the first part and delete or skip over it entirely.

CULTURE STRATEGY

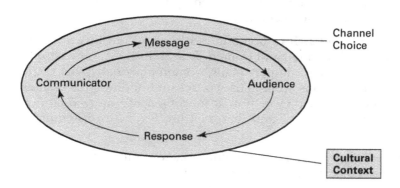

Every aspect of communication strategy we have discussed so far will be greatly influenced by the cultural context in which you are communicating. These cultural differences could result from different countries, regions, industries, organizations, genders, ethnic groups, or work groups. The danger in cultural analysis is stereotyping: saying all the people in a group behave a certain way all the time, and using negative phrasing, such as "all British people are cold." A more useful approach is to think in terms of cultural norms: saying most people in a group behave a certain way most of the time, expressed as a behavior, not as a judgment, such as "the British tend to use formal greetings."

Communicator strategy   The culture in which you communicate will affect all three aspects of communicator strategy.

Communication objective   Rethink your communication objective in terms of the culture. (1) *Time:* Consider cultural attitudes toward time: you may want to set a different objective in a culture that is relative, relaxed, and tradition-oriented about time than you would in a culture that is precise and future-oriented toward time. (2) *Attitude:* Think also about the cultural attitude toward fate: the objective you set in a culture believing in deterministic fate may be different from one set in a culture believing in human control over fate.

Communication style   Different communication styles will tend to work better in different cultures. Group-oriented cultures may favor consult/join styles; individualistic cultures may favor tell/sell styles. Autocratic cultures may favor tell styles; democratic cultures may favor consult styles.

Credibility   Different cultures value the five aspects of credibility differently. For instance, goodwill credibility is more important in cultures that value personal relations; expert credibility is more important in cultures that value hard facts and task orientation. Similarly, some cultures value rank, titles, and authority more than others.

Audience strategy   The culture will also influence your audience strategy.

Audience selection   You may need to include additional primary audiences (people who receive your message directly), and leaders (key decision makers), depending on cultural expectations about rank, authority, and group definition. Also, remember that different cultures have different attitudes toward age, sex, and educational level.

Audience persuasion   Different audience persuasion techniques will work more effectively in different cultures. Although some cultures value material wealth and acquisition, others place greater value on work relationships, challenges, or status. Some cultures value Western logic more than others. The relative importance of individual relationships and credibility varies, as does the relative importance of group relationships and identity. Finally, persuasive values and ideals vary tremendously among cultures.

Gender-based tendencies   Sometimes it's useful to think about the cultural differences between men and women. Research shows, for example, that men tend to take arguments impersonally, women personally; that men seek quick authoritative decisions, women use consensus building; that men use stronger language even when they're not sure, women use more qualified language even when they are sure; and that men use less active listening, women use more.

Message strategy   In addition, cultural factors will influence your choice of message structure. Cultures valuing slow, ritualistic negotiations may favor indirect structure; cultures valuing fast, efficient negotiations may favor direct structure. Authoritarian cultures may favor direct structure downward and indirect structure upward.

Channel strategy   Different cultures may have different norms for channel and form—for example, a technical department versus a marketing department or a traditional organization versus a start-up venture. These norms may range from standardized one-page memos to face-to-face hallway discussions. In addition, cultures valuing personal trust more than hard facts tend to prefer oral communication and oral agreements; cultures valuing facts and efficiency tend to prefer written communication and written agreements.

Nonverbal considerations   In addition to the other strategic variables we have discussed in this chapter, nonverbal differences present another set of challenges in cross-cultural communication.

Body and voice   Consider cultural norms regarding body and voice: posture, gestures, eye contact and direction of gaze, facial expression, touching behaviors, pitch, volume, rate, and attitude toward silence. Avoid gestures considered rude or insulting in that culture; resist applying your own culture's nonverbal meanings to other cultures. For example, Vietnamese may look down to show respect, but that doesn't mean they are "shifty." Northeasterners may speak fast, but that doesn't mean they are "arrogant."

Space and objects   Also consider norms regarding space and objects: how much personal space people expect or need, how much institutional space people receive (who works where, with how much space, and with what material objects), how people dress, and how rigid dress codes are. For example, Latin Americans may prefer closer social space; Swedes may prefer more distant social space.

Greetings and hospitality   Finally, consider cultural norms regarding greetings and hospitality. Knowing these norms can go a long way toward increasing your rapport and credibility.

Communication Strategy Checklist

Communicator Strategy

See pages 206–209.

1. What is your communication objective: "As a result of this communication, my audience will . . ."?
2. What communication style do you choose: tell, sell, consult, or join?
3. What is your credibility: rank, goodwill, expertise, image, common ground?

Audience Strategy

See pages 209–214.

1. Who are they? Who should be included and how can you find out about them?
2. What do they know: necessary background information and new information; expectations for style, channel, and format?
3. What do they feel: emotions, interest, bias, hard or easy for them?
4. How can you persuade them using audience benefits, credibility, and message structure?

Message Strategy

See pages 215–218.

1. How can you emphasize: direct or indirect?
2. How can you organize a strategic message?

Channel Choice Strategy

See pages 218–222.

1. Writing: traditional, fax, email, or web page?
2. Speaking to a group face-to-face: tell/sell presentation or consult/join meeting?
3. Speaking to a group electronically: videoconference, conference call, broadcast or webcast, electronic meeting, or email meeting?
4. Speaking to an individual: face-to-face, telephone, or voicemail?

Culture Strategy

See pages 223–224.

1. How does the culture affect the communicator strategy: objective, style, credibility?
2. How does the culture affect the audience strategy: selection and persuasion?
3. How does the culture affect the message strategy: direct or indirect?
4. How does the culture affect the channel choice strategy?
5. What nonverbal considerations should you keep in mind?

CHAPTER 19

Writing: Composing Efficiently

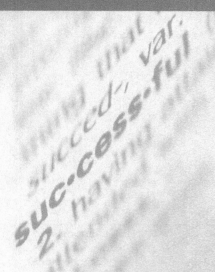

To many business people, writing does not seem as exciting or important as speaking—perhaps because writers are not actually face-to-face with their audience. However, in some ways, writing is more important than speaking because writing is (1) *often a "career sifter"*—that is, a specific report or memo may make or break a promotion or permanent hiring, (2) *permanent* and may be used for or against you long into the future, and (3) *increasingly prevalent* because of word processing and email.

Given its importance, writing (especially email) is all too often tossed off thoughtlessly because business writers are under severe time pressures. Therefore, this chapter concentrates on how to write under time pressure, how to compose more efficiently—that is, faster—(1) under normal circumstances, and (2) under special circumstances—including writer's block, email, and group writing.

Writing: Composing Efficiently

Section in this chapter:	Composing Under Normal Circumstances	Composing Under Special Circumstances
Goal:	To write faster	To overcome special writing challenges

Outline

1. Composing under normal circumstances
   Gather information
   Organize your thoughts
   Focus the message
   Draft the document
   Edit the document

2. Composing under special circumstances
   Overcoming writer's block
   Using email
   Writing in groups

COMPOSING UNDER NORMAL CIRCUMSTANCES

Writing: Composing Efficiently

Section in this chapter:	Composing Under Normal Circumstances	Composing Under Special Circumstances
Goal:	To write faster	To overcome special writing challenges

Before you sit down and start writing, make some decisions and set some expectations for yourself.

- **Setting your strategy first:** Before you write, always set, review, and keep in mind your communication strategy, as explained in the previous chapter.

- **Deciding whether to write or not:** As a part of that strategy, give some thought to a basic strategic issue: should you write or not? (1) Do you have an important reason to write? (2) Is writing too rigid? Do you want to solidify what may be temporary feelings on the matter? (3) Is writing too risky? Are you sure you want a permanent record? (4) Do you need to see your audience's reactions immediately? (5) Given your audience's situation, is this the right time to be writing? (6) Are you the right person to be writing this document?

- **Differentiating activities:** Once you decide it is appropriate to write, you will be more efficient if you can differentiate the five activities in the writing process: (1) gathering, (2) organizing, (3) focusing, (4) drafting, and (5) editing. Each of these activities calls for different skills.

- **Expecting overlap:** At the same time that you differentiate these stages, do not expect them to occur in lockstep order. Instead, during any one of these stages, be prepared to loop back, to rethink, to make changes. For example, once you've focused your ideas, you may find you need to collect more information for certain topics; or, once you've completed a draft, you may discover you need to reorganize some of your ideas. If you expect this kind of intelligent flexibility, you will take it in stride when the need for it occurs.

A helpful way to visualize the composition process, adopted from writing expert Donald Murray, is shown in the following illustration. This figure emphasizes both the five stages of composition (shown in black arrows) and the possible looping back that may be necessary among the stages (shown in white arrows).

THE WRITING COMPOSITION PROCESS

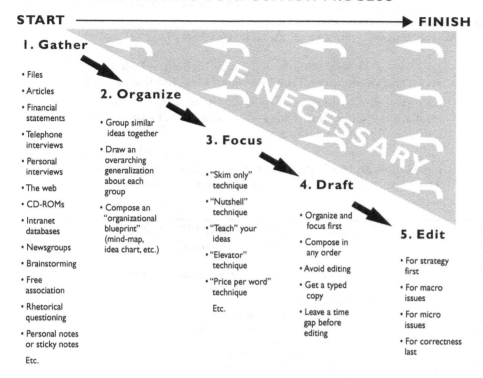

START ⟶ **FINISH**

I. Gather

- Files
- Articles
- Financial statements
- Telephone interviews
- Personal interviews
- The web
- CD-ROMs
- Intranet databases
- Newsgroups
- Brainstorming
- Free association
- Rhetorical questioning
- Personal notes or sticky notes

Etc.

2. Organize

- Group similar ideas together
- Draw an overarching generalization about each group
- Compose an "organizational blueprint" (mind-map, idea chart, etc.)

3. Focus

- "Skim only" technique
- "Nutshell" technique
- "Teach" your ideas
- "Elevator" technique
- "Price per word" technique

Etc.

4. Draft

- Organize and focus first
- Compose in any order
- Avoid editing
- Get a typed copy
- Leave a time gap before editing

5. Edit

- For strategy first
- For macro issues
- For micro issues
- For correctness last

IF NECESSARY

GATHER INFORMATION

As you can see from the illustration above, the first step in the writing process is to gather information. One way to do so is to collect information from various sources (ranging from hard copy to the Internet to interviews). Another set of methods is more intuitive (brainstorming alone or with others, or free writing for a certain amount of time even if it doesn't make sense). Before you move on to the next step, however, think about your "scope"—the breadth of your subject and how deeply you should cover it. Do you need to add more or different information based on (1) your audience analysis and (2) your communication objective?

ORGANIZE YOUR THOUGHTS

Stand back from all the information you have gathered and reapply your message strategy (as explained on pages 215–218), especially your use of the direct approach most of the time.

Then, start grouping similar ideas together, drawing an overarching generalization about each group and composing some kind of "organizational blueprint." This blueprint might take a variety of forms: (1) *a linear outline,* with Roman numerals, capital letters, and so forth; (2) *a circular mind map,* with the main point in the middle and subordinate points drawn like spokes around the circle using different images, colors, print sizes, arrows, and so forth; (3) *a sideways idea chart,* with subordinate points displayed to the side of each main point; (4) *a pyramid-shaped idea chart,* with subordinate points displayed below each main point; or (5) *other:* index cards, sticky notes, computer outlining software, or any other form that works for you. Refer to the Buzan book on mind mapping or the Minto book on the pyramid principle, both in the bibliography, for further details.

Most composition experts recommend that your "organizational blueprint" be in the form of a visual idea chart, instead of linear traditional outline, so you can

(1) literally see the different levels of ideas and how parts fit together, (2) modify it easily, and (3) be more likely to come up with new ideas. The example on the facing page shows such a visual idea chart.

As you compose your idea chart, make sure that . . .

- **Each top-level idea summarizes:** Every higher-level idea should generalize about and summarize all the lower-level ideas branching out below it.

- **All same-level branches are equivalent:** Check that all branches at the same level are the same kind of idea—for example, all reasons, all steps, all problems, or all recommendations.

- **Same-level branches are limited in number:** Your audience's short-term working memory and their attention span can handle only five to seven main points. Therefore, include no more than seven main branches on any given level.

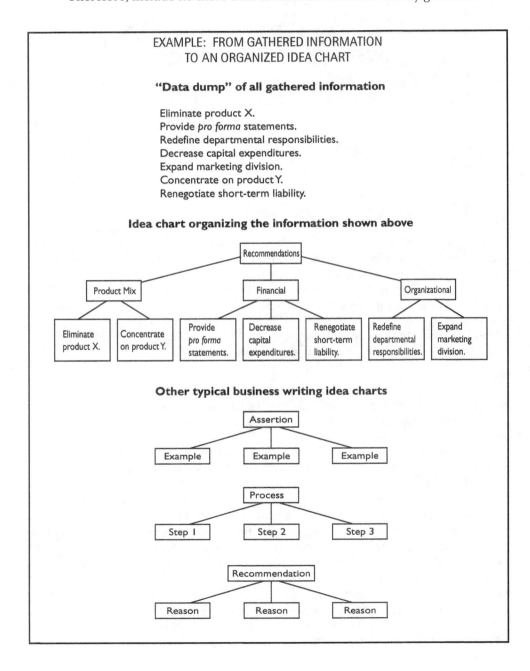

FOCUS THE MESSAGE

Now, step back from the details and try to see the essence of the message in terms of your communication objective and your audience analysis. Here are some techniques to focus your ideas.

- **Imagine the reader skimming:** Ask yourself, "What does my audience need to know most? If they only skim my message, what is the absolute minimum they should learn?"
- **"Nutshell" your ideas:** In the words of writing expert Linda Flower, "nutshell" your ideas. In a few sentences—that is, in a nutshell—lay out your main ideas. Distinguish major and minor ideas and decide how they are all related.
- **"Teach" your ideas:** Once you can express your ideas in a nutshell to yourself, think about how you would teach those ideas to someone else. Like nutshelling, figuring out how you would teach your ideas helps you form concepts in such a way that your audience gets the point, not just a list of facts.
- **Simulate the "elevator pitch":** Another way to focus your ideas is to imagine meeting your audience in the top-floor elevator. You have only the time it takes the elevator to descend to explain your main ideas. What would you say?
- **Use the "busy boss" technique:** Imagine your boss or client catches you in the hall and says "I have to leave for the airport and I don't have time to read your document. Tell me the main ideas in two minutes."

At this stage in the process, you will have an organized, focused list. For example, you might have a list of three to five steps in a procedure, examples supporting a conclusion, component parts of a process, a chronological list of events, reasons why they should buy this product, or recommendations for approval. Upon analyzing this focused list, you may find you need to go back and gather additional information.

Although the writing process is recursive, be sure to complete the first stages, generally referred to as "prewriting" (setting your strategy, gathering, organizing, and focusing), before you start composing. Experts observe that effective writers spend about 50% of their time on prewriting activities, as opposed to drafting and editing.

DRAFT THE DOCUMENT

The key to effective drafting is to let your creativity flow. Don't try to draft and edit at the same time. Don't be a perfectionist; don't try to write a perfect product the first time. Here are some techniques to help you in the drafting stage.

Compose in any order.   Rather than forcing yourself to write from the beginning of your document straight through to the end, write the sections you are most comfortable with first. You don't need to write your introduction first. Writing the introduction may be a formidable task, and you often end up having to change it anyway, if you modify your ideas or organization as you compose the rest of the draft. Therefore, many writing experts advise writing your introduction last.

Avoid editing.   Drafting should be creative, not overly analytical. Do not worry about specific problems as you write your draft. Do not edit. If you cannot think of a word, leave a blank space. If you cannot decide between two words, write them both down. Circle or put a check mark in the margin next to awkward or unclear sections, and come back to them later.

Print a hard copy.   Get your draft onto typed copy—one side only, double-spaced, with wide margins. You will draft faster if you avoid writing by hand: you write in longhand at about 15 words per minute; you can type at 20 to 60 words per minute; you can dictate into a machine or voice recognition software at 65 to 95 words per minute. Furthermore, you will edit faster working from typed copy. Print a hard copy, so you will overcome the prevalent problem of microediting only the section you can see at one time on your computer monitor instead of editing the document as a whole.

Schedule a time gap.   You will do a better job of editing if you leave some time between the creative drafting and analytical editing stages, so your thoughts can incubate subconsciously. For important or complex documents, separate the two stages by an overnight break. Even if you are under severe time constraints or composing a routine document, leave yourself a short gap: for example, begin editing after a lunch break or even a five- to ten-minute break.

EDIT THE DOCUMENT

When you begin editing, don't immediately begin to agonize over commas and word choices. Instead, complete the four-step plan that follows—using a hard copy of the entire document, not just what you can see at one time on your computer screen. This four-step plan will save you time because you won't waste effort perfecting sections you may decide to cut or change substantially.

Step 1: Edit for strategy.   Before you begin fine-tuning, review the document for the communication strategy issues discussed in Chapter 18: (1) channel choice strategy, (2) communicator strategy, (3) audience strategy, (4) message strategy, and (5) culture strategy.

Step 2: Edit for macro issues.   Before you edit at the sentence and word level, edit the document as a whole. Specifically, (1) document design for "high skim value," (2) signposts to show connection, and (3) effective paragraphs or sections.

Step 3: Edit for micro issues.   Once you have edited at the strategic and macro levels, then edit your sentences and words: (1) avoiding wordiness and overlong sentences, and (2) using an appropriate style. In addition, check your format for consistency.

Step 4: Edit for correctness.   Finally, edit for correctness. Effective writers do this task last; ineffective writers do this first. If you have any specific questions on grammar or punctuation, refer to the appendices at the end of this book.

Proofread carefully. Don't confuse computer proofreading for human proofreading. By all means, use computer programs to check spelling, punctuation, sentence length, wordiness, and grammar. However, computers cannot check for logic, flow, emphasis, tone, or computer-generated errors such as transferring only a part of a section or not deleting a phrase you changed. Computers cannot even check all spelling errors (for example, *you* when you meant to write *your* or *on* when you meant to write *of*). Finally, computers cannot catch missing words or phrases.

Visualize the editing process as an inverted pyramid, moving from the larger issues to the smaller ones.

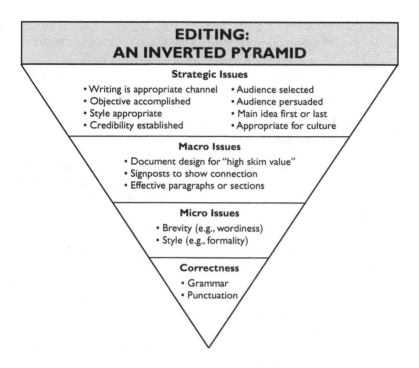

COMPOSING UNDER SPECIAL CIRCUMSTANCES

Writing: Composing Efficiently

Section in this chapter:	Composing Under Normal Circumstances	Composing Under Special Circumstances
Goal:	To write faster	To overcome special writing challenges

This section offers some ideas on how to deal with three special challenges in writing: (1) overcoming writer's block, (2) using email, and (3) writing in collaboration with a group.

OVERCOMING WRITER'S BLOCK

Writer's block is a temporary inability to write: you sit there facing the blank screen or the blank page and can't get any words out. Virtually everyone has experienced writer's block at one time or another. Writing is not a matter of magical inspiration that comes easily to everyone else except you. If you're stuck, try one or more of these techniques.

Change your writing task.   One set of techniques centers on changing the writing task you are working on at that particular moment.

- **Write another section first.** If you are stuck on one section, put it aside and write another section first. Don't force yourself to write from beginning to end. Write any section that seems easier first—even if it's the conclusion.

- **Write your headings first.** Try writing your headings, subheadings, or bullet points first. Then, go back and flesh out each one.

- **Resketch your idea chart.** Some people think better visually than they do verbally. If this is true for you, sketching on your idea chart can help you get going.
- **Work on nontext issues.** Work on some other part of the writing task, such as formatting or graphics, so you can have some sense of accomplishment before returning to text writing.

Change your activity. Another set of techniques has to do with changing the kind of activity you are engaged in.

- **Take a break.** If you are bogged down with your ideas or expression, taking a break often helps. Walk away. Do something else. Allow time for the problems to incubate in your mind subconsciously. When you return after this rest period, you will often be able to work more effectively.
- **"Talk" to your readers.** Sit back and imagine that you are talking to your readers. Then, write what you would say to them. Often, wording will flow more easily and less awkwardly when you talk out loud than when you write silently.
- **Talk about your ideas.** To use this technique, talk with someone else about your writing. Discuss your ideas, or your overall organization, or specific points—whatever seems to be eluding you.
- **Read or talk about something else.** Read something else. Talk to someone about something else. Some people find that changing activities in this way allows their thoughts to develop.

Change your perceptions. A final set of techniques involves changing your perceptions about yourself and about writing.

- **Relax your commitment to rules.** Sometimes writers are blocked by what they perceive as hard-and-fast "rules," such as "Never use the word *I* in business writing." Reject these rules, especially during the drafting stage. You can always edit later on.
- **Break down the project.** Reorganize the entire writing project into a series of more manageable parts.
- **Print draft at the top of each page.** Print the word *draft* at the top of each page, or lightly in the background of each page to remind yourself that you don't have to be perfect.
- **Relax your expectations.** Avoid being too self-critical. Lower unrealistic expectations for yourself.
- **Don't fall in love with your prose.** Just get something down. It doesn't have to be perfect; you may have to edit it anyway.
- **Expect complexity.** Writing is so complex that you should not expect it to go logically and smoothly, but rather to involve continual rethinking and changing. Keep in mind the writing composition process, illustrated on page 229.

USING EMAIL

Email can be a tremendously efficient and useful tool for writing. If not used effectively, however, it can be unclear, inappropriate, and burdensome. To avoid such problems in your email, use the following tips, based in part on the work of writing experts Jone Rymer and Priscilla Rogers.

Do not use email when you . . .

- **Are angry or in radical disagreement.** Avoid "flaming"—that is, responding to an email in an inappropriately uninhibited, irresponsible, or destructive way—by giving yourself time to calm down before you send an email.

- Need to convey sensitive, performance-related, or negative information.
- Need to interact, see, or hear your audience. Email lacks nonverbal interaction and immediate "give-and-take" and is ineffective for confrontation or consensus building.
- Need confidentiality or privacy. Nothing on email is completely confidential or private. Your message might be printed, distributed, forwarded, or saved by the recipient; monitored; or subpoenaed.

Compose your subject line carefully.

- Be specific about the subject. For example, rather than "Marketing staff," write "New additions to Marketing staff" or "Marketing staff: new additions."
- Use a verb if reader action is needed—for example, "Vote on new policy" or "Send reactions to new policy."

Compose your first screen carefully.   Assume your readers may look at the first screen of your message only.

- Move requests up front. If you want your reader to do something, say so in the first sentence.
- Give overview and number multiple points. Without such an overview, readers might not scroll down. State, for example . . .

> This email explains the five-step process you need to install the new software program.
>
> Here are four arguments in favor of the proposal.

Use "high skim value."   Because readers may only skim their email, use document design techniques to ensure they will notice your important points.

- Use headings. After you have written a long email, go back and insert headings and subheadings at the beginning of each main idea.
- Use lists and typography (for example, all caps for headings or a dashed line between main points) to make your email easier to follow.
- Break your message into short chunks. Because readers tend to glance over email quickly, help them to access your messages by using short lines, relatively short sentences, and short paragraphs. Double-space between paragraphs to add white space and make it easier for readers to see organizational breaks.

Make up for the lack of nonverbal cues.   Email lacks the gestures, facial expressions, and tone of voice that help your audience interpret your meaning in face-to-face conversation.

- Consider using "politeness markers," such as "please," and "I'm sorry to say." Some email writers use "emoticons" such as :-) and :-(to add nonverbal cues. With some audiences, use of emoticons may be seen as too cute and even harm your credibility.
- Be careful with jokes. Jokes in email may offend readers; ironic comments may be taken at face value. Be careful about carrying over into email the kind of joking and the casual, even off-color, language that might be accepted in face-to-face conversation.

Pause before you send. Do not send . . .

- To the wrong recipient or mistakenly to "Reply to all."
- If you feel angry or highly emotional. Email is conducive to rapid response in the heat of the moment, so never send it if you still feel upset. You can

always send the message later after reflection, but you can't bring it back once it's posted.

- **If you wouldn't want others to read it.** Don't email anything that you would be uncomfortable with your colleagues, your boss, or a reporter reading. Assume that anything you email can be printed, forwarded, or downloaded and shown anywhere.

WRITING IN GROUPS

Group writing is increasingly prevalent in business. Collaborating means compromising; however, it also means benefiting from a wealth of talents and differing degrees of credibility. Here are some suggestions for writing effectively and efficiently in groups.

Agree on group guidelines.   Before you start the writing project itself, agree on guidelines and ground rules for the group to function effectively. Decide who will facilitate the meetings, how you will make decisions for various items, how you will deal with emotional "ownership" of wording, and how you will deal with infractions of group agreements and refusals to change. Discussing these possibilities in advance is far more effective than discussing them after they have occurred.

Agree on the tasks and time line.   Once you have agreed on general guidelines for the group, set the specific time line and writing tasks. Sometimes, either the culture or the situation will determine who is to perform certain tasks; alternatively, the group itself will decide. As you delineate the tasks and time line, decide if and how you might use groupware (for example, to edit various drafts of the document). Specify deadlines, yet try to build in some leeway. Finally, remember to specify what milestones you will use to identify progress and modify the time line, if necessary. The six tasks to include on your time line follow.

Task 1: Setting the strategy   Agree on a time frame for, and specify who will be involved in, setting the communication strategy—communicator strategy, audience strategy, message strategy, and culture strategy—as summarized on the checklist on pages 223–224.

Task 2: Gathering information   Most groups divide the research tasks based on the interests and expertise of each member. Remember to set times for periodic meetings during the research phase to pool ideas, avoid unnecessary overlap, and move together toward conclusions and recommendations.

Task 3: Organizing and focusing the information   Set a time to organize and focus the information, as described on pages 229–230. With group writing, it is especially important to do so extremely clearly before you start writing. As a group, collaborate on the outline or idea chart and main headings before anyone starts drafting.

Task 4: Drafting the document   Next on the time line comes the drafting stage. Consider two options here.

- **Use various draft writers.** One choice is to have different people write different sections. This option is most appropriate if you want to spread the responsibility, if the writers' styles are similar, or if people want to write the section of their expertise. If you use multiple draft writers, be sure to (1) agree about formality, directness, and other style issues in advance, (2) allow enough time to edit for consistency after all the drafts are complete, and (3) avoid a "smorgasbord" in which every item that every team member has learned is tossed into the final document.

- Use one writer. A second option is to use one writer, who writes the entire document from scratch. This option assures you of a more consistent style throughout, avoids ownership issues with various sections, and takes advantage of a gifted writer; however, it centralizes power and responsibility with one person. If you are using one writer, be sure to (1) include him or her in the research progress meetings throughout the process, and (2) allow enough time to incorporate group revisions after the draft.

Task 5: Editing the document   Be sure to allow enough time for editing the document for consistent style and content. Some groups waste time arguing about every detail of editing; others don't leave enough time to edit at all. Instead, consider these two options.

- Use a single editor. One choice is to use one editor—either a group member, a colleague, or a professional. If you do so, schedule enough time for him or her to edit. Agree clearly whether you want (1) a copy editor for typos, spelling, and grammar only, or (2) a style editor for consistency in style and format only, or (3) an analytic editor for strategy and content changes.

- Use a group of editors. A second choice is to edit as a group. Circulate hard copy or electronic copy for each group member to read and annotate. Then, (1) the group can meet face-to-face or electronically to discuss all editing issues, (2) one person can read all the comments and decide what to incorporate, or (3) the group can discuss strategy and content issues only, delegating style editing and copy editing to one person.

Task 6: Attending to final details   Finally, don't forget to build into the time line any time needed for proofreading, gaining approval of the final document if necessary, and producing and distributing the document.

CHAPTER 20

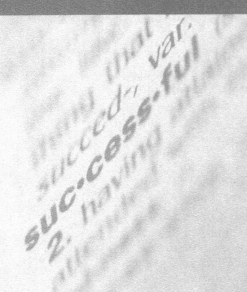

Correspondence Memos and Letters

Objectives

When you complete this chapter, you will be able to do the following:

1. Understand the differences between memos and letters.
2. Follow all-purpose templates to write memos and letters.
3. Use memo samples as guidelines for memo components, organization, writing style and tone.
4. Evaluate your memos and letters with checklists.
5. Correctly use the eight essential letter components: the writer's address, the date, an inside address for the recipient, a salutation, the body of the letter, a complimentary close, and the writer's signed and typed names.
6. Write different types of letters, including the following:
   - Inquiry
   - Cover (Transmittal)
   - Complaint
   - Adjustment
   - Sales
7. Follow the writing process—prewriting, writing, and rewriting—to create memos and letters.
8. Test your knowledge of correspondence through end-of-chapter activities:
   - Case Studies
   - Individual and Team Projects
   - Problem Solving Think Pieces
   - Web Workshop

COMMUNICATION AT WORK

In this scenario, a biotechnology company frequently corresponds through letters and memos.

CompuMed CompuMed, a wholesale provider of biotechnology equipment, is home-based in Reno, NV. CompuMed's CEO, Jim Goodwin, plans to capitalize on emerging nanotechnology to manufacture and sell the following:

- Extremely lightweight and portable heart monitors and ventilators.
- Pacemakers and hearing aids, 1/10 the size of current products on the market.
- Microscopic bio-robotics that can be injected in the body to manage, monitor, and/or destroy blood clots, metastatic activities, arterial blockages, alveoli damage due to carcinogens or pollutants, and scar tissues creating muscular or skeletal immobility.

CompuMed is a growing company with over 5,000 employees located in 24 cities and 3 states. To manage this business, supervisors and employees write on average over 20 letters and 15 memos a day.

The letters are written to many different audiences and serve various purposes. CompuMed must write letters for employee files, to customers, to job applicants, to outside auditors, to governmental agencies involved in biotechnology regulation, to insurance companies, and more. They write

- *Letters of inquiry* to retailers seeking product information (technical specifications, pricing, warranties, guarantees, credentials of service staff, and so forth).
- *Cover letters* prefacing CompuMed's proposals.
- *Complaint letters* written to parts manufacturers if and when faulty equipment and materials are received in shipping and *adjustment letters* to compensate retailers when problems occur.
- *Sales letters* to computer and biotechnology retailers.

CompuMed's managers and employees also write memos to accomplish a variety of goals:

- document work accomplished
- call meetings and establish meeting agendas
- request equipment from purchasing
- preface internal proposals
- highlight productivity and problems

Writing memos and letters are two important types of workplace communication at CompuMed.

THE DIFFERENCES BETWEEN MEMOS AND LETTERS

This chapter focuses on traditional correspondence—memos and letters. To give you an overview of the differences and similarities between memos and letters, look at Table 20.1.

TABLE 20.1   Memos vs. Letters

Characteristics	Memos	Letters
Destination	Internal: correspondence written to colleagues within a company.	External: correspondence written to people outside the business.
Format	Identification lines include "Date," "To," "From," and "Subject." The message follows.	Includes letterhead address, date, reader's address, salutation, text, complimentary close, and signatures.
Audience	Generally specialists or semi-specialists, mostly business colleagues.	Generally semi-specialists and lay readers, such as vendors, clients, stakeholders, and stockholders.
Topic	Generally topics related to internal corporate decisions; abbreviations and acronyms often allowed.	Generally topics related to vendor, client, stakeholder, and stockholder interests; abbreviations and acronyms usually defined.
Tone	Informal due to peer audience.	More formal due to audience of vendors, clients, stakeholders, and stockholders.
Attachments or Enclosures	Hard-copy attachments can be stapled to the memo. Complimentary copies (cc) can be sent to other readers.	Additional information can be enclosed within the envelope. Complimentary copies (cc) can be sent to other readers.
Delivery Time	Determined by a company's in-house mail procedure.	Determined by the destination (within the city, state, or country). Letters could be delivered within 3 days but may take more than a week.
Security	If a company's mail delivery system is reliable, the memo will be placed in the reader's mailbox. Then, what the reader sees on the hard copy page will be exactly what the writer wrote. Security depends on the ethics of coworkers and whether the memo was sent in an envelope.	The U.S. Postal Service is very reliable. Once the reader opens the envelope, he or she sees exactly what the writer wrote. Privacy laws protect the letter's content.

MEMOS

REASONS FOR WRITING MEMOS

Memos are an important means by which employees communicate with each other. Memos, hard-copy correspondence written within your company, are important for several reasons. In 2004, The National Commission on Writing substantiated the importance of correspondence (memos and letters). Their survey of 120 major companies employing approximately 8 million workers found that 70 percent of the companies require the writing of memos and letters ("Writing: A Ticket to Work").

Next, you will write memos to a wide range of readers. This includes your supervisors, coworkers, subordinates, and multiple combinations of these audiences. Since memos usually are copied (cc: complimentary copies) to many readers, a memo sent to your boss could be read by an entire department, the boss's boss, and colleagues in other departments.

Because of their frequency and widespread audiences, memos could represent a major component of your interpersonal communication skills within your work environment.

Furthermore, memos are very flexible and can be written for many different purposes. Consider these options.

- Documentation. Expenses, incidents, accidents, problems encountered, projected costs, study findings, hirings, firings, reallocations of staff or equipment, etc.

- Confirmation. A meeting agenda, date, time, and location; decisions to purchase or sell; topics for discussion at upcoming teleconferences; conclusions arrived at; fees, costs, or expenditures, etc.

- Procedures. How to set up accounts, research on the company intranet, operate new machinery, use new software, apply online for job opportunities through the company intranet, create a new company Web site, solve a problem, etc.

- Recommendations. Reasons to purchase new equipment, fire or hire personnel, contract with new providers, merge with other companies, revise current practices, renew contracts, etc.

- Feasibility. Studying the possibility of changes in the workplace (practices, procedures, locations, staffing, equipment, missions/visions), etc.

- Status. Daily, weekly, monthly, quarterly, biannually, yearly statements about where you, the department, or the company is regarding many topics (sales, staffing, travel, practices, procedures, finances, etc.)

- Directive (delegation of responsibilities). Informing subordinates of their designated tasks.

- Inquiry. Asking questions about upcoming processes or procedures.

- Cover. Prefacing an internal proposal, long report, or other attachments.

CRITERIA FOR WRITING MEMOS

Memos contain the following key components:

- Memo Identification Lines—Date, To, From, and Subject
- Introduction
- Discussion
- Conclusion
- Audience Recognition
- Appropriate Memo Style and Tone

Figure 20.1 shows an ideal, all-purpose organizational template that works well for memos.

Subject Line. The subject line summarizes the memo's content. One-word subject lines do not communicate effectively, as in the following flawed subject line. The "before" sample has a *topic* (a what) but is missing a *focus* (a what about the what).

before	after
Subject: Sales	Subject: Report on Quarterly Sales

Introduction. Once you have communicated your intent in the subject line, get to the point in the introductory sentence(s). Write one or two clear introductory sentences that tell your readers *what* topic you are writing about and *why* you are writing. The following example invites the reader to a meeting, thereby communicating *what* the writer's intentions are. It also tells the reader that the meeting is one of a series of meetings, thus communicating *why* the meeting is being called.

FIGURE 20.1
All-Purpose
Memo Template

DATE:
TO:
FROM:
SUBJECT: Focus + Topic

Introduction: A lead-in or overview stating *why* you are writing and *what* you are writing about.

Discussion: Detailed development, made accessible through highlighting techniques, explaining *exactly what* you want to say.
  •
  •
  •

Conclusion: State *what* is next, *when* this will occur, and *why* the date is important.

Example

In the third of our series of sales quota meetings this quarter, I'd like to review our productivity.

Discussion. The discussion section allows you to develop your content specifically. Readers might not read every line of your memo (tending instead to skip and skim). Thus, traditional blocks of data (paragraphing) are not necessarily effective. The longer the paragraph, the more likely your audience is to avoid reading. Make your text more reader-friendly by itemizing, using white space, boldfacing, creating headings, or inserting graphics.

before

Unfriendly Text

This year began with an increase, as we sold 4.5 million units in January compared to 3.7 for January 2005. In February we continued to improve with 4.6, compared with 3.6 for the same time in 2005. March was not quite so good, as we sold 4.3 against the March 2005 figure of 3.9. April was about the same with 4.2, compared to 3.8 for April 2005.

after

Reader-Friendly Text

Comparative Quarterly Sales (in Millions)

	2005	2006	Increase/Decrease
Jan.	3.7	4.5	0.8+
Feb.	3.6	4.6	1.0+
Mar.	3.9	4.3	0.4+
Apr.	3.8	4.2	0.4+

Conclusion. Conclude your memo with "thanks" and/or a directive action. A pleasant conclusion could motivate your readers, as in the following example. A directive close tells your readers exactly what you want them to do next or what your plans are (and provides dated action).

If our quarterly sales continue to improve at the current rate, we will double our sales expectations by 2006. Congratulations! Next Wednesday (12/22/06), please provide next quarter's sales projections and a summary of your sales team's accomplishments.

Audience Recognition.   Since letters go outside your company, your audience is usually a semi-specialist or lay, demanding that you define your terms specifically. In memos your in-house audience is easy to address (usually a specialist or semi-specialist). You often can use more acronyms and internal abbreviations in memos than you can in letters.

You will write the message to "Distribution" (listing a group of readers) or send the memo to one reader but "cc" (send a "carbon copy" or "complimentary copy") to other readers. Thus, you might be writing simultaneously to your immediate supervisor (specialist), to his or her boss (semi-specialist), to your colleagues (specialists), and to a CEO (semi-specialist). To accommodate multiple audiences, use parenthetical definitions, such as Cash In Advance (CIA) or Continuing Property Records (CPR).

Style and Tone.   Because memos are usually only one page long, use simple words, short sentences, specific detail, and highlighting techniques. In addition, strive for an informal, friendly tone. Memos are part of your interpersonal communication abilities, so a friendly tone will help build rapport with colleagues.

In memos, audience determines tone. For example, you cannot write directive correspondence to supervisors mandating action on their part. It might seem obvious that you can write directives to subordinates, but you should not use a dictatorial tone. Though the subordinates are under your authority, they must still be treated with respect. You will determine the tone of your memo by deciding if you are writing vertically (up to management or down to subordinates) or laterally (to coworkers), as shown in Figure 20.2.

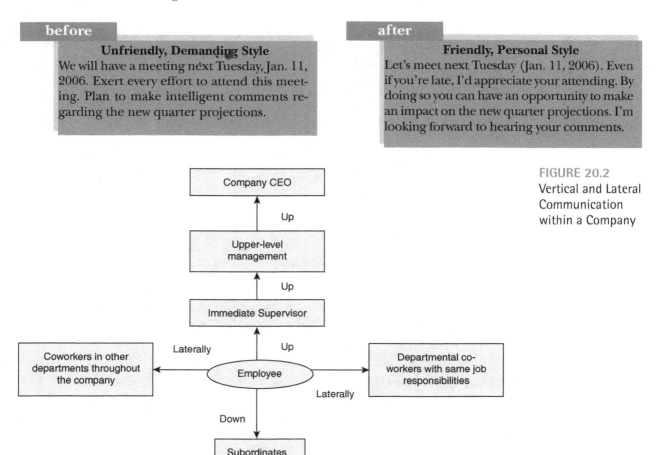

before	after
Unfriendly, Demanding Style We will have a meeting next Tuesday, Jan. 11, 2006. Exert every effort to attend this meeting. Plan to make intelligent comments regarding the new quarter projections.	**Friendly, Personal Style** Let's meet next Tuesday (Jan. 11, 2006). Even if you're late, I'd appreciate your attending. By doing so you can have an opportunity to make an impact on the new quarter projections. I'm looking forward to hearing your comments.

FIGURE 20.2
Vertical and Lateral Communication within a Company

SAMPLE MEMOS

See Figures 20.3 and 20.4 for sample memos.

"Distribution" indicates that the memo is being sent to a number of employees. Notice that at the bottom of the memo, a distribution list is provided.

The introduction states the purpose of this memo, providing dates, personnel, options, and intended action.

The memo's discussion analyzes the criteria used to decide which radio to purchase. Tables are used to ensure reader-friendly ease of access.

The conclusion summarizes the importance of the action. It also ends in a personalized and positive tone to ensure reader involvement and to build rapport.

MEMORANDUM

DATE: December 12, 2006
TO: Distribution
FROM: Luann Brunson
SUBJECT: Replacement of Maintenance Radios

On December 5, the manufacturing department supervisor informed the purchasing department that our company's maintenance radios were malfunctioning. Purchasing was asked to evaluate three radio options (the RPAD, XPO 1690, and MX16 radios). Based on my findings, I have issued a purchase order for 12 RPAD radios.

The following points summarize my findings.

1. *Performance*
During a one-week test period, I found that the RPAD outperformed our current XPO's reception. The RPAD could send and receive within a range of 5 miles with minimal interference. The XPO's range was limited to 2 miles, and transmissions from distant parts of our building broke up due to electrical interference.

2. *Specifications*
Both the RPAD and the MX16 were easier to carry, because of their reduced weight and size, than our current XPO 1690s.

	RPAD	XPO 1690	MX16
Weight	1 lb.	2 lbs.	1 lb.
Size	5″ × 2″	8″ × 4″	6″ × 1″

3. *Cost*
The RPAD is our most cost-effective option because of quantity cost breaks and maintenance guarantees.

	RPAD	XPO 1690	MX16
Cost per unit	$70.00	$215.00	$100.00
Cost per doz.	$750.00	$2,580.00	$1,100.00
Guarantees	1 year	6 months	1 year

Purchase of the RPAD will give us improved performance and comfort. In addition, we can buy 12 RPAD radios for approximately the cost of 4 XPOs. If I can provide you with additional information, please call. I'd be happy to meet with you at your convenience.

Distribution: M. Ellis   M. Rhinehart   T. Schroeder
                 P. Michelson   R. Travers   R. Xidis

FIGURE 20.3   Comparison/Contrast Memo Recommending Action

Memo

DATE: November 11, 2006
TO: CompuMed Management
FROM: Bill Baker, Human Resources Director
SUBJECT: Information about Proposed Changes to Employee Benefits Package

Compu *M* **ed**

As of January 1, 2007, CompuMed will change insurance carriers. This will affect all 5,000 employees' benefits packages. I have attached a proposal, including the following:

1.	Reasons for changing from our current carrier.	page 2
2.	Criteria for our selection of a new insurance company.	pages 3–4
3.	Monthly cost for each employee.	pages 5–6
4.	Overall cost to CompuMed.	page 7
5.	Benefits derived from the new healthcare plan.	page 8

Please review the proposal, survey your employees' responses to our suggestions, and provide your feedback. We need your input by December 1, 2006. This will give the human resources department time to consider your suggestions and work with insurance companies to meet employee needs.

Enclosure: Proposal

FIGURE 20.4   Cover Memo Prefacing Attachments

MEMO CHECKLIST

The Memo Checklist will give you the opportunity for self-assessment and peer evaluation of your writing.

MEMO CHECKLIST

MEMO CHECKLIST

___ 1. Does the memo contain identification lines (Date, To, From, and Subject)?

___ 2. Does the subject line contain a topic and a focus?

___ 3. Does the introduction clearly state
- Why this memo has been written?
- What topic the memo is discussing?

___ 4. Does the body explain exactly what you want to say?

___ 5. Does the conclusion
- tell when you plan a follow-up or when you want a response?
- explain why this dated action is important?

___ 6. Are highlighting techniques used effectively for document design?

___ 7. Is the memo concise?

___ 8. Is the memo clear,
- achieving specificity of detail?
- answering reporter's questions?

___ 9. Does the memo recognize audience,
- defining acronyms or abbreviations where necessary for various levels of readers (specialists, semi-specialists, and lay)?

___ 10. Did you avoid grammatical errors? Errors will hurt your professionalism. See Appendix A for grammar rules.

LETTERS

REASONS FOR WRITING LETTERS

Letters are external correspondence that you send from your company to a colleague working at another company, to a vendor, to a customer, to a prospective employee, and to stakeholders and stockholders. Letters leave your work site (as opposed to memos, which stay within the company).

Because letters are sent to readers in other locations, your letters not only reflect your communication abilities but also are a reflection of your company. This chapter provides letter components, formats, criteria, and examples to help you write the following kinds of letters: inquiry, cover (transmittal), complaint, adjustment, and sales.

ESSENTIAL COMPONENTS OF LETTERS

Your letter should be typed or printed on $8^1/_2'' \times 11''$ paper. Leave $1''$ to $1^1/_2''$ margins at the top and on both sides. Choose an appropriately businesslike font (size and style), such as Times New Roman or Arial (12 point). Though "designer fonts," such as Comic Sans and Shelley Volante, are interesting, they tend to be harder to read and less professional.

Your letter should contain the essential components shown in Figure 20.5.

Writer's Address.   This section contains either your personal address or your company's address. If the heading consists of your address, you will include your street address; the city, state, and zip code. The state may be abbreviated with the appropriate two-letter abbreviation.

If the heading consists of your company's address, you will include the company's name; street address; and city, state, and zip code.

Date.   Document the month, day, and year when you write your letter. You can write your date in one of two ways: May 31, 2006, or 31 May 2006. Place the date one or two spaces below the writer's address.

Reader's Address.   Place the reader's address two lines below the date.

- Reader's name (If you do not know the name of this person, begin the reader's address with a job title or the name of the department.)
- Reader's title (optional)
- Company name
- Street address
- City, state, and zip code

Salutation.   The traditional salutation, placed two spaces beneath the inside address, is *Dear* and your reader's last name, followed by a colon (Dear Mr. Smith:).

You can also address your reader by his or her first name if you are on a first-name basis with this person (Dear John:). If you are writing to a woman and are unfamiliar with her marital status, address the letter Dear Ms. Jones. However, if you know the woman's marital status, you can address the letter accordingly: Dear Miss Jones: *or* Dear Mrs. Jones: *or* Dear Dr. Jones:

Letter Body.   Begin the body of the letter two spaces below the salutation. The body includes your introductory paragraph, discussion paragraph(s), and concluding paragraph. The body should be single spaced with double spacing between paragraphs. Whether you indent the beginning of paragraphs or leave them flush with the left margin is determined by the letter format you employ.

FIGURE 20.5
Essential Letter
Components

UNITED SPECTOGRAPH

19015 Lakeview Avenue   ← ——————— Writer's address
Columbus, OH 43212

June 10, 2006   ← ——————— Date

Kristy Pieburn
Corporate Communications, Inc. ← ——————— Reader's address
1245 Grant
Chicago, IL 60611

Dear Ms. Pieburn: ← ——————— Salutation

Here is the schedule for your presentation during our Basic Information
Training for Supervisors (BITS) seminar. You will hold your sessions in our
Training Center at 19015 Lakeview Avenue.

The schedule and important information regarding your two, 8-hour
seminars are as follows:

- Group 1, consisting of 15 employees, will meet Monday, July 6, 2006,
  from 8:00 A.M. to 5:00 P.M.
- Group 2, consisting of 18 employees, will meet Tuesday, July 7, 2006, from
  8:00 A.M. to 5:00 P.M.   Letter text

As you requested, the training room will have an overhead projector,
screen, flip chart, and pad. During the morning sessions, coffee, juice, and
rolls will be served. In the afternoon, seminar participants will be offered
cold drinks and cookies. We look forward to working with you again. If I
can answer any questions, please let me know.

Sincerely,   ← ——————— Complimentary
                            close

Martha Lee   ← ——————— Signed name

Martha Lee   ← ——————— Typed name

Complimentary Close.   Place the complimentary close, followed by a comma,
two spaces below the concluding paragraph. Typical complimentary closes include "Sincerely," "Yours truly," and "Sincerely yours."

Signed Name.   Sign your name legibly beneath the complimentary close.

Typed Name.   Type your name four spaces below the complimentary close.
You can type your title one space beneath your typed name. You also can include your title on the same line as your typed name, with a comma after your
name.

OPTIONAL COMPONENTS OF LETTERS

In addition to the letter essentials, you can include the following optional components.

Subject Line.   Place a subject line two spaces below the reader's address and two spaces above the salutation.

Dr. Ron Schaefer
Linguistics Department
Southern Illinois University
Edwardsville, IL 66205

Subject: Linguistics Conference Registration Payment

Dear Dr. Schaefer:

You also could use a subject line instead of a salutation.

Linguistics Department
Southern Illinois University
Edwardsville, IL 66205

Subject: Linguistics Conference Registration Payment

A subject line not only helps readers understand the letter's intent but also (if you are uncertain of your reader's name) helps you avoid such awkward salutations as "To Whom It May Concern," "Dear Sirs," and "Ladies and Gentlemen." In the simplified format, both the salutation and the complimentary close are omitted, and a subject line is included.

New Page Notations.   If your letter is longer than one page, cite your name, the page number, and the date on all pages after page 1. Place this notation either flush with the left margin at the top of subsequent pages or across the top of subsequent pages. (You must have at least two lines of text on the next page to justify another page.)

Left margin, subsequent
page notation

Across top of
subsequent pages

Mabel Tinjaca
Page 2
May 31, 2006

Mabel Tinjaca 2   May 31, 2006

Writer's and Typist's Initials. If the letter was typed by someone other than the writer, include both the writer's and the typist's initials two spaces below the typed signature. The writer's initials are capitalized, the typist's initials are typed in lowercase, and the two sets of initials are separated by a colon. If the typist and the writer are the same person, this notation is not necessary.

> Sincerely,
>
> W. T. Winnery
> WTW:mm

Enclosure Notation. If your letter prefaces enclosed information, such as an invoice or report, mention this enclosure in the letter and then type an enclosure notation two spaces below the typed signature (or two spaces below the writer and typist initials). The enclosure notation can be abbreviated "Enc."; written out as "Enclosure"; show the number of enclosures, such as "Enclosures (2)"; or specify what has been enclosed—"Enclosure: January Invoice."

Copy Notation. If you have sent a copy of your letter to other readers, show this in a copy notation. A complimentary copy is designated by a lowercase "cc." List the other readers' names following the copy notation. Type the copy notation two spaces below the typed signature or two spaces below either the writer's and typist's initials or the enclosure notation.

> Sincerely,
>
> Brian Altman
> Enclosure: August Status Report
> cc: Marcia Rittmaster and Larry Rochelle

FORMATTING LETTERS

Three common types of letter formats include **full block** (Figure 20.6), **full block with subject line** (Figure 20.7), and **simplified** (Figure 20.8). Two popular and professional formats used in business are full block and full block with subject line. With both formats, you type all information at the left margin without indenting paragraphs, the date, the complimentary close, or signature. The full block with subject line differs only with the inclusion of a subject line.

Another option is the simplified format. This type of letter layout is similar to the full block format in that *all text is typed margin left. The two significant omissions include no salutation* ("Dear _____:") *and no complimentary close* ("Sincerely,"). Omitting a salutation is useful in the following instances:

- You do not know your reader's name (NOTE: avoid the trite salutation "To Whom It May Concern:")

- You are writing to someone with a non-gender-specific name (Jesse, Terry, Stacy, Chris, etc.) and you do not know whether to use "Mr.," "Mrs.," or "Ms."

⇕ 1–1¹⁄₂″ margins on all sides of the letter

State Health Department
1890 Clark Road
Jefferson City, MO 67220

⇕

June 6, 2006   *double space above and below the date*

⇕

Dale McGraw, Manager
Elmwood Mobile Home Park
Elmwood, MO 64003

⇕

Dear Mr. McGraw: *double space above and below the salutation*

⇕

Single space within the paragraphs.

Double space between the paragraphs.

On April 19, 2006, Ryan Duran and I, environmental specialists from the health department, conducted an inspection of the Elmwood Mobile Home Park Wastewater Treatment Facility. The purpose was to assess compliance with the following: the state's Clean Water Law, Clean Water Commission regulations, and your facility's plan for pollution control. The inspection also would allow the state to promote proper operation of wastewater facilities and to provide technical assistance where needed to the Elmwood Mobile Home management.

Though the Elmwood Mobile Home pollution control plan had expired in 2005, a consent judgment was issued by the state's attorney general's office. The county court stipulated a timeline for correction by connection to an available sewer system. Your mobile home park's wastewater system has continually discharged to the Little Osage River. A copy of the abatement order, which requires that monthly discharge monitoring reports (DMRs) be submitted by the 28th of the month following the reporting periods, is attached. All DMRs for the previous twelve months have been received, and reported pollution parameters are not within limits. Due to the plant's performance, the stream was placed on the 1998 303 (d) stream for impairment by the Elmwood Mobile Home.

As part of the inspection, a review of the facility's DMR was conducted. Twenty-four-hour composite samples were collected using a composite sampler. Enclosed are the results of the 24-hour composite samples collected on April 20, 2006. Every one of the problems documented is an infraction that must be addressed.

Within 30 days of receipt of this letter, please submit to the health department written documentation describing steps taken to correct each of the concerns identified in the enclosure. Also include engineering reports, and submit a timeframe to eliminate the problems. Thank you for your cooperation.

⇕

Sincerely,   *double space before "Sincerely"*

⇕

Harvey Haddix   *4 spaces between "Sincerely" and the typed signature*
Environmental Manager

Enclosure

FIGURE 20.6   Full Block Format

State Health Department
1890 Clark Road   Jefferson City, MO 67220

June 6, 2006

Dale McGraw, Manager
Elmwood Mobile Home Park
Elmwood, MO 64003

Subject: Pollution Control Inspection

Dear Mr. McGraw:

On April 19, 2006, Ryan Duran and I, environmental specialists from the health department, conducted an inspection of the Elmwood Mobile Home Park Wastewater Treatment Facility. The purpose was to assess compliance with the following: the state's Clean Water Law, Clean Water Commission regulations, and your facility's plan for pollution control. The inspection also would allow the state to promote proper operation of wastewater facilities and to provide technical assistance where needed to the Elmwood Mobile Home management.

Though the Elmwood Mobile Home pollution control plan had expired in 2005, a consent judgment was issued by the state's attorney general's office. The county court stipulated a timeline for correction by connection to an available sewer system. Your mobile home park's wastewater system has continually discharged to the Little Osage River. A copy of the abatement order, which requires that monthly discharge monitoring reports (DMRs) be submitted by the 28th of the month following the reporting periods, is attached. All DMRs for the previous twelve months have been received, and reported pollution parameters are not within limits. Due to the plant's performance, the stream was placed on the 1998 303 (d) stream for impairment by the Elmwood Mobile Home.

As part of the inspection, a review of the facility's DMR was conducted. Twenty-four-hour composite samples were collected using a composite sampler. Enclosed are the results of the 24-hour composite samples collected on April 20, 2006. Every one of the problems documented is an infraction that must be addressed.

<u>Within 30 days</u> of receipt of this letter, please submit to the health department written documentation describing steps taken to correct each of the concerns identified in the enclosure. Also include engineering reports, and submit a timeframe to eliminate the problems. Thank you for your cooperation.

Sincerely,

Harvey Haddix
Environmental Manager

Enclosure

FIGURE 20.7   Full Block Format with Subject Line

State Health Department
1890 Clark Road
Jefferson City, MO 67220

June 6, 2006

Dale McGraw, Manager
Elmwood Mobile Home Park
Elmwood, MO 64003

Subject: Pollution Control Inspection

On April 19, 2006, Ryan Duran and I, environmental specialists from the health department, conducted an inspection of the Elmwood Mobile Home Park Wastewater Treatment Facility. The purpose was to assess compliance with the following: the state's Clean Water Law, Clean Water Commission regulations, and your facility's plan for pollution control. The inspection also would allow the state to promote proper operation of wastewater facilities and to provide technical assistance where needed to the Elmwood Mobile Homes management.

Though the Elmwood Mobile Home pollution control plan had expired in 2005, a consent judgment was issued by the state's attorney general's office. The county court stipulated a timeline for correction by connection to an available sewer system. Your mobile home park's wastewater system has continually discharged to the Little Osage River. A copy of the abatement order, which requires that monthly discharge monitoring reports (DMRs) be submitted by the 28th of the month following the reporting periods, is attached. All DMRs for the previous twelve months have been received, and reported pollution parameters are not within limits. Due to the plant's performance, the stream was placed on the 1998 303 (d) stream for impairment by the Elmwood Mobile Home.

As part of the inspection, a review of the facility's DMR was conducted. Twenty-four-hour composite samples were collected using a composite sampler. Enclosed are the results of the 24-hour composite samples collected on April 20, 2006. Every one of the problems documented is an infraction that must be addressed.

<u>Within 30 days</u> of receipt of this letter, please submit to the health department written documentation describing steps taken to correct each of the concerns identified in the enclosure. Also include engineering reports, and submit a timeframe to eliminate the problems. Thank you for your cooperation.

Harvey Haddix
Environmental Manager

Enclosure

FIGURE 20.8 Simplified Format Omitting "Dear . . ." and "Sincerely"

The Administrative Management Society (AMS) suggests that if you omit the salutation, you also should omit the complimentary close. Some people feel that omitting the salutation and the omplimentary close will make the letter cold and unfriendly. However, the AMS says that if your letter is warm and friendly, these omissions will not be missed. More importantly, if your letter's content is negative, beginning with "Dear" and ending with "Sincerely" will not improve the letter's tone or your reader's attitude toward your comments.

The simplified format includes a subject line to aid the letter's clarity.

CRITERIA FOR DIFFERENT TYPES OF LETTERS

Though you might write different types of letters, including letters of inquiry, cover, complaint, response, adjustment, or sales, consider using the all-purpose letter template (Figure 20.9) to format your correspondence.

Writer's Address

Date

Reader's Address

Salutation:

A lead-in or overview stating *why* you are writing and *what* you are writing about.

Detailed development, made accessible through highlighting techniques, explaining *exactly what* you want to say.
-
-
-

State *what* is next, *when* this will occur, and *why* the date is important.

Complimentary close,

Signed Name

Typed Name

FIGURE 20.9
All-Purpose Letter Template

LETTER OF INQUIRY

If you want information about degree requirements, equipment costs, performance records, turnaround time, employee credentials, or any other matter of interest to you or your company, you write a letter requesting that data. Letters of inquiry require that you be specific. For example, if you write, "Please send me any information you have on your computer systems," you are in trouble. You will either receive any information the reader chooses to give you or none at all. Look at the following flawed letter of inquiry from a biochemical waste disposal company.

---

before

Dear Mr. Jernigan:

Please send us information about the following filter pools:

1. East Lime Pool
2. West Sulphate Pool
3. East Aggregate Pool

Thank you.

The reader replied to the "before" sample as follows:

Dear Mr. Scholl:

I would be happy to provide you with any information you would like. However, you need to tell me what information you require about the pools.

I look forward to your response.

The first writer, recognizing the error, rewrote the letter as follows:

---

after

Dear Mr. Jernigan:

My company, Jackson County Hazardous Waste Disposal, Inc., needs to purchase new waste receptacles. One of our clients used your products in the past and recommended you. Please send us information about the following:

1. Lime Pool: costs, warranties, time of installation, and dimensions
2. Sulphate Pool: costs, material, and levels of acidity
3. Aggregate Pool: costs, flammability, maintenance, and discoloration

We plan to install our pools by March 12. We would appreciate your response by February 20. Thank you.

Providing specific details makes your letter of inquiry effective. You will save your reader's time by quantifying your request.

To compose your letter of inquiry, include the following:

Introduction.   Clarify your intent in the introduction. Until you tell your readers why you are writing, they do not know. It is your responsibility to clarify your intent and explain your rationale for writing. Also tell your reader immediately what you are writing about (the subject matter of your inquiry). You can state your intent and subject matter in one to three sentences.

Discussion.   Specify your needs in the discussion. To ensure that you get the response you want, ask precise questions or list specific topics of inquiry. You must quantify. For example, rather than vaguely asking about machinery specifications, you should ask more precisely about "specifications for the 12R403B Copier." Rather than asking, "Will the roofing material cover a large surface?" you need to quantify—"Will the roofing material cover $150' \times 180'$?"

Conclusion.   Conclude precisely. First, explain when you need a response. Do not write "Please respond as soon as possible." Provide dated action and tell the reader exactly when you need your answers. Second, to sell your readers on the importance of this date, explain why you need answers by the date given.

Figure 20.10 will help you understand the requirements for effective letters of inquiry.

COVER (TRANSMITTAL) LETTERS

In business, you are often required to send information to a client, vendor, or colleague. You might send multipage copies of reports, invoices, drawings, maps, letters, specifications, instructions, questionnaires, or proposals.

A cover letter accomplishes two goals. First, it lets you tell readers up front what they are receiving. Second, it helps you focus your reader's attention on key points within the enclosures. Thus, the cover letter is a reader-friendly gesture geared toward assisting your audience. To compose your cover letter, include the following:

Introduction.   In the introductory paragraph, tell your reader why you are writing and what you are writing about. What if the reader has asked you to send the documentation? Do you still need to explain why you are writing? The answer is yes. Although the reader requested the information, time has passed, other correspondence has been written, and your reader might have forgotten the initial request.

Discussion.   In the body of the letter, you can accomplish two things. You either will tell your reader exactly what you have enclosed or exactly what of value is within the enclosures. In both instances, you should provide an itemized list or easily accessible, short paragraphs.

Conclusion.   Your conclusion should tell your readers what you want to happen next, when you want this to happen, and why the date is important.

See Figure 20.11 for an example of a cover letter from a healthcare provider.

COMPLAINT LETTERS

You are purchasing director at an electronics firm. Although you ordinarily receive excellent products and support from a local manufacturing firm, two of your recent orders have been filled incorrectly and included defective merchandise. You don't want to have to look for a new supplier. You should express your complaint as pleasantly as possible.

FIGURE 20.10
Letter of Inquiry
Using the Simplified
Format

Compu Med

8713 Hillview   Reno, NV 32901   1-800-551-9000   Fax: 1-816-555-0000

September 12, 2006

Sales Manager
OfficeToGo
7622 Raintree
St. Louis, MO 66772

Writer's Insight

Jim says, "When I write letters of inquiry, I make sure that I itemize the body questions so my readers can easily access them. More than that, I get as specific as I can so I don't have to waste my time—or theirs—with follow-up e-mail questions. A real grammar challenge for me is making the bulleted items parallel!"

Subject: Request for Product Pricing and Shipping Schedules

In the introduction, explain why you are writing.

My medical technology company has worked well with OfficeToGo (OTG) for the past five years. However, in August I received a letter informing me that OTG had been purchased by a larger corporation. I need to determine if OTG remains competitive with other major office equipment suppliers in the Reno area.

Please provide the following information:

In the discussion, specify your needs. To ensure accuracy of response, ask precise questions.

1. What discounts will be offered for bulk purchases?
2. Which freight company will OTG now be using?
3. Who will pay to insure the items ordered?
4. What is the turnaround time from order placement to delivery?
5. Will OTG be able to deliver to all my satellite sites?
6. Will OTG technicians set up the equipment delivered, including desks, file cabinets, bookshelves, and chairs?
7. Will OTG be able to personalize office stationery on site, or will it have to be outsourced?

In the conclusion, state when you need a response and explain why this date is important. Providing contact information will help the reader respond.

Please respond to these questions by September 30 so I can prepare my quarterly orders in a timely manner. I continue to expand my company and want assurances that you can fill my growing office supply needs. You can contact me at the phone number provided above or by e-mail (jgood@CompuMed.com). Thank you for your help.

Jim Goodwin
Owner and CEO

To compose your complaint letter, include the following:

Introduction. In the introduction, politely state the problem. Although you might be angry over the service you have received, you want to suppress that anger. Blatantly negative comments do not lead to communication; they lead to combat. Because angry readers will not necessarily go out of their way to help you, your best approach is diplomacy.

To strengthen your assertions, in the introduction, include supporting details, such as the following: serial numbers, dates of purchase, invoice numbers, check numbers, names of salespeople involved in the purchase, and/or receipts. When possible, include copies documenting your claims.

AMERICAN HEALTHCARE
1401 Laurel Drive
Denton, TX 76201
November 11, 2006

Jan Pascal
Director of Outpatient Care
St. Michael's Hospital
Westlake Village, CA 91362

Dear Ms. Pascal:

Thank you for your recent request for information about our specialized outpatient care equipment. American Healthcare's stair lifts, bath lifts, and vertical wheelchair lifts can help your patients. To show how we can serve you, we have enclosed a brochure including the following information:

	Page
• Maintenance, warranty, and guarantee information	1–3
• Technical specifications for our products, including sizes, weight limitations, colors, and installation instructions	4–6
• Visuals and price lists for our products	7–8
• An American Healthcare order form	9
• Our 24-hour hotline for immediate service	10

Early next month, I will call to make an appointment at your convenience. Then we can discuss any questions you might have. Thank you for considering American Healthcare, a company that has provided exceptional outpatient care for over 30 years.

Sincerely,

Toby Sommers

Enclosure

FIGURE 20.11
Cover Letter in Block Format

A positive tone in the introduction builds rapport and informs the reader why this letter is being written: in response to a request.

An itemized body clarifies what is in the enclosure. Adding page numbers in the list helps readers find the information in the enclosed material.

Discussion.   In the discussion paragraph(s), explain in detail the problems experienced. This could include dates, contact names, information about shipping, breakage information, an itemized listing of defect, or poor service.

Be specific. Generalized information will not sway your readers to accept your point of view. In a complaint letter, you suffer the burden of proof. Help your audience understand the extent of the problem. After documenting your claims, state what you want done and why.

Conclusion.   End your letter positively. Remember, you want to ensure cooperation with the vendor or customer. You also want to be courteous, reflecting your company's professionalism. Your goal should be to achieve a continued rapport with your reader. In this concluding paragraph, include your contact information and the times you can best be reached.

Creating a Positive Tone.   Audiences respond favorably to positive words. If you use negative words, you could offend your reader. In contrast, positive words will

TABLE 20.2 Positive Words

advantage	efficient	meaningful
asset	enjoyable	please
benefit	favorable	positive
certain	good	profit
confident	grateful	quality
constructive	happy	successful
contribution	helpful	thank you
effective	improvement	value

help you control your readers' reactions, build goodwill, and persuade your audience to accept your point of view.

Choose your words carefully. Even when an audience expects bad news, they still need a polite and positive response. The positive words in Table 20.2 and positive verbs in Table 20.3 will help you create a pleasant tone and build audience rapport.

Table 20.4 gives you a "before and after" view of negative sentences rewritten using a positive tone.

TABLE 20.3 Positive Verbs

accomplish	improve
achieve	increase
assist	initiate
assure	insure (ensure)
build	maintain
coordinate	organize
create	plan
develop	produce
encourage	promote
establish	satisfy
help	train
implement	value

TABLE 20.4 Negative vs. Positive Sentences

Before	*After*
1. The error is your fault. You scheduled incorrectly and cannot complain about our deliveries. If you would cooperate with us, we would work with you to solve this problem.	1. To improve deliveries, let's work togetheron our companies' scheduling practices.
2. I regret to inform you that we will not replace the motor in your dryer unless we have proof of purchase.	2. When you provide us proof of purchase, we will be happy to replace the motor in your dryer.
3. The accounting records your company submitted are incorrect. You have obviously miscalculated the figures.	3. After reviewing your company's accounting records, please recalculate the numbers to ensure that they correspond to the new X44 tax laws (enclosed).
4. Your letter suggesting an improvement for the system has been rejected. The reconfigurations you suggest are too large for the area specifications. We need you to resubmit if you can solve your problem.	4. Thank you for your suggestions. Though you offer excellent ideas, the configurations you suggest are too large for our area specifications. Please resubmit your proposal based on the figures provided online.
5. You have not paid your bill yet. Failure to do will result in termination of services.	5. Prompt payment of bills ensures continued service.

See Figure 20.12 for a sample complaint letter to an automotive supplies company.

ADJUSTMENT LETTERS

Responses to letters of complaint, also called adjustment letters, can take three different forms.

1. 100% Yes: You could agree 100 percent with the writer of the complaint letter.
2. 100% No: You could disagree 100 percent with the writer of the complaint letter.
3. Partial Adjustment: You could agree with some of the writer's complaints but disagree with other aspects of the complaint.

Table 20.5 shows you the differences among these three types of adjustment letters.

1234 18th Street
Galveston, TX 77001
May 10, 2006

Mr. Holbert Lang
Customer Service Manager
Gulfstream Auto
1101 21st Street
Galveston, TX 77001

Dear Mr. Lang:

On February 12, 2006, I purchased two shock absorbers in your automotive department. Enclosed are copies of the receipt and the warranty for that purchase. One of those shocks has since proved defective.

I attempted to exchange the defective shock at your store on May 2, 2006. The mechanic on duty, Vernon Blanton, informed me that the warranty was invalid because your service staff did not install the part. I believe that your company should honor the warranty agreement and replace the part for the following reasons:

1. The warranty states that the shock is covered for 48 months and 48,000 miles.
2. The warranty does not state that installation by someone other than the dealership will result in warranty invalidation.
3. The defective shock absorber is causing potentially expensive damage to the tire and suspension system.

I can be reached between 1 P.M. and 6 P.M. on weekdays at 763-9280 or at 763-9821 anytime on weekends. I look forward to hearing from you. Thank you for helping me with this misunderstanding.

Sincerely,

Carlos De La Torre

Enclosures (2)

FIGURE 20.12
Complaint Letter in Block Format

The introduction includes the date of purchase (to substantiate the claim) and the problem encountered.

In the body, explain what happened, state what you want done, and justify your demand. This letter develops its claim with warranty information.

Conclude your letter by providing contact information and an upbeat, pleasant tone.

TABLE 20.5   Differences Among Adjustment Letters

	100% Yes	*100% No*	*Partial Adjustment*
Introduction	State the good news.	Begin with a buffer, a comment agreeable to both reader and writer.	State the good news.
Discussion	Explain what happened and what the reader should do and/or what the company plans to do next.	Explain what happened, state the bad news, and provide possible alternatives.	Explain what happened, state the bad news, and provide possible alternatives—what the reader or company should do next.
Conclusion	End upbeat and positive.	Resell (provide discounts, coupons, follow-up contact names and numbers, etc.) to maintain goodwill.	Resell (provide discounts, coupons, etc.) to maintain goodwill.

Writing a 100% Yes response to a complaint is easy. You are telling your audience what they want to hear. The challenge, in contrast, is writing a 100% No response or a Partial Adjustment. In these letters, you must convey bad news, but you do not want to convey bad news too abruptly. Doing so might offend, anger, or cause hurt feelings. Using a buffer statement delays bad news in written communication and gives you an opportunity to explain your position.

Buffers to Cushion the Blow.   Use the following techniques to buffer the bad news:

- Establish rapport with the audience through positive words to create a pleasant tone. Instead of writing "We received your complaint," be positive and say, "We always appreciate hearing from customers."
- Sway your reader to accept the bad news to come with persuasive facts. "In the last quarter, our productivity has decreased by 16 percent, necessitating cost-cutting measures."
- Provide information that both you and your audience can agree upon. "With the decline of dotcom jobs, many information technology positions have been lost."
- Compliment your reader or show appreciation. "Thank you for your June 9 letter commenting on fiscal year 2005."
- Make your buffer concise with one to two sentences. "Thank you for writing. Customer comments give us an opportunity to improve service."
- Be sure your buffer leads logically to the explanation that follows. Consider mentioning the topic, as in the following example about billing practices. "Several of our clients have noted changes in our corporate billing policies. Your letter was one of several addressing this issue."
- Avoid placing blame or offending the reader. Rather than stating, "Your bookkeeping error cost us $9,890.00," write, "Mistakes happen in business. We are refining our bookkeeping policies to ensure accuracy."

See Figures 20.13 through 20.15 for sample adjustment letters.

1101 21st Street
Galveston, TX 77001
(712) 451-1010
May 31, 2006

Gulfstream Auto

Mr. Carlos De La Torre
1234 18th Street
Galveston, TX 77001

Dear Mr. De La Torre:

Thank you for your recent letter. Gulfstream will replace your defective shock absorber according to the warranty agreement.

The Trailhandler Performance XT shock absorber that you purchased was discontinued in October 2006. Mr. Blanton, the mechanic to whom you spoke, incorrectly assumed that Gulfstream was no longer honoring the warranty on that product. Because we no longer carry that product, we either will replace it with a comparable model or refund the purchase price. Ask for Mrs. Cottrell at the automotive desk on your next visit to our store. She is expecting you and will handle the exchange.

We appreciate your business, Mr. De La Torre. I'm glad you brought this problem to my attention. If I can help you in the future, please contact me.

Sincerely,

Holbert Lang
Sales Manager

cc: Jordan Cottrell, Supervisor
    Jim Gaspar, CEO

FIGURE 20.13
100% Yes
Adjustment Letter,
Complete with
Letter Essentials

Positive word usage ("Thank you") achieves audience rapport.

The introduction immediately states the good news.

The discussion explains what created the problem and provides an instruction telling the customer what to do next.

The conclusion ("We appreciate your business") resells to maintain customer satisfaction.

SALES LETTERS

You have just manufactured a new product (an electronic testing device, a fuel injection mechanism, a fiber optic cable, or a high-tech, state-of-the-art heart monitor). Perhaps you have just created a new service (computer maintenance, automotive diagnosis, home repair, or computer security). You must market your product or service. Connect with your end users, and let the public know that you exist by writing a sales letter. To compose your sales letter, include the following:

Introduction. The introductory paragraph of your sales letter tells your readers why you are writing (you want to increase their happiness or reduce their anxieties, for example). Your introduction should highlight a reader problem, need, or desire. If the readers do not need your services, then they will not be motivated to purchase your merchandise. The introductory sentences also should mention the product or service you are marketing, stating that this is the solution to their problems. Arouse your readers' interest with anecdotes, questions, quotations, or facts.

FIGURE 20.14
100% No
Adjustment Letter

The introduction
begins with a buffer.
The writer
establishes rapport
with the audience
through positive
words to create a
pleasant tone.

The discussion
explains the
company's position,
states the bad news,
and offers an
alternative.

1101 21st Street
Galveston, TX 77001
(712) 451-1010
May 31, 2006

Gulfstream Auto

Mr. Carlos De La Torre
1234 18th Street
Galveston, TX 77001

Dear Mr. De La Torre:

Thank you for your May 10 letter. Gulfstream Auto always appreciates hearing from its customers.

The Trailhandler Performance XT shock absorber that you purchased was discontinued in October 2006. Mr. Blanton, the mechanic to whom you spoke, correctly stated that Gulfstream was no longer honoring the warranty on that product. Because we no longer carry that product, we can not replace it with a comparable model or refund the purchase price. Although we can not replace the shock absorber, we want to offer you a 10 percent discount off of a replacement.

We appreciate your business, Mr. De La Torre. I'm glad you brought this problem to my attention. If I can help you in the future, please contact me.

Sincerely,

Holbert Lang,
Sales Manager

cc: Jordan Cottrell, Supervisor
    Jim Gaspar, CEO

Discussion. In the discussion paragraph(s), specify exactly what you offer to benefit your audience or how you will solve your readers' problems. You can do this in a traditional paragraph. In contrast, you might want to itemize your suggestions in a numbered or bulleted list. Whichever option you choose, the discussion should provide data to document your assertions, give testimony from satisfied customers, or document your credentials.

Conclusion. Make your readers act. If your conclusion says, "We hope to hear from you soon," you have made a mistake. The concluding paragraph of a sales letter should motivate the reader to act. Conclude your sales letter in any of the following ways:

- Give directions (with a map) to your business location.
- Provide a tear-out to send back for further information.
- Supply a self-addressed, stamped envelope for customer response.
- Offer a discount if the customer responds within a given period of time.
- Give your name or a customer-contact name and a phone number (toll-free if possible).

FIGURE 20.15
Partial Adjustment
Letter

1101 21st Street
Galveston, TX 77001
(712) 451-1010
May 31, 2006

Gulfstream Auto

Mr. Carlos De La Torre
1234 18th Street
Galveston, TX 77001

Dear Mr. De La Torre:

Thank you for your recent letter. Gulfstream will replace your defective shock absorber according to the warranty agreement.

Begin your letter with the good news.

The Trailhandler Performance XT shock absorber that you purchased was discontinued in October 2006. Mr. Blanton, the mechanic to whom you spoke, incorrectly assumed that Gulfstream was no longer honoring the warranty on that product. However, we no longer carry that product. We will replace the shock absorber with a comparable model, but you will have to pay for installation.

Explain what happened, state the bad news, and provide a possible alternative.

We appreciate your business, Mr. De La Torre. I'm glad you brought this problem to my attention. If I can help you in the future, please contact me.

Sincerely,

Holbert Lang,
Sales Manager

cc: Jordan Cottrell, Supervisor
    Jim Gaspar, CEO

See Figure 20.16 for a successful sales letter from a computer hardware/software company.

LETTERS CHECKLIST

The Letters Checklist (on page 265) will give you the opportunity for self-assessment and peer evaluation of your writing.

THE WRITING PROCESS AT WORK

Prewriting → Writing → Rewriting

4520 Shawnee Dr. Tulsa, OK 86221 721-555-2121

November 12, 2006

Bill Schneider
Office Manager
REM Technologies
2198 Silicon Way
Tulsa, OK 86112

The introduction arouses reader interest by asking questions.
The questions highlight reader problems: profits, costs, productivity,
and breakdowns.

Dear Mr. Schneider:

Are hardware and software upgrades making your profits plummet? Would you like to reduce your company's computer purchase and maintenance costs? Do computer breakdowns hurt your business productivity? Don't let technology breakdowns harm your bottom line. Many companies have taken advantage of **Office Station's** computer prices, service guarantees, and certified technicians.

The last sentence shows how Office Station will
solve the problems.

Office Station, located in your neighborhood, offers you the following benefits:

The letter uses
positive words
to persuade:
advantage,
guarantees,
certified, benefits,
satisfied, prompt,
and courteous.

- Purchase prices at least 10 percent lower than our competitors.

- IBM-trained technicians, available on a yearly contract or per-call basis.

- An average response time to service calls of under two hours.

- Repair loaners to keep your business up and running.

- Over 5000 satisfied customers, like IBM, Ford, Chevrolet, and Boeing.

- All-inclusive agreements that cover travel, expenses, parts, and shop work.

- State-of-the-art technologies, featuring the latest hardware and software.

The body provides
specific proof to
sway the reader:
10 percent lower,
IBM-trained
technicians, two-
hour response, and
satisfied customers.

Our service is prompt, our technicians are courteous, and our prices are unbeatable. For further information and a written proposal, please call us at **721-555-2121** or e-mail your sales contact, Steve Hudson (shudson@os.com). He's waiting to hear from you. Take advantage of our *Holiday Season Discounts!*

The conclusion urges action by giving contact
names and numbers and seasonal discounts.

Sincerely,

Rachel Adams,
Sales Manager

Office Station
Authorized Sales and Service for
Gateway   3M   Microsoft   HP   Apple   Dell   Swingline

FIGURE 20.16   Sales Letter in Block Format

LETTERS CHECKLIST

___ 1. **Letter Essentials:** Does your letter include the eight essential components (writer's address, date, reader's address, salutation, text, complimentary close, writer's signed name, and writer's typed name)?

___ 2. **Introduction:** Does the introduction state *what* you are writing about and *why* you are writing?

___ 3. **Discussion:** Does your discussion clearly state the details of your topic depending on the type of letter?

___ 4. **Highlighting/Page Layout:** Is your text accessible? To achieve reader-friendly ease of access, use headings, boldface, italics, bullets, numbers, underlining, or graphics (tables and figures). These add interest and help your readers navigate your letter.

___ 5. **Organization:** Have you helped your readers follow your train of thought by using appropriate modes of organization? These include chronology, importance, problem/solution, or comparison/contrast.

___ 6. **Conclusion:** Does your conclusion give directive action (tell what you want the reader to do next and when) and end positively?

___ 7. **Clarity:** Is your letter clear, answering reporter's questions and providing specific details that inform, instruct, or persuade?

___ 8. **Conciseness:** Have you limited the length of your words, sentences, and paragraphs?

___ 9. **Audience Recognition:** Have you written appropriately to your audience? This includes avoiding biased language, considering the multicultural/cross-cultural nature of your readers, and your audience's role (supervisors, subordinates, coworkers, customers, or vendors). Have you created a positive tone to build rapport?

___10. **Correctness:** Is your text grammatically correct? Errors will hurt your professionalism. See Appendix A for grammar rules.

Effective writing follows a process of prewriting, writing, and rewriting. Each of these steps is sequential and yet continuous. The writing process is dynamic, with the three steps frequently overlapping. To clarify the importance of the writing process, look at how Jim Goodwin, the CEO of CompuMed, used prewriting, writing, and rewriting to write a memo to his employees.

PREWRITING

No single method of prewriting is more effective than another. Throughout this textbook, you will learn many different types of prewriting techniques, geared uniquely for different types of communication. The goal of all prewriting is to help you overcome the blank page syndrome (writer's block). Prewriting will allow you to spend time before writing your memo or letter, gathering as much information as you can about your subject matter. In addition, prewriting lets you determine your objectives.

Jim used mind mapping/clustering to gather data and determine objectives (Figure 20.17).

WRITING

Once you have gathered your data and determined your objectives in prewriting, your next step is to draft your memo or letter. In doing so, consider the following techniques:

Jim factored in his coworker's suggestions and rewrote the memo. See Figure 20.20 for the finished product.

FIGURE 20.20
Finished Bad-News, Problem-Solution Memo Incorporating Revision Suggestions

Date	October 14, 2006
To:	CompuMed Employees
From:	Jim Goodwin
Subject:	Suggestions for Improving Corporate Finances

CompuMed is experiencing lower profits and declining stock value. Consequently, stockholders are displeased with company performance. I have been meeting with the Board of Directors and division managers to determine the best course of action. Here are ideas to improve our company's financial situation.

1. Consolidating departments: By merging our marketing and advertising departments, for example, we can reduce redundancies. This could save CompuMed approximately $275,000 over a six-month period.
2. Reducing staff: We need to cut back employees by 15 percent. This does not necessarily mean that layoffs are inevitable. One way, for instance, to reduce staff is through voluntary retirements. We will be encouraging employees with over 20 years vested in the company to take our generous early-retirement package.
3. Freezing wages: For the next fiscal quarter, no raise increases will go into effect. Internal auditors will review the possibility of reestablishing raises after the first quarter.
4. Freezing travel: Conference attendance will be stopped for six months.

I encourage you to visit with me and your division managers with questions or suggestions. CompuMed is a strong company and will bounce back with your help. Thank you for your patience and understanding.

Writer's Insight

Jim says, "I find it extremely difficult and painful to communicate bad news to people I care about—my employees. However, to run a business successfully, you sometimes have to make difficult choices that will negatively affect many people. The best way to convey bad news is to state it clearly and follow up with options. I always try to end positively to maintain good relations. Having someone else read my correspondence helps me focus on what needs to be changed and what's successful."

DEVELOPING WORKPLACE SKILLS

CASE STUDIES

After reading the following case studies, write the appropriate correspondence required for each assignment.

1. As director of human resources at CompuMed biotechnology company, Andrew McWard helps employees create and implement their Individual Development Plans (IDPs). Employees attend 360-Degree Assessment Workshops where they learn how to get feedback on their job performance from their supervisors, coworkers, and subordinates. They also provide self-evaluations.

   Once the 360-Degree Assessments are complete, employees submit them to Andrew, who, with the help of his staff, develops IDPs.

   Andrew sends the IDPs to the employees, prefaced by a cover letter. In this cover letter, he tells them why he is writing and what he is writing about. In the letter's body, he focuses their attention on the attachment's contents: supervisor's development profile, the schedule of activities that helps employees implement their plans, the courses designed to increase their productivity, the costs of each program, and guides to long-term professional development.

   In the cover letter's conclusion, Andrew ends upbeat by emphasizing how the employees' IDPs help them resolve conflicts and make better decisions.

   Based on the information provided, write this cover letter for Andrew McWard. He is sending the letter to Sharon Baker, Account Executive, 1092 Turtle Hill Road, Evening Star, GA 20091.

2. Mark Shabbot works for Apex, Inc., at 1919 W. 23rd Street, Denver, CO 80204. Apex, a retailer of computer hardware, wants to purchase 125 new flat-screen monitors from a vendor, Omnico, located at 30467 Sheraton, Phoenix, AZ 85023. The monitors will be sold to Northwest Hills Educational Cooperative. However, before Apex purchases these monitors, Mark needs information regarding bulk rates, shipping schedules, maintenance agreements, equipment specifications, and technician certifications. Northwest Hills needs this equipment before the new term (August 15). Write a letter of inquiry for Mr. Shabbot based on the preceding information.

3. Gregory Peña (121 Mockingbird Lane, San Marcos, TX 77037) has written a letter of complaint to Donya Kahlili, the manager of TechnoRad (4236 Silicon Dr., San Marcos, TX 77044). Mr. Peña purchased a computer from a TechnoRad outlet in San Marcos. The *San Marcos Tattler* advertised that the computer "came loaded with all the software you'll need to write effective letters and perform basic accounting functions." (Mr. Peña has a copy of this advertisement.) When Mr. Peña booted up his computer, he expected to access word processing software, multiple fonts, a graphics package, a grammar check, and a spreadsheet. All he got was a word processing package and a spreadsheet. Mr. Peña wants Ms. Kahlili to upgrade his software to include fonts, graphics, and a grammar check; he wants a computer technician from TechnoRad to load the software on his computer; and he wants TechnoRad to reimburse him $400 (the full price of the software) for his trouble.

   Ms. Kahlili agrees that the advertisement is misleading and will provide Mr. Peña software including the fonts, graphics, and grammar check (complete with instructions for loading the software). Write Ms. Kahlili's 100% Yes Adjustment to Mr. Peña based on the information provided.

4. TechToolshop provides automotive sales and service. They install and repair automotive equipment at service sites nationwide; through an online catalog and storefront sites, they sell automotive equipment both wholesale and retail.

   TechToolshop's home office is in Big Springs, Iowa, at 11324 Elm, where over 1,200 employees work. Their phone number at this site is 212-345-6666, and their email address is *ToolHelp@TechTools.com*. TechToolshop's new local address in your city is 5110 Nueces Avenue. Their phone number is 345-782-8776.

   TechToolshop offers free product support 24 hours a day at 1-800-TechHelp. They also can guarantee arrival at your site within two hours of any automotive service emergency call. Plus—their greatest innovation—TechToolshop has installed service kiosks in every mall, library, and bank in your city where you can look up answers to frequently asked automotive questions. They warrant all products and services—money back—for 90 days, covering defects in material and workmanship.

   Write a sales letter marketing TechToolshop's.

5. Bob Ward, an account manager at HomeCare Health Equipment, has not gotten the raise that he thinks he deserves. When Bob met with his boss, Helene Koren,

(Continued)

last Thursday for his annual evaluation, she told him that he had missed too many days of work (eight days during the year), was unwilling to work beyond his 40-hour workweek to complete rush jobs, and had not attended two mandatory training sessions on the company's new computerized inventory system.

Bob agrees that he missed the training sessions, but he was out of town on a job-related assignment for one of those sessions. He missed eight days of work, but he was allowed five days of sick leave as part of his contract. The other three days missed were due to his having to stay home to take care of his children when they were sick. He believed that these absences were covered by the company's parental leave policy. Finally, he does not agree that employees should be required to work beyond their contractual 40 hours.

Write a memo to Helene Koren, stating Bob's case.

INDIVIDUAL AND TEAM PROJECTS

1. Write a letter of inquiry. You might want to write to a college or university requesting information about a degree program or to a manufacturer for information about a product or service. Whatever the subject matter, be specific in your request.

2. Write a cover letter. Perhaps your cover letter will preface a report you are working on in school, a report you are writing at work, or documentation you will need to send to a client.

3. Write a letter of complaint. You might want to write to a retail store, a manufacturing company, a restaurant, or a governmental organization. Whatever the subject matter, be specific in your complaint.

4. Write an adjustment letter. Envision that a client has written a complaint letter about a problem he or she has encountered with your product or service. Write a 100% Yes letter in response to the complaint.

5. Write a sales letter. You plan to sell a new product, portable computer zip drives, that are small enough to fit on key chains.

6. Write a memo requesting office equipment. Your company plans to purchase new office equipment. Your memo will explain your office's needs. Specifically state what equipment and furniture you want and why these purchases are important.

7. Write a memo reporting on a project's progress. Draw from your experiences in one of your classes. How are you progressing on an assignment? What work have you accomplished? What problems have you encountered? What work remains on this project? In a memo to your instructor, detail this status.

8. Write a memo inviting coworkers to your company's annual picnic. In this memo, tell why the picnic is being held, when the celebration will occur, what special events are planned, where the picnic will take place, and what the guests should bring (equipment, clothing, etc.) to enjoy their outing.

9. Write a good news memo. One of your coworkers has done an outstanding job (with customer service, sales, training, or helping other colleagues in the department). You want to write a memo to your manager commending this employee.

10. Write a bad news memo. One of your subordinates has not been performing well on the job. Maybe this employee has been rude to customers, has not performed tasks up to the company's standards, has been shirking responsibilities,